Caught on Tape

Caught on Tape

White Masculinity and Obscene Enjoyment

CASEY RYAN KELLY

OXFORD
UNIVERSITY PRESS

OXFORD
UNIVERSITY PRESS

Oxford University Press is a department of the University of Oxford. It furthers
the University's objective of excellence in research, scholarship, and education
by publishing worldwide. Oxford is a registered trade mark of Oxford University
Press in the UK and certain other countries.

Published in the United States of America by Oxford University Press
198 Madison Avenue, New York, NY 10016, United States of America.

Library of Congress Control Number: 2023932443

ISBN 978-0-19-767787-2 (pbk.)
ISBN 978-0-19-767786-5 (hbk.)

DOI: 10.1093/oso/9780197677865.001.0001

Paperback printed by Marquis Book Printing, Canada
Hardback printed by Bridgeport National Bindery, Inc., United States of America

Contents

Acknowledgments

Throughout the review and production process, Norm Hirschy and Oxford University Press have been outstanding supporters of this book, and I am eternally grateful that this project will appear in their catalogue. Of course, the anonymous reviewers took great care with this manuscript as well, and I am indebted to their wisdom and valuable criticism. I am also grateful for the enthusiastic and unwavering support of my colleagues in the Department of Communication Studies at the University of Nebraska-Lincoln, without which this book may never have been written. I am fortunate enough to have the support of many colleagues across the field of rhetoric who have helped refine the arguments that appear herein. I am especially indebted to the many conversations and helpful feedback I have received from my friends and colleagues Paul Elliot Johnson, Calum L. Matheson, Eric King Watts, and Ryan Neville-Shepard. I would like to thank Jay Childers for the invitation to present this work at the 2022 Biennial Public Address conference at the University of Kansas and the thoughtful commentary of the plenary respondents Claire Sisco King, Tom Nakayama, and Amanda Nell Edgar.

A special thank you goes to my brother-in-law Kent Hoerl for introducing me to parts of YouTube that are featured in Chapter 3. Finally, thank you to my spouse Kristen Hoerl for enduring way too many conversations about the obscene material featured in this book but, most importantly, for her love and encouragement.

Introduction

On Obscene Enjoyment

George Orwell's novel *Nineteen Eighty-Four* (otherwise known as *1984*) imagined a dystopian future in which the state ("Big Brother") exercised absolute control over the citizens of Oceania. The ubiquity of cameras and other watchful eyes meant that every individual behaved as if they were constantly being watched. Although Orwell's nightmare was illustrative of the emerging dangers of omniscient authoritarian control, his story was perhaps less prescient concerning the diffuse, decentralized, and participatory nature of the contemporary surveillance society. As surveillance scholar David Lyon writes, "[W]atching itself has become a way of life," meaning that contemporary surveillance culture is underwritten by the active consent of the governed.[1] Michel Foucault's theorization of panoptic power also reminds us that individuals often do much of the hard labor to watch and police themselves in the absence of juridical authority.[2] Although it may be distressing to many of us, engaging with cameras and recording devices has become a fairly banal experience: smartphones, CCTV, home camcorders, body cams, dash cams, traffic cams, doorbell cams, GoPro cams, airborne drone cams, satellite cams, toilet cams, and nanny cams among others. There are an estimated 1 billion surveillance cameras in operation worldwide.[3] In the United States, approximately 85 percent of the population owns a smartphone device with both photographic and audio-visual recording capabilities. Websites and applications that support user-generated image-based (Instagram, Flicker, Tumblr) and video content (YouTube, TikTok, Vimeo) are frequented daily by billions of users worldwide. Watching and eavesdropping on others have been somewhat delinked from more lurid association with voyeurism, now constituting an acceptable form of participation in public life.

The widespread applicability and accessibility of surveillance technologies have certainly normalized being watched and eavesdropped on—an inescapable fact of modern technological progress, we are told. Yet, a vast majority of us are enthusiastic and voluntary participants in surveillance regimes.

Caught on Tape. Casey Ryan Kelly, Oxford University Press. © Oxford University Press 2023.
DOI: 10.1093/oso/9780197677865.003.0001

We post images and videos to social networks that disclose our geolocation, track our activity, refine facial recognition software, and feed algorithms that amass behavioral data to create personalized digital profiles.[4] Many of the most successful forms of popular entertainment are television programs that make use of surveillance devices to purportedly show unscripted reality (with titles such as *Big Brother* no less!).[5] Even NBC's hit show *To Catch a Predator* made use of hidden cameras and private Internet chat logs to transform outing pedophiles into prime time entertainment. But our participation in surveillance regimes also serves civic functions: doorbell and nanny cameras monitor neighborhood property crimes, body cameras putatively restrain police brutality, smartphone videos capture offensive public outbursts, voice memos record the lurid conversations of the powerful and wealthy, and drone and satellite cameras can help law enforcement track down criminals and evil-doers *in the act.*

But with new surveillance regimes come new cultural fantasies. For instance, one promise of the surveillance society is that cameras might expose crimes and police violations of the public's trust. Thought of this way, one could argue that public and personal surveillance helps hold individuals accountable and, in doing so, realize the democratic promise of total transparency, or a society in which dirty secrets and hidden agendas are inevitably exposed. We now possess the means to throw open every locked door and shed light on every dark recess of society. But as Jodi Dean observes, democratic cultures have long fetishized the dialectic of secrecy and revelation in order to sustain the fantasy that openness and transparency realize the promise of democracy, fait accompli.[6] "The secret," she writes, "promises that a democratic public is within reach—as soon as everything is known. All that is necessary to realize the ideal of the public is to uncover these secrets, to bring them to light."[7] A strategically placed hot mic or hidden camera can expose a politician's corruption or a celebrity's racism as much as it can capture a stranger's racist outburst or a neighbor's lewd behavior. In civic surveillance regimes, the ideal citizen is both a producer and consumer: they film, photograph, record, eavesdrop, witness, watch, and monitor others as part of a civic and technological imperative.

Following Dean, there are many reasons to be skeptical of the liberating potential of publicity, particularly when we consider that U.S. media culture is organized around spectacles.[8] Spectacles are mass produced "images, commodities, and staged events" that dazzle, stupefy, and attract attention.[9] As Kevin DeLuca and Jennifer Peeples announced at the outset of the twenty-first century, we live in the age of visual spectacle, acutely marked by the prominence of the "image event" and where life is mediated primarily through screens.[10] On the public screen, only shocking images are capable of halting and holding the public's attention. Particularly when attention is scarce and information is abundant, spectacles are the only means to draw eyes and ears to matters of public concern.[11] Now in the digital age, spectacles are also interactive and participatory. For instance, at the January 6, 2021, insurrection at the U.S. Capitol, many of the assailants used Facebook Live, Instagram, and Parler to share their criminal mayhem with various publics.[12] Although the insurrection was certainly newsworthy, there are also many spectacular media events that are hardly deserving of public attention: a new royal baby, billionaires launching themselves into space, a leaked celebrity sex tape, or fisticuffs at the Oscars. At the same time, matters of grave public concern are stripped of their complexity and converted into entertainment products: wars, elections, social strife, economic crises, and national tragedies. In a culture organized around screens, spectacularizing events is the precondition for national circulation.

Media spectacles incentivize the broadcasting and sharing of obscene, scandalous, and extreme content. Douglas Kellner and Henry Giroux have respectively documented how U.S. media culture presents a shocking tableau of violence and depravity that tends to normalize cruelty. As Giroux writes, "[A] culture of depravity has become commonplace in a society in which pain, humiliation and abuse are condensed into digestible spectacles of violence endlessly circulated through extreme sports, reality TV, video games, YouTube postings and proliferating forms of the new and old media."[13] He concludes that "images that attempt to shock might well reinforce a media-induced habituation to and comfort with 'the horror of certain images.'"[14] Adding to Giroux's list of stultifying spectacles, consider how the media culture of depravity is supplemented by a ceaseless flow of scandalous mediated gossip: the president-elect caught bragging about sexual assault, a billionaire NBA team owner confessing to his distaste for consorting with Black players, an a-list Hollywood actor growling threats of sexual violence, and even ordinary people caught on video shouting hate speech in a local grocery store.

With the ever-improving means to document and expose once private transgressions, U.S. media culture is now inundated with scandalous revelations of the most depraved and obscene kind.[15] The past decade has wrought a deluge of high-profile figures—mostly wealthy white men—who have been recorded making vile, racist, and misogynistic statements: President Donald J. Trump, Mel Gibson, Donald Sterling, Hulk Hogan, Shia Lebouf, and Michael Richards just to name a few. In 2017, the *New Yorker* released obtained NYPD recordings of Hollywood producer Harvey Weinstein attempting to coerce and sexually assault a young actress. In 2019, portions of a 1971 conversation between then President Richard Nixon and future President Ronald Reagan were made available by the National Archives in which the two shared a laugh when referring to African delegates at the United Nations as "monkeys" who were "uncomfortable in shoes."[16] New media platforms are now repositories of everyday racist tirades, public freak outs, crime, corruption, violence, and ordinary people acting out in public. Given this ever-growing archive of the obscene, has our ability to document and dissect private obscenity in public brought us any closer to realizing the democratic promise of transparency? What are the cultural entailments of repetitive encounters with our worst transgression? What kind of public and media culture arises from this form of spectatorship? I suggest that the answer to these questions lies in the videos and recordings themselves: the kinds of symbolic and imaginary world they conjure for audiences and the relationships they forge between the spectators and the powerful white men who are exposed for their crimes. As Jacques Derrida observed, the mediation of tragedies "makes archiving an active interpretation, one that is selective, productive qua reproductive, productive of a 'making known' narrative as much as reproductive of images."[17] Put another way, recordings and videos are not so much archives that accompany events as they are active ways of seeing or "making known" that invite certain modes of perception and interpretation. Though there are many ways that spectators might interpret or value what is contained within this archive, available readings are delimited to the act of archiving itself.

Thus, motivated by this insight, this book addresses the cultural and political implications of a contemporary genre of publicity: *the public revelation*. Here, I am also guided by Michael Warner's statement about the rhetorical effects of publicity, that "the direction of our glance can constitute our social world."[18] What, then, is the social world constituted in and through the direction of our eyes and ears toward our worst secrets, misbehaviors, and wrongdoings—our failures to live up to our most progressive ideals? *Caught on Tape* is an inquiry into the forms of spectatorship and audience dynamics that are forged through the habituated exhibition and consumption of obscene acts of transgression. This book is specifically interested in our consumption of racist and misogynistic acts that violate the rules of decorum and the ideological sensibilities of a putatively colorblind, postfeminist, and democratic society. I characterize the revelation as a form of public address that "makes known," or visual and auditory statements that direct public attention to an aberration or imperfection thwarting the fulfillment of a postracial and postfeminist society.

In this context, I argue that public revelations prefigure racism and misogyny as historical anachronisms whose elimination is only made possible by shocking acts of publicity. All that is hidden and secretive is sinister; therefore, revelations shine the light of publicity as a democratic form of disinfectant. At the same time, there is a sense in which irruptions of racist and misogynistic speech become the very condition of possibility for postracial and postfeminist culture. By *irruption*, I mean the sudden, arresting, and forcible incursion of hate speech into public life. Irruptions create tears in the fabric of social reality that must be stitched closed to maintain a semblance of order and coherence. At the same time, Lauren Berlant's concept of "cruel optimism" reminds us that sometimes such stitches keep us invested in the very social systems that debilitate us.[19] Following Berlant, I suggest that the circulation of racist and misogynistic transgressions via video and sound recording invites spectators to become invested in the mythological optimism of postracialism and postfeminism; namely, that race and gender oppression are matters of personal prejudice and that the exposure of "bad apples" will bring about progressive multiculturalism. But for all our capacity to reveal obscene behaviors and beliefs, we lack the acumen to make sense of transgressions as symptoms of structural and systemic oppression. Thus, racism and misogyny represent what Sigmund Freud characterized as the *return of the repressed* whereby traumatic and threatening experiences return again and again despite our best attempts to block and keep those experiences at bay.[20] Hateful and offensive speech—once thought to be relegated to the margins by social progress—perpetually returns only to be disavowed and repressed again and again with renewed declarations of commitments to equality and justice. But as part of a media spectacle of depravity, such revelations conceal the underlying dynamics of structural racism and misogyny that guarantee their return.

Examining both quotidian and high-profile public revelations—from the infamous *Access Hollywood* tape to leaked recordings of Donald Sterling's racist tirades—the pages that follow explore how the ritual publication of secret tapes and hidden recordings constitutes a cultural site of *obscene enjoyment*: an experience of ecstatic and excessive pleasure-in-pain that arises from encounters with that which disturbs, traumatizes, and interrupts illusory notions of our coherent selves. By enjoyment I refer to neither joy nor entertainment, but instead Jacques Lacan's theorization of *jouissance*: a compulsion or drive to repetitively transgress the law, social conventions, and cultural prohibitions.[21] The central argument of this book is that the spectators are the ones "caught on tape," meaning that audiences can become trapped in a compulsively repetitive encounter with forms of depravity that postracial and postfeminist mythology assures us have been banished by the march of progress.

As a rhetorical critic, I am interested in how these tapes constitute a symbolic and imaginary world for the public. What is it that this obscene archive "makes known"? Although this project is influenced by cultural studies' insistence that popular texts are apertures into the conjunctural and contextual, *Caught on Tape* is a rhetorical inquiry that explores the textual and suasory dynamics of public revelations.[22] That is, while I am concerned with historical shifts in spectatorship and white masculinity, I elaborate on such contextual fields through close attention to the content, style, and form of the recordings themselves in order to explain how obscene texts position audiences to make sense of racism and sexism in U.S. public life. Thus, I ask: What do these tapes reveal *and* conceal about the "secret" life of racism and misogyny? I wager that part of the reason that these videos and recordings fail to achieve the desired outcome is that obscene transgressions are folded back into the structural dynamics of spectatorship wherein it is easy to succumb to the illusion that viewing and listening produce a sense of mastery over threatening social forces. It is, thus, also easy to confuse publicity and spectatorship with antiracism and feminism. Yet, racism and gender violence return again and again; traumatizing, horrifying, and titillating all at once. The revelation crafts a public and media culture organized around the obscene enjoyment of transgressions—racist and misogynistic *jouissance*—that subsequently becomes the means by which white supremacy and white masculine hegemony are consolidated. That is to say that transgressive performances of white masculinity are consistent with the spectacle of depravity that is normalized throughout U.S. media culture.

Each chapter to come demonstrates how a culture of public revelations is based on a series of problematic assumptions: that white masculine power is solely exercised in secret, that sleuthing out secret bigots will make progressive equality possible, that the offended spectator bears no relation or accrues no benefit from hate speech, and that looking and listening offer mastery over racism and misogyny. Drawing from the insights of psychoanalysis, cultural studies, and rhetorical theory, this book examines the fantasies engendered by the public revelation and illustrates how spectatorship thwarts our ability to create a culture of accountability. I conclude that these awful texts actually sustain democratic fantasies by foiling a structural analysis of the relationship between democracy and white masculine violence,[23] thus creating the conditions for racism and misogyny to be "enjoyed."

Revelations in a Convergence Culture

Observing the cultural transformations brought about by the invention of television, Raymond William argued that "we have never as a society . . . acted so much or watched so many others acting." Although, he argued drama "is built into the rhythms of everyday life" broadcasting technology rendered "drama as habitual experience: more in a week, in many cases, than most human beings would previously have seen in a lifetime."[24] While one can only surmise what Williams would make of forms such as reality television and viral videos, it is safe to say that he might find in the decentralization and personalization of media production an intensification of the dramatic structuring of everyday life. The difference, however, is that the distinction between scripted and extemporaneous drama is increasingly difficult to discern, particularly where everyday life becomes both the scene and source material for new media. As reality television scholars Rachel Dubrofsky and Emily Ryalls note, one hallmark of contemporary media culture is the act of "performing not-performing," whereby belabored and staged dramatic performances are made to look effortless, organic, and completely unscripted.[25] A surveillance society makes everyone a potential dramatic actor—whether an ordinary person stars in the next new reality competition show or shares a livestream of themselves storming the U.S. Capitol.[26] Both are scripted performances insofar as media have particular affordances that organize how subjects might take up, use, and consume content.[27]

The dramatic affordances of scripted film and television were once limited by both the centralized technological capacities of broadcasting and film production as well as corporate entities and professional societies that acted as gatekeepers to ordinary citizens seeking fame. The production of celebrities (otherwise known as the "star system") was at one time tethered to the industrial infrastructure of the Hollywood studio system, talent agents, publicists, acting guilds, financiers, insiders, and journalists, among others.[28] Of course, reality television, YouTube, and Instagram have not completely supplanted the star system; however, they have infused the logics of celebrity into everyday media networks and created a parallel populist system of celebrity. Ordinary people now have the capacity and know-how to build a personal brand and gain followers within social networks in ways that mirror the old logics of celebrity.[29] On the one hand, social networks can make celebrities out of ordinary people, sometimes even inadvertently when a video "goes viral." On the other hand, the proliferation of tabloid and gossip media knocks down Hollywood celebrities by exposing their personal embarrassments, human foibles, and taboo desires. As Martin Conboy contends, "[T]abloid values have come to permeate our general media culture and in so doing have generated a cultural continuum that critics of culture might have to consider a variant of 'common culture,' with all the implications of the word 'common' from vernacular, to the everyday, to the vulgar."[30] It is not a stretch of the concept, as I argue in Chapter 4, to suggest that the populist turn in celebrity and new media enabled someone like Donald Trump to reach the White House.

Perhaps more than any other tabloid, Harvey Levin's TMZ (Thirty-Mile Zone) perfectly exemplifies the changing dynamics of spectatorship entailed in the permutation of a celebrity and surveillance society, where every embarrassing moment can be captured, rapidly disseminated, and monetized. *Exposure* is one of the organizing principles of new media.[31] New, shocking revelations generate not just viewers and readers, but also likes, shares, retweets, parody videos, memes, reaction GIFs, and livestream commentary. With this transformation in celebrity, it should come as no surprise that the modes of spectatorship that emerge within new media forms *demand* exposure—the more obscene and disgraceful, the more affective intensity it will garner. Relatively new and interactive media forms, including reality television, social networking apps, microblogging sites, viral videos, image boards, and other mediums, traffic in the exposure of private life in public.

Rather than drawing distinctions between old and new media paradigms, Henry Jenkins contends that these new mediums constitute a *convergence* or *participatory* culture in which audiences are active and interactive, consume and produce media, and traffic across a variety of mediums to make sense of everyday life.[32] The evolution of celebrity in a convergence culture has actively transformed what constitutes public intimacy by cultivating expectations of not simply exposure but of accessibility. Noting the radical transformation in publicity and celebrity, Sharon Marcus observes that "new media have redefined what it means to be a person, both in private and in public."[33] New mediums afford unprecedented levels of public self-disclosure and access to the private lives of others—not just access to celebrities and politicians but also friends, family members, colleagues, and even casual acquaintances or complete strangers. As P. David Marshall explains,

> The level of exposure—the capacity of our technologies to record and to transmit images, text, and sound—and an online culture that has new expectations of exposure have helped expand our comfort with public intimacy. To understand the extent of this public intimacy, one only has to look at the quite remarkable availability and accessibility of online video pornography.[34]

Indeed, Marshall's example of Internet pornography exemplifies the kind of transgressive and sometimes obscene nature of public intimacy in new media. For instance, social networking, image boards, and microblogging sites invite us to share our most intimate thoughts, feelings, images, and experiences in (virtual) public while also giving us a commensurate level of access to the lives of others (and, as Marshall suggests, even their boudoirs). Viral videos on sites like YouTube and TikTok transform everyday life and quotidian experiences into entertainment and opportunities for virtual connectivity. Reality television gives audiences unprecedented access to the private lives of ordinary people and celebrities alike.[35] New media technologies along with the runaway accumulation of personal data have acclimated the public and invited them to participate in their own exposure.[36] Although new media forms also frame and filter content through the public screen, they tend to render their own production processes opaque.[37] In so doing, convergence culture imparts a sense of realness, authenticity, and proximity to genuine raw emotion—even though this sense is manufactured and belabored for its effect.[38] Surveillance promises us an encounter with the "real" life that happens backstage, not the phoniness that is explicitly coded as a scripted performance in public.

In sum, the unique dynamics of (micro)celebrity, spectatorship, and public exposure create the conditions for obscene enjoyment to operate as the underlying economy of a convergence culture. Put differently, convergence culture organizes spectators' enjoyment in shocking revelations of private intimacies. As I argue in the next section, this dynamic is structurally at odds with holding perpetrators accountable. As exposure of private lives in public becomes the precondition for participating in the new culture of public intimacy, the more transgressive and obscene the behavior, the more likely it is to operate as a signifier of realness. In this context, spectators are invited to encounter obscene enjoyment so as to reveal the hidden dynamics of power that explain and remedy their woes. Convergence culture set the stage for racism and misogyny to be folded into the logics of spectatorship.

Transgressive White Masculinity

Caught on Tape is largely a study of white masculinity, given that the transgressions examined throughout quite frequently purport to reveal the inner workings of white men's indiscretions that take place in those private enclaves and intimate interiors where "boys will be boys." At the same time, this book addresses white masculinity as a subject position, a signifier, or an imaginary identification that is often synonymous with power and authority, rather than specific individuals who identify as white and male. In other words, the book makes neither generalizable statements about individual white men nor does it suggest that only white men transgress cultural prohibitions against obscene speech. Thus, when I use terms like *white masculinity* or *whiteness*, I am referring to pernicious structural and symbolic phenomena that arbitrarily confer privileges and benefits based on race and gender.

One of the central problems with the public revelation is that it rests on the assumption that publicity summons accountability and maintains new taboos against white masculine depravity; that is, unless of course, transgressing taboos can be seen as an expression of authentic, unbridled masculinity. Those looking for new media to reestablish taboos against obscene transgressions will likely find themselves wanting. In the present age, the performance of white masculinity is strikingly spectacular and transgressive. Consider a few contemporary examples. In 2017, white men openly marched in Charlottesville, Virginia, carrying lit tiki torches and chanting, "Jews will not replace us!" and "white lives matter." One man struck a counterprotestor (Heather Heyer) with his vehicle, fatally wounding her. During his 2018 Senate confirmation hearing, then Supreme Court nominee Brett Kavanaugh responded to claims that he had sexually assaulted Dr. Christine Blasey-Ford with an unprecedented rage-filled tantrum—something previously beyond the pale of such hearings. In 2020, anti-mask and COVID-19 lockdown protests featured images of white men yelling obscenities and taunting police with impunity. That same year, 17-year old Kyle Rittenhouse fatally shot two and injured one during a counterprotest over the police shooting of an unarmed Black man (Jacob Blake). He was later acquitted after a melodramatic and tear-laden outburst while testifying in his own defense. In 2021, the Capitol rioters filmed and photographed themselves vandalizing the hallowed halls of Congress. These striking examples evince a larger pattern in the performance of white masculinity; namely, a proclivity to openly violate cultural taboos and stand in defiance of norms, conventions, and the rule of law. Although rebelliousness and exemption from the rule of law have long been white masculine privileges, this more generalized tendency toward spectacular transgressions has become one of the defining attributes of Trump-era white masculinity.[39]

As the above examples illustrate, white masculinity has taken on an increasingly transgressive and (self-) destructive character. Claire Sisco King observed this churning current of abject white masculinity in the media culture of the early twenty-first century.[40] She explained that white masculinity had come to reconstitute its hegemony in the face of progressive challenges by "sacrificing its fictions in order to absorb, assimilate, and make room for Otherness, for instance, cherished narratives of masculine strength, aggression, and invulnerability in order to indulge in femininity, passivity, and lack."[41] As a hegemonic ideological formation, there is no homogenous or singular definition that permits white masculinity to be pinned down as any one thing in particular other than what it needs to be.[42] Resounding with King's notion of abject hegemony, Hamilton Carroll characterized the elusive character of white masculinity as *labile*, which for him is an identity formation that quickly shifts, alters, and displaces itself in reaction to disruptive social transformations.[43] At its most extreme, "acting out" means enacting necropolitical violence, defined by an onslaught of mass shooters, vigilantes, and serial killers, white supremacists marching openly across the country, and violent Trump-inspired insurrectionists ransacking the U.S. Capitol.[44] These examples of transgressive masculine violence are all connected by the assailant's willingness to commit crimes in the open—even to the point of posting incriminating videos of themself on social media platforms.

The election and presidency of Donald J. Trump perfectly exemplified the ethos of open rebellion that had come to define the emergent politics of white male aggrievement.[45] Part of Trump's appeal was his unwillingness to abide social conventions: accusing President Obama of being a foreign citizen, calling Mexicans rapists, bragging about the size of his penis during a presidential debate, openly calling for foreign adversaries to intervene in the 2016 election, referring to white supremacists as "very fine people," attempting to overturn the results of a free and fair election, and expressing "love" for an insurrectionist mob that tried to enact his wishes. As I examine more closely in Chapter 4, Trump was elected despite revelations of a 2005 video in which the president boasted that celebrities like himself have free reign to sexually violate women, including "grab[bing] them by the p****." Trump did not invent transgressive white masculinity, but his presidency did evince a structural transformation in public discourse that manifests in a disdain for "the system," social conventions, and taboos against explicit indulgence in racism, misogyny, and violence.[46] For those who desired a reprieve from seemingly oppressive rules and conventions, or at the very least to renegotiate the rules of political engagement, Trump's indiscretions on the *Access Across America* bus were simply a reflection of The Donald being The Donald.[47]

In part, Trump's refusal of norms reflects a broader political transformation as well. For instance, the evolution of conservative populism hinges on an authentic conception of "the people" that lies outside the messy entailment of a rules-based democratic order. As Paul E. Johnson argues, conservative populism reflects "masculinist fear of democracy, a worry that some other force or forces might get to draw the contours of the body politic, and in so doing might also effect a change upon the American self."[48] Thus, progressive movements for racial and gender equality, even in their most modest of demands for democratic accountability, become "signs of the historical trauma of liberty foreclosed" to the white conservative subject.[49] For instance, during the Obama presidency, the conservative Tea Party movement fomented a racist campaign to characterize President Obama as an anti-white racist threat while comparing taxes and universal healthcare to chattel slavery and the ovens of Auschwitz.[50] At its core, the right's transgressions against the democratic rule of law express a desire to be free of the contending social forces that impinge the unbridled exercise of white masculine personhood.

With growing conservative animosity toward a perceived slide in the direction of progressive multiculturalism, white supremacists, men's rights activists, and far right groups organized alienated white men throughout emerging digital networks into a loose political collective that sought to bring the fringe rhetoric of white supremacy into the public realm of legitimate controversy.[51] The transgressive *alt-right* repudiated mainstream moral conservativism in favor of a more chaotic and countercultural politics in which ethnonationalism was recast as a hip and irreverent alternative to traditionalist Republicanism.[52] Their brand of quasi-ironic humor, primarily expressed through racist and misogynistic memes, was designed to deliberately offend outsiders and entertain the in-group.[53] Trump's irreverent candidacy tapped into this culture of white male aggrievement while also refusing to obey the stuffy conventions of beltway politics. Trump-era white masculinity has been marked by a willingness to openly flaunt social conventions, embrace cruelty and violence, flirt with white supremacy, and express naked hostility toward marginalized groups.[54] It is also characterized by political incorrectness, braggadocio, and garish revelry in the profane. This new chauvinism is aimed at repudiating the progressive politics of race and gender while restoring white men to their so-called rightful and natural place in the social order. The movement's apocalyptic tone is conveyed by its willingness to destroy cherished institutions and conventions; to remake society altogether rather than see their privileges and entitlements soiled by "diversity." The point, as Johnson reminds us, is that no other group should be allowed to enjoy the power to reshape the body politic.

Finally, Trump and transgressive white masculinity are ultimately symptoms of a deeper transformation in the psychical structures of U.S. public life. Hence, this book observes that there is a peculiar alignment between transgressive performances of white masculinity and the structures of enjoyment that underwrite U.S. media culture. As Joshua Gunn argues, the aberration of Trumpism actually reflects that the cultural predominance of *perversion*, a psychical structure marked by an eroding abidance of social conventions and the refusal of consensus reality, brought about changing modes of communication and spectatorship.[55] He highlights how the accelerating pace of communication in a social media age has hastened the demise of consensus reality, otherwise characterized by Slavoj Žižek as the decline of "symbolic efficiency."[56] This argument relies on Lacan's three clinical structures—neurosis, psychosis, and perversion—to illustrate how Trump's obscene behavior and disdain for norms are a reflection of cultural patterns of enjoyment reaped from persistent violation of taboos.

Take, for instance, the structures of gratification that underwrite the two predominant genres of entertainment in the early twenty-first century: reality television and social media (two forms, not incidentally, that Trump appears to have mastered).[57] Both afford a refusal of consensus reality and an ethos of cruelty, narcissism, excess, and impulsive gratification.[58] For example, Trump's reality television career on *The Apprentice* crafted a celebrity persona of a garish and politically incorrect business mogul whose success was predicated on shameless self-promotion and transgressive indulgence (from sleeping with porn stars to defecating into a gilded toilet). Prior to being banned from the platform (which Elon Musk recently undid), Trump's Twitter account offered a steady stream of disinformation and reckless falsehoods as well as braggadocio, caustic attacks, rage, and bigotry. In all, Trump's perversion is most clearly reflected in his perceived mastery of this transgressive media ecology: he knows it is wrong but does it anyway.

Gunn's study in political perversity illustrates how transformations in mediated forms paved the way for new forms of white masculine depravity to operate as a spectacle. Transgressive white masculinity enters a new media culture that is already organized by the enjoyment of depravity. In other words, new surveillance regimes plug white masculine depravity into the cultural circuits in which audiences are acclimated to observing obscene behavior under the assumption that it domesticates and polices such behaviors. Thus, this book makes an argument about the structural affinity between transgressive white masculinity and the modes of spectatorship cultivated by new media forms. That is, I posit that a culture of surveillance engages in the compulsive repetition of appalling beliefs and experiences, but *not* because it gives spectators a sense of control and mastery. Rather, watching and listening to transgressions of cultural taboos help spectators stage an encounter with something forbidden, overwhelming, and incapacitating. This argument diverges from some of the conventional wisdom concerning spectatorship; namely, that screen audiences are invited to adopt a powerful male gaze that asserts sadistic control over the bodies depicted on screen.[59] A more thoroughly Lacanian view of the gaze suggests the opposite: that spectators actually seek out a *loss of control* in their elusive pursuit of *jouissance*.

Racist and Misogynistic *Jouissance*

Caught on Tape attends to the polysemic and polyvalent tensions presented by public revelations.[60] That is to say that different audiences come to these texts with different political and ideological investments as well as from diverse social locations concerning race and gender. The meaning of public revelations is not indeterminant; thus, texts enter a social field and media ecology that constrains and enables divergent yet bounded relations to these texts. One the one hand, the logics of spectatorship invite progressive audiences to conflate witnessing and disseminating hateful and discriminatory speech with anti-racism and anti-sexism. In this way, the logics of spectatorship can immobilize and disempower audiences that are dependent on the next transgression to realize the promise of democracy. On the other hand, for those interested in renegotiating the rules of public decorum, obscene transgressions relieve them of the burdens of propriety and promise an encounter with something forbidden.

Another piece of this puzzle concerns how postracial and postfeminist ideals contain the range of available interpretations for racist and sexist incidents. In this context, public revelations offer both audiences an opportunity to disavow such transgressions as aberrations. In a putatively postracial and postfeminist culture, there is virtual prohibition against hate speech but also any discourse that acknowledges the structural and systematic nature of race and gender oppression.[61] Whereas postracial rhetoric insists on the pastness of racism and the obsolescence of race,[62] postfeminist rhetoric celebrates women's accomplishments devoid of any analysis of patriarchy, sexism, heterosexism, or misogyny.[63] If racial and gender oppression rear their ugly head, it is only due to aberrant individuals rather than structural factors. As Eric King Watts argues, postracialism conflates the elimination of racial signifiers from public life with the elimination of racism.[64] But because race is synonymous with negative difference, the persistence of race "registers a recurring traumatic condition triggered by ruptures or fractures in what Lauren Berlant calls the 'sovereign sensorium' of a society, felt as threats to the imaginary and symbolic status of masculine whiteness."[65]

In light of bold declarations concerning the end of race and gender oppression, postracial and postfeminist ideologies must contend with their sudden reappearance in public. After all, such myths do not only serve overt racists and chauvinists but also progressive multicultural liberals who believe in the concept of equality but are perhaps unwilling to recognize the need for systemic social change.[66] Insofar as postracial and postfeminist discourse confuses the absence of difference with the absence of discriminatory attitudes and practices, each creates the conditions for the return of the repressed. As a result of our incapacity to adequately address racism and misogyny, its sudden reemergence in a monstrous form entails a patterned response in which we either quickly scapegoat the obscene individual and attempt to exile them from public life or assimilate the violation by explaining away its power or redirecting criticism at the offended for enforcing stifling rules on public discourse. In either case, the underlying structure of racism and misogyny remains undisturbed.

Of the many and varied ways these texts might position spectators, this book is preeminently concerned with the peculiar affect of *jouissance*. What does it mean to say that public revelations teach spectators to *enjoy* racism and misogyny? Here, I draw from psychoanalytical theory to help explain the kind of perverse gratifications that subjects reap from painful and traumatizing experiences. For Lacan, *jouissance* names an excess of gratification that lies beyond Freud's pleasure principle, something a subject encounters in their attempts to transgress the prohibitions and rules introduced by language. *Jouissance* is precisely what is foreclosed and forbidden from a subject when they transition from being a bundle of nerves and cells in their infancy into an individuated and seemingly coherent ego-image that has the capacity to differentiate itself from others—its primary caregivers specifically—and live by the rules of consensus reality. Lacan posits that the introduction of the signifier (i.e., the acquisition of language) cuts off subjects from the kind of instantaneous and complete gratification they experienced as an infant. Drawing from Freud's Oedipus complex and related theories of sexual difference, Lacan observes that we can more appropriately read the paternal figure's interdiction into the mother–child dyad and his threat of castration as the function of the signifier.[67] As Gunn explains, "[U]nderstood symbolically, the father's prohibition of the infant's romantic love for the mother actually represents the demand that the child become a social subject and civic being."[68] The paternal signifier castrates insofar as the introduction of language forces the newly formed subject to give up access to unmediated and forbidden gratification. The signifier installs social reality and compels subjects to comport their desires with a Symbolic realm that is alien and full of other people's desires.[69]

Despite its foreclosure, subjects still compulsively repeat painful experiences in an attempt to repossess the *jouissance* robbed from them by the signifier. Freud observed that subjects endlessly repeat past behaviors and restage difficult experiences in an attempt to bind and assert mastery over traumatic affects.[70] He posed the existence of an instinct (which later psychoanalytical theorist reformulated as a "drive") independent of the libido that prepared subjects to return to the nothingness from which they came. Though it can manifest as self-destruction or aggression, the death drive is not so much a desire for death as much as it is a compulsion to recover a sense of wholeness or ultimate gratification that preceded the subject.

The Lacanian notion of *jouissance* approaches the death drive as a substitute for the loss of unicity—a kind of absence or "lack" that compels subjects to desire.[71] The death drive is an unconscious impulse to stage an encounter with "the lost object," or what Lacan refers to as *objet petit a*. Todd McGowan characterizes *objet petit a* as an object that only exists insofar as it lost, which simply means we might imagine that we were once complete in our uninterrupted experience with *jouissance*, but it was something we never actually experienced (nor would it be a good thing to exist in such a state).[72] In cultural terms, the death drive helps account for gratifications that are beyond pleasure though ultimately unattainable—a place where we relive and build attachments to traumatic experiences. In our minor transgressions against the reality engendered by language, we stage an encounter with something mysterious that surpasses our grasp.

What, then, is *obscene* enjoyment? I use the term *obscene* to denote an excessive preoccupation or revelry in depraved transgressions that reap ruinous gratification; a pursuit of nearly lethal *jouissance* that tears at the very fabric of taken-for-granted rules and norms. I mean neither the colloquial nor legal definition of obscenity as speech or representations that appeal primarily to one's prurient interests and lack any scientific, literary, artistic, or political value.[73] Instead, I wish to distinguish a kind of *jouissance* that is repulsive and abhorrent—not simply because it offends etiquette, decorum, and virtue—but because it is an insurrection against conventions and meaning itself. As George Bataille writes, "[O]bscenity is our name for the uneasiness which upsets the physical state associated with self-possession, with the possession of a recognized and stable individuality."[74] In other words, obscenity might be more fittingly described as that which unseats the lawful neurotic's grasp on reality and selfhood. Obscene enjoyment is experienced as an assault on reality because excessive transgressions thumb their nose at the very law that was instituted by the paternal signifier. As Terry Eagleton writes, with obscene enjoyment "there is a twisted sort of satisfaction in being freed from the burden of meaningfulness."[75] Obscene enjoyment dispossesses the lawful subject of their capacity to call on cultural norms and prohibitions to stabilize social reality.

Consider, for example, when *Fox News* aired two segments of *Tucker Carlson Tonight* concerning two separate white terrorist attacks: one on a Christchurch mosque and the other at an El Paso Walmart. Rather than unequivocally renounce the racist-motivated mass murder, Carlson snickered that each of the shooter's manifestos made a few good points about white people being "replaced" by racial minorities. Dog whistles and racist con-spiracy theories are, to be sure, not beyond the pale of conservative media; however, espousing overt white supremacist and pro-genocide talking points on a nationally television broadcast without censure was so jolting, profane, and incomprehensible there is hardly a moral sanction one can summon in response. Such is not a routine or minor transgression, but a contemp-tuous, menacing smirk at our taken-for-granted sense of reality and human decency. This is an example of unsublimated racism that no longer hides behind the law to evade accountability. Carlson entertained forbidden and destructive ideas for the sake of destabilizing disapproving liberal moralists. Eagleton characterizes such extreme transgressions as the "ultimate case of *jouissance*," a virtual hell whose inhabitants "would not wish for a moment to be snatched from them. For it is not only what gives them an edge over cred-ulous idealists of every stripe; it is also misery that assures them that they still exist."[76]

Obscene enjoyment is also tied to the act of spectatorship, meaning that there is an audience dynamic that is constituted in and through the observ-ance of excessive transgression. Specifically, the notion that public revelations automatically empower the democratic subject is what guarantees an audi-ence for obscene performances. If revelation is a democratically constitu-tive act, the fundamental role of rhetoric in civic culture is to disclose and witness.[77] And, furthermore, if the democratic subject is indeed an exhib-itor and spectator, then we can expect that hegemonic "ways of seeing" and "listening" to shape how subjects are invited to relate to the obscene.[78] For instance, Laura Mulvey theorized that cinematic spectators are courted to identify with a controlling masculine gaze that consummates fantasies of power over women's bodies on screen.[79] Yet, if mastery and control were to be fulfilled, there would be no desire to perpetually reveal more secrets— the very thing that sustains democracy as an *aim* always perpetually around the bend.

Democratic scopophilia is a term I use throughout this book to denote the misguided assumption that surveillance (looking and listening) automat-ically empowers the democratic subject and engenders a sense of mastery over cultural transgressions. In actuality, watching and eavesdropping can be sought out to experience a *loss of control* in that the spectator submits them-self to an encounter with something intrusive and *verboten*. In the language of psychoanalysis, the spectator is introduced to a traumatic encounter with the Real, or what Lacan describes as that which is ineffable and escapes the grasp of signification. Stultify irruptions of hate speech are sometimes incomprehensible and resist binding, integration, or assimilation. Lacanian-influenced film theorists make a similar point about the gaze unseating the spectator's sense of mastery in revealing their sheer inability to look at a safe distance. As McGowan observes, "[T]he gaze is not the look of the subject at the object, but the point at which the object looks back. The gaze thus involves the spectator in the image, disrupting her/his ability to remain all-perceiving and unperceived in the cinema."[80] The spectator is actually invited to experience a loss of control, an encounter that reveals their inability to wield the gaze with agency and omniscience.

As such, it is in the *failure* of mastery that the spectator encounters as lack or absence where the mystery of *jouissance* is located in the Other and is thus able to sustain rather than satiate desire. Similarly, spectatorship introduces the subject to a surplus or excess, located in the field of the Other, that circumvents the homeostatic control of the ego and is, thus, at odds with a controlling and pleasurable gaze. For example, the television sitcom *Mythic Quest*, a show that satirizes the video game industry, featured a stand-alone episode about a couple that invents a video game called *Dark Quiet Death*. The game seems counterintuitive at first as the protagonist can never actually vanquish the monsters in the game, only keep them at bay with light. The game's incredible success was originally predicated on the player's failure of mastery, the mystery sustained by the protagonist's limited field of vision, and their inability to achieve ultimate fulfillment. The fictional game simply makes explicit the unconscious desire of spectators to thwart their own fulfillment—the notion that desire seeks only to sustain desire. This is precisely the kind of enjoyment garnered from recursive viewing of obscene videos and recordings: it introduces a stumbling block to the fulfillment of democratic fantasies; hence, the need to perpetually reveal more.

Rhetoric, Trope, and the Available Means of *Perception*

Though borrowing from a variety of intellectual fields, this book primarily draws from the discipline of rhetoric to theorize the symbolic and imaginary registers of public secrets and mediated gossip. Given the somewhat unconventional nature of the texts I examine, the above heading is a deliberate misappropriation of Aristotle's definition of rhetoric as "the faculty of observing in any given case the available means of persuasion."[81] Given this definition, scholarship indebted to the Greco-Roman tradition has naturally focused on discrete forms of public oratory, political speeches, and other modes of civic address. Such work was perhaps best suited for a time in which oratory and literature were the predominant media for civic engagement, public deliberation, and even popular entertainment. Since the so-called critical turn in the academy, it is easy to find this definition of rhetoric wanting insofar as it overlooks transformations in mediums of communication but also because it codifies the norms of a predominantly white male bourgeois class that has long enjoyed taken-for-granted access to public life.[82] Excluded were the vernacular texts, quotidian practices, and experiences of marginalized populations.[83] Moreover, the traditional definition of rhetoric was at odds with the ways in which publics were increasingly being addressed, including film, television, photography, the Internet, mobile phones, and so forth. One of Michael Calvin McGee's most important interventions in rhetorical studies was to illustrate that the fragmentation of postmodern culture meant that there were few if any discrete texts widely engaged by the same public.[84] The role of the rhetorical critic, then, is to assemble a text worthy of criticism out of the fragments and snippets of messages that form patterns and thus constitute our social imaginary.

With a more capacious definition, we find that rhetoric is mediated, sensory, visual, auditory, embodied, performative, and quotidian. The *available means of perception* simply foregrounds a contemporary conception of rhetoric in which the influence and suasory force, asserted by new media, play a primary role. I suggest that audiences or publics are trained and socialized how to make sense of revelations of obscene behavior by the media forms they encounter and use daily.[85] Rhetoric, then, is the effect of fragmented though patterned forms of discourse, shaped by mediated forms that allow and disallow certain kinds of content to circulate, and circumscribe how audiences are invited to relate to and interpret content. While I do not make assertions about how specific audiences interpret texts, a rhetorical perspective on audience starts with the notion that ideal or imagined audiences are constructed from within texts themselves. In response to the influence of positivism and social science on the humanities, Edwin Black argued that it was in the invitational gesture of rhetoric where we find the audience, a "second persona" or implied "you" sought out or hailed by a text.[86] Thus, critics can make judgments concerning audience by discerning how a text offers cues as to what it would have us do or become.

But there still remains a tendency within rhetorical studies to reify publicness as a vaunted and separate space of discursive activity, leading to the de facto relegation of the private or personal sphere. As this book suggests, in a surveillance culture, private matters are a perennial public concern chiefly because any speech act or deed performed in private can make its way to a public. I contend that the transformations in mediated forms invite us to consider what counts as rhetoric and/or public address when audiences are hailed by a deluge of private transgressions. In their landmark essay "Sex in Public," Lauren Berlant and Michael Warner begin with a fitting provocation on this point: "There is nothing more public than privacy."[87] Although their primary concern was how heterosexuality cloaks its desires to legislate queer sex and intimacy out of public existence, their claim rings true in another sense. That is, in much the same ways that heteronormative publics wield privacy to banish what they perceive as threatening, they also cannot help broadcasting their own private transgressions and misfortunes—and they certainly have the means to do so with regularity. As Berlant and Warner observe,

> Every day, in many countries now, people testify to their failure to sustain or be sustained by institutions of privacy on talk shows, in scandal journalism, even in the ordinary course of mainstream journalism addressed to middlebrow culture. We can learn a lot from these stories of love plots that have gone astray: about the ways quotidian violence is linked to complex pressures from money, racism, histories of sexual violence, cross-generational tensions. We can learn a lot from listening to the increasing demands on love to deliver the good life it promises. And we can learn from the extremely punitive responses that tend to emerge when people seem not to suffer enough for their transgressions and failures.[88]

Perhaps it behooves critics to listen to what the private realm is trying to tell us about our public commitments. This passage is striking (not to mention prescient) for its emphasis on the civic lessons offered by a culture of private disclosures; that such incidents make implicit arguments about popular ideologies and social structures. The publicity of private mishaps shapes how publics are invited to think about issues of public concern. Such disclosures may mystify and obscure as much as they reveal, meaning that they assert public influence but by highlighting certain aspects of reality while lowlighting others.[89]

As the controversies explored within illustrate, scandal mongering is perhaps the predominant language of contemporary U.S. media culture. As Laura Kipnis observes, "[W]e need [scandals] as much [as] they need us." Scandals are "free public theater" wherein "the curtain opens on a bizarre private world of breached taboos, chaos, and misjudgment; through some brew of inadvertency or compulsion or recklessness, an unspeakable blunder is brought to light. And who's the audience for these performances? All the rest of us: commenting on the action like a Greek chorus, dissecting motives like amateur psychoanalysts, maybe nervously pondering our own susceptibilities to life-wrecking inchoateness."[90] Public scandals invite audiences to ponder the messiness and cruelty of libidinal desires, the embarrassment of secrets, and the perverse pleasure of taking part in the spectacle. To quote Black again, "[O]ne who conducts an exposé, who seeks disclosure of secrets in the belief that such exposure will work to the detriment of whatever is revealed—that the secret, which is simultaneously concealed because it is evil and evil because it is concealed, will shrivel in the luminosity of revelation."[91] In other words, disclosure is guided by the erroneous assumption that publicity is a pure space of morality, where illuminations will yield critical and self-reflexive judgments of the good. What, then, would revelations have us do or become?

To address this question, psychoanalysis offers a wealth of resources to make sense of the patterns of the psyche that manifest in broader cultural patterns; patterns of discourse and spectatorship that germinated from the mental apparatus yet do not remain closed within the interiority of any individual subject. As Alenka Zupančič argues, "[T]he object of psychoanalysis is . . . where the biological or somatic is *already* mental or cultural and where, at the same time, culture springs from the very impasse of the somatic functions which it tries to resolve (yet, in doing so, it creates new ones)."[92] In the realm of cultural theory, psychoanalysis is concerned neither with finding solutions to individual pathologies nor offering amateur clinical diagnosis. Instead, psychoanalysis pertains to how subjects are "inscribed, from the very outset, into the socio-symbolic field that Lacan calls 'the Other.'"[93] One of Lacan's most important rhetorical insights concerns the role of language in the production of individuated subjects. Because we are born into a system of language that is alienating, incapable of adequately translating affects, and filled with other people's desire, it is the exterior terrain of the Symbolic where subjects belabor and feign coherence. Calum Lister Matheson observes that Lacan's biggest innovation is the "transformation of the unconscious from a hidden interiority within the subject to a rhetorically mediated field that functions as the necessary condition for speech."[94] Psychoanalysis suggests that signifiers speak through subjects, which means that individual cases directly pertain to the kind of cultural meanings and social formations that are made durable by the habitual pairing of signifiers with referents.

Psychoanalysis is particularly illustrative on the rhetorical function of *trope*, or the symbolic pathways by which signifiers become attached to arbitrary meanings. Racism and misogyny are tropological in that subjective markers of race and gender such as physiology, phenotypes, and anatomy are habitually assigned and invested with arbitrary meaning.[95] Christian Lundberg argues that because rhetoric takes place under conditions of "failed unicity" in which there is neither automatic nor necessary correlation between signifiers, representations, and the objects to which they refer, tropes form the basis of intersubjective communication.[96] It is precisely because of this contingency that we must "feign unicity," or act as if these connections between signifiers are coherent and durable even though they are the product of accident and contingency. It is feigned unicity that anchors the subject in reality, which itself is made up of imagined relationships and investments in the connections between signifiers, representations, and referents. Because language cannot offer metaphysical guarantees, subjects must "labor" and "invest" in the arbitrary and accidental connections between signifiers. Thus, Lundberg suggests that Lacan's most significant contribution to rhetorical studies lies in the concept of *trope*.

Trope denotes a linguistic turn toward something that directs the relationship between signifier and signified. While tropes have formal qualities, their effect is generated through the power of ritual and repetition that generates affective investment in subjects who use them. Trope, then, is the effect of failed unicity where subjects must labor to forge and maintain connections between signifiers (without being overdetermined by structure as the relation between signifiers is not natural or determined in advance). Lundberg offers an "economic" approach to trope, insofar as tropes differentiate, connect, and assemble signifiers into chains of equivalence. The labor of trope—of belaboring that signifiers have durable meanings—is what enchants signifiers with meaning (meanings that subjects invest in to anchor themselves to reality).

The general working of trope as a function of language need not stop critics from analyzing specific economies of tropes. Lundberg notes there are specific economies or "discrete configurations of tropes that individuals and groups take up in assuming public identitarian commitments. The specific economy names the space where subjects invest in texts and narratives about their relation to other subjects, where public discourses circulate, and where a subject takes on specific imagined modes of relation to others."[97] It is therefore possible to make sense of the particular and historic modulations of symbols and forms. Barbara Biesecker finds that this is precisely the function of *rhetoric*, or what she calls "a technology of (re)subjectivation whose constitutive but conjunctural effects contribute to the consolidation and stabilization of particular epistemological and political regimes."[98] The racist and misogynist tropes examined throughout this project do rhetorical work within the Symbolic to make oppressive social formations durable by forging arbitrary though historically repetitive associations between difference and inferiority. For example, racist tropes that assert people of color's connection to criminality, animality, and hypersexuality provide rhetorical scaffolding for white supremacy by transforming meaningless physical attributes into signs of inferiority and threatening difference. Similarly, misogynistic tropes that affirm women's welcomeness of powerful men's sexual advances belie a sex/gender system underwritten by masculine dominance and sexual violence. Thus, I examine the racist and misogynistic tropes that organize obscene texts, attending to how they sustain particular investments in white supremacy and patriarchy despite the fact that they are held up as exemplars of unacceptable speech and behavior.

What Is to Come

To be sure, many rhetoric scholars have turned to psychoanalysis to explain the effect of the unconscious on public life,[99] the affective charge of rhetorical demands,[100] the cultural politics of suffering,[101] the rhetorical function of genres,[102] manifestations of cultural psychosis,[103] anxiety,[104] apocalyptic rhetoric,[105] the imaginary function of archetypes,[106] and political subjectivity in late modernity.[107] Building on this well-established mode of rhetorical criticism and theorization, this book's contribution concerns how new media's emphasis on *revelation* generates perverse public attachments to the tropological economy of hate speech. Ultimately, this book shows how the imperative to reveal secret racism and misogyny becomes, in Atilla Hallsby's words, "its own form of self-defeating enjoyment."[108] The revelation presupposes the secret as something hidden; however, racism and misogyny might best be understood as phenomena that hide in plain sight: they do not disguise their operation as much as publics are invited to look and listen absent comprehension of precisely how oppressive social structures operate. Thus, this book shows how revelations are their own form of concealment that render racism and misogyny more difficult to address.

In the chapters to come, I explore a series of case studies in obscene *jouissance* that evince how white supremacy and misogyny organize U.S. public life. Chapter 1 begins with an examination of a series of racist celebrity tirades by actor Mel Gibson, comedian Michael Richards, and WWE Wrestling and reality television star Hulk Hogan. I argue that these three racist events restage the primal scene of U.S. colonialism, or the racist psychosexual dynamics of the nation's origins. Rather than unmask and indict overt racism, the wide circulation of such outbursts does the work of postracial culture by staging an encounter with lack but with significant distance between *hearing* and *understanding* of the primal scene of U.S. racism.

Chapter 2 continues to explore the rhetorical unconscious of white supremacy by situating racist disclosures within the confines of a symbolic economy inherited from the history of chattel slavery. This chapter examines leaked audio of phone conversations between NBA team owner Donald Sterling and his girlfriend V. Stiviano. In conversations between the two, Sterling admonishes Stiviano for consorting with Black friends and acquaintances in public, begging her to keep her associations with Black people private. The tapes illustrate how whiteness rhetorically manages its anxiety over boundary violations within racial capitalism—between the labor of people of color and leisure of white people. Chapter 3 explores the diffusion of obscene enjoyment into everyday life by examining the scaling down of public scandal in "racist freak out" videos on YouTube.com. The racist freak out video (otherwise labeled as "racist rant" or "racist tirade" videos) is a genre of viral video, captured by smartphone technology, that features ordinary white people expressing racist rage in public: harassing people of color, yelling racial epithets, and even threatening violence. The ubiquity of such videos suggests that beneath the surface of postracial culture is a seething yet sometimes unacknowledged rage lurking within the white imaginary. Although the abundance of such videos helps document the extent to which racism remains lodged in the white psyche, this chapter argues that racist freak out videos circulate as part of a libidinal economy that pathologizes and individualizes racism, thus obscuring the structural and systemic nature of white supremacy.

Chapter 4 examines the infamous *Access Hollywood* tape as a key moment in the rearticulation of white masculinity around a refusal of sexual prohibitions and moral authority. Reading the tape through Freud's parable of the primal horde in *Totem and Taboo*, I argue that Trump introduced traumatic paralysis into the body politic by announcing the gross refiguration of white masculinity as beyond reproach, its function merged and conflated with the paternal signifier. The tape offers a theory of masculine power that is organized around what Gayle Rubin termed the "traffic in women."[109] Finally, I conclude by illustrating what it would entail for us to, in Žižek's words "traverse the fantasy" of postracial and postfeminist culture to bring about a productive reckoning with the horrors, fissures, and failures of the Symbolic—to cease situating that the Other possesses *objet petit a* and to transform white masculinity's relationship to the death drive.[110] In the Epilogue, I consider the implications of calling back the law of the paternal signifier in relation to the Other's enjoyment. Part of the problem with prescribing political alternatives is that prohibition is the ultimate source of enjoyment for the transgressor. I suggest that one healthy route is to create space for indifference to the Other's enjoyment—not so much a matter of ignoring the law as much as it is a refusal to look so as to change our psychical orientation toward the death drive. Between 24-hour news, social media platforms, and reality television, contemporary media culture suffocates spectators with a ceaseless stream of the Other's enjoyment. New forms of prohibition are perhaps less constructive than detaching from narcissistic and self-annihilating patterns of the psyche. I ask, then, what would accountability look like when it is detached from the sovereignty of the death drive and white masculinity?

Why This Book?

Why do we need another sustained meditation on the rhetoric of obscene white masculinity? What is to be gained by paying *more* attention to white men? One reason that I persist in this endeavor is that it is tempting to believe that white masculinity is uncomplicated, straightforward, or simply an absence of racial, gender, or sexual identity. Indeed, white masculinity has often operated from a space of invisibility and benefited from a presumption of universal humanness, even as it increasingly commands our attention through spectacle. The history and identity of white men are rarely named as particularity. In other words, there is no history of white men, there is simply history.[111] As I have argued elsewhere, when white men do take up identity frames, they frequently do so to articulate victimhood, reverse discrimination, and aggrievement.[112] Richard Dyer dreaded the possibility that white scholars might see the call to study whiteness as an excuse for simply dropping any pretense of objectivity and neutrality.

Or, alternatively, white scholars might lacerate themselves with unproductive guilt. In much the same way the Dyer's project has been to make whiteness "strange," my goal is to pay white masculinity the kind of scholarly attention that pins down its particularity.[113]

Thus, one of the primary purposes of this book is to destabilize the false equivalence between white masculinity and universal humanness. White masculinity has long covered its tracks, so to speak, by subjecting women, people of color, indigenous people, and queer people to systems of classification that deprive humanity to anyone other than bourgeois white men.[114] María Lugones observes that such classifications constitute a "process of active reduction of people, the dehumanization that fits them for the classification, the process of subjectification, the attempts to turn the colonized into less than human beings."[115] In addition to naked brutality, colonization and slavery inflicted particularity, subjection, and symbolic violence onto raced and gendered Others, all the while furnishing theories of possessive individualism that imbued white masculinity with its own ontological if not spiritual unicity.[116] It is for this reason that Fred Moten surmised that "to be figured as the exemplary human—and as the very opening through which access to the human is given—is perhaps the greatest index of racism."[117] This book understands obscene enjoyment as white masculinity's response, but not necessarily a conscious one, to not only demands for transparency and accountability but also to those who question its colorless exemplification of the category of human.

My purpose in engaging in critical inquiry herein is to provide space, or rather distance, from the suffocating presence of the Other's enjoyment. Here, I take inspiration from Matthew Houdek and Ersula Ore, who have argued that whiteness is suffocating—both literally stealing breath from the bodies of persons of color but also in a metaphoric sense of stifling opportunities to rethink how we can survive and thrive together. They argue that the need for building "breathable futures" has "renewed urgency against the backdrop of COVID-19 and the suffocating forces of state and settler violence it revealed, exacerbated, or rearticulated."[118] In extending their metaphor, I suggest that this book demonstrates that the Other's enjoyment is suffocating—the oxygen needed for the life blood of a healthy society is sucked out of the cultural atmosphere by these figures of obscenity and our repetitive encounters with their hate speech. Creating critical distance from the Other's enjoyment entails traversing the fantasies that orbit around obscene enjoyment and give us breathing room for healthier and more self-reflexive alternatives to emerge.

1

Leaked Celebrity Tirades and the Primal Scene of Racism

In the summer of 2010, the gossip website RadarOnline posted leaked audio of phone conversations between actor Mel Gibson and his romantic partner, singer-songwriter Oksana Grigorieva. The salacious celebrity tattler boasted, "Mel Gibson's INSANE Racist, Screaming Rants EXPOSED!"[1] In the midst of a bitter 2006 custody battle over their daughter, the tapes captured Gibson during an obscene fit of rage. A growling, heavy-breathing, and incoherent Gibson violently excoriated Grigorieva, bellowing all manner of offensive and degrading racist and misogynistic insults. Multiple times he threatened to come over and "burn the goddamn house down," but not before she would "blow [him] first." In a crescendo of racist and sexual violence, Gibson exclaimed: "You go out in public, and it's a fucking embarrassment to me. You look like a fucking bitch in heat, and if you get raped by a pack of [expletive], it'll be your fault. All right? Because you provoked it." Although Gibson's racism, anti-Semitism, misogyny, and homophobia are not well-kept Hollywood secrets, his indulgence in racist rape fantasies exemplifies the worst compulsions of fragile white masculinity and summons a long history of race and gender violence that traces back to the nation's colonialist foundations. The tapes are now part of an ever-growing public archive of hate—made up of threats, taunts, insults, and sexist and racist tropes that serve as traumatic reminders to people of color that their humanity is, at best, provisional. Although such revelations undoubtably damaged Gibson's career, he continues to produce films distributed by major studios, including Lionsgate.[2] Even as his films (*Passion of the Christ*, *Apocalypto*) also receive blistering criticism for their racist and anti-Semitic content, it is clear that a combination of talent, fame, and white privilege tends to thwart efforts to hold celebrities accountable.[3]

Although Gibson's outburst was shocking, it was not entirely out of character. Straightforward as his transgressions may seem, the fact that his comments are preserved in perpetuity on a grainy tape recording makes his

Caught on Tape. Casey Ryan Kelly, Oxford University Press. © Oxford University Press 2023.
DOI: 10.1093/oso/9780197677865.003.0002

obscene rant all the more complicated. For instance, it is noteworthy that each person is invisible to listeners; however, the tape enables spectators to imagine a clash of embodied vocal identities: one calm and confounded, the other erratic and malevolent. The ecstatic voice heard on these tapes departs from the family-friendly vocal tone of Rocky in *Chicken Run* (2000) and John Smith in *Pocahontas* (1995)—both voiced by Gibson. At the same time, his on-screen appearances provide listeners with a visual reference point to imagine his body seething with anger as he has so many times before in films such as *Braveheart* and throughout the *Lethal Weapon* franchise (not to mention his likeness parodied on *South Park*). This time, his corpus generates the discordant excess of bodily and symbolic violence. The event conjures *a scene*, a hauntingly familiar tableaux of sexual and racial melodrama. Disconnected from his body, Gibson's voice stands as an emissary of white male power structures. As Amanda Nell Edgar writes, "[W]hite supremacy, misogyny, homophobia, and other oppressive systems imprint themselves onto the voice."[4] In this regard, Gibson's spectacular tirade is shocking yet strangely familiar. Such poisonous words, delivered with malice, have been uttered by domestic abusers, rapists, stalkers, sexual harassers, and sociopaths long before him and in an endless number of permutations. As Claire Sisco King and Joshua Gunn have suggested, the implications of this particular tantrum, but also others like it, stretch "across screens and scenes of everyday life, a point made plain by Gibson's (seemingly unscripted) hate speech."[5] Gibson's rant illustrates additional registers of obscene enjoyment, namely in his use of tropes that call forth scenes of sexual and racial trauma as part and parcel of the securitization of white masculinity.

The much broader concern of this chapter is whether such highly publicized exposure and shaming of obscene behavior thwart white masculine violence and afford protection and comfort to the victims. In contrast to other efforts to document systemic racism and sexism, the logics of *exposure* demand that we orient a progressive politic around a series of *terrible objects*, relics of oppressive discourse, epithets, and tropes that we must perpetually confront and overcome so that they may be rendered anachronisms and aberrations. Doing so affords us spatial and temporal distance from the scene of the original utterance while presenting what appears to be a narrative arc of progress—even where material reality might suggest otherwise (after all, Gibson is still making films and has an estimated net worth of $425 million). Although counterhegemonic re-appropriations illustrate how hate speech is not inexorably tethered to the original scene of utterance,[6] the irony of this unmasking is that it requires a continual restaging of a violent scene as a precondition for social progress. Albeit in a new and critical context, the democratic subject must return to the original sin of racism and misogyny to bear witness to its traumatic undoing of the self and, in the process, dispel its power. John Durham Peters characterizes this approach to hate speech as a form of "homeopathic machismo," an exercise in the refinement of liberal civic temperament through the "the daily imbibing of poisons in small doses so that large drafts will not hurt."[7] Exposure is entangled in the tethers of melancholia wherein one must continually relive without adequately mourning past traumas—a process that mirrors the death drive's compulsive repetition.[8] In short, it is the overcoming that matters. As Robin James contends, rhetorics of resilience engender melancholic investments in the transformational power of overcoming past damage—that pain, loss, and strife are catalysts for self-empowerment and improvement.[9] These terrible objects, then, must be recycled and incorporated into the body politic as a collective reexperience of original trauma, a substitute for the (national) lost object.[10]

This chapter concentrates on how the ever-growing number of racist tirades becomes subject to a kind of double movement. On the one hand, this archive creates narrative distance between the scene of hate and its overcoming—a move fundamental to the fantasy of progress. On the other hand, because trauma predicates the transformation of overcoming, it must therefore be reexperienced not as something that happen*ed* in the past but also as something happen*ing* in the present. In postracial culture, racism (a threat to people of color) is something that happened in the past, whereas race (a threat to white people) is a threat that is happening in the present. This chapter addresses shared serial encounters with powerful public figures, household names, and beloved celebrities within the context of a postracial culture. To be sure, there is no shortage of secret recordings of racist tirades by white Hollywood celebrities. Here, I will attend to three highly publicized yet powerfully resonate celebrity outbursts captured on tape: those of Mel Gibson, actor and comedian Michael Richards, and WWE wrestler and reality television star Hulk Hogan (Terry Bollea). In 2006, *Seinfeld* co-star Michael Richards erupted during an onstage performance at *The Comedy Store* in Los Angeles. When challenged by a heckler, Richards threatened that "fifty years ago we'd have you upside down with a fucking fork up your ass!"[11] He then proceeded with a barrage of racial epithets I will not reproduce here.[12] In another notable incident six years later, the now defunct celebrity gossip website Gawker released a sex tape of Hulk Hogan and Heather Clem in which Hogan complained about his daughter Brooke dating Black men. He was recorded saying, "I'd rather if she was going to fuck some [expletive]. . . . I'd rather have her marry an 8-foot-tall [expletive] worth a hundred million dollars! Like a basketball player![13] Although both Richards and Hogan claimed these comments did not reflect "who they are," such irruptions evince an underlying symbolic economy of racism that from time to time breaches the placid surface of postracial culture and violently channels its venom through purportedly unknowing white subjects, many of whom seem confounded by their own words in retrospect. But in restaging an encounter with violent racism, postracial culture folds racial damage into national identity without rectifying the nation's original sin. Ultimately, race *not racism* becomes the object of scorn.

In these outbursts, racial difference appears suddenly in the form of abject bodily excess: an animalistic horde of rapists, a lynched and emasculated corpse, a monstrously gifted biological specimen. In this chapter, I argue that each of these events articulates and reproduces white anxiety about racial homogeneity and miscegenation—or the *primal scene* of U.S. colonialism. By primal scene, I refer to traumatic origins concealed by fantasies that attempt to answer the question: "Where do we come from"?[14] Freud's primal scene was something experienced (or believed to have been experienced) but only understood retroactively through fantasies.[15] Jean Laplanche and Jean-Bertrand Pontalis describe primal *fantasies* as "fantasies of origins . . . of the individual," which entail "fantasies of seduction, the origin and upsurge of sexuality; fantasies of castration, the origin of the difference between the sexes."[16] In the context of colonialism, Frantz Fanon and Homi Bhabha each understood the primal scene as a setting of violent racial and sexual desire— a scene in which colonizers systematically raped Black, indigenous, and women of color.[17] Fantasies of origins give coherence to the colonizer's identity while erasing the primal violence on which that identity was founded. As Bhabha writes, the primal scene is "not itself the object of desire but its setting, not an ascription of prior identities but their production in the syntax of the scenario of racist discourse."[18] The scene is restaged as a parallel Oedipal fantasy that conceals this original trauma by reversing the racial and sexual power dynamics. Miscegenation, then, casts men of color as the hypersexual predator who threatens white women's purity. In this scenario, white violence is, by definition, defensive. As Luz Calvo argues, "[M]iscegenation constitutes such a fantasy, the setting of inter-racial desire in a scenario that produces racialized subjects both inhibited by the constraints of purity and aroused by their transgression."[19]

The racist tropology assembled in these three exemplars constitutes *pornotropes*, or signifying practices that reduce bodies to flesh and constitute racial Others through violence.[20] Returning to the primal scene of U.S. racism (characterized by scenes of slavery, lynching, indigenous, internment, borders, and brutal policing among others) re-stages the relationship of enmity to racial Otherness wherein the existence of difference is imagined to be existential to white purity and power. The telos of such primal fantasies is the elimination of difference altogether. Thus, I argue that these three events restage the primal scene of racism, with references to miscegenation concealing the colonial violence that marked the original scene. Conjuring the threat of miscegenation enables white subjects to avoid knowledge that implicates fragile white identities in the racist violence that constituted the nation. Hence, these mediated performances are folded into postracial fantasies that shelter the white imaginary from this traumatic knowledge of racist complicity. The exposure, then, constitutes part of the process by which the original trauma is collectively repressed within the white imaginary. In the aftermath of such events, the following questions remain: Who must sacrifice themselves for the betterment of the white civic temperament? Who must withstand the brunt of obscene enjoyment for the fictions of a postracial culture? Who, in the process, is shielded from the traumatic knowledge of the nation's traumatic origins?

Miscegenation and the (Post)racist Scene

A cornerstone of the racist imaginary, the trope of miscegenation organizes the white subject's ambivalent relation to the Other through fantasies of interracial sexuality. In other words, the threat of race mixing and the "mongrelization" of white stock has always been accompanied by a powerful erotic charge—a sexual excess that marks a fundamental difference between racialized subjects.[21] The attribution of hypersexuality to people of color is, above all, a projection of white desire onto a subjugated Other whose demands are unintelligible and beyond control.[22] Legal and extralegal violence helped externalize white lack onto people of color so that it might be enjoyed. As punishment for white men's own desires, lynching projected lack onto people of color to make them physically and symbolically bear the burden of castration.[23] The threat or violation of white women's purity was and remains *casus belli* for white masculine violence against racial Others. Protective or defensive violence, however, also comes at a great cost for white women. "Good women"—chaste, pious, and moral—must show obedience and deference to white male authority to prove themselves worthy of the protections of the *cult of true womanhood.*[24] "Bad" or "fallen" women who question white men's authority or violate tradition sexual morality invite the lust of morally inferior men and therefore forfeit such protections.[25]

Patricia Hill Collins's concomitant catalogue of "controlling images" indexes the tropes and archetypes of Black femininity similarly deployed to legitimize the rape of Black women.[26] The Black jezebel was enchanted with mystical seductive powers that explained the ubiquity of mixed-race children without attributing desire or culpability to white men.[27] Women of color are cast as seductive but also castrating insofar as they threaten to emasculate white men through sexual aggression. Meanwhile, the rules of hypodescent excluded the progeny of miscegenation from the privileges of whiteness and protected fantasies of white racial purity from its own racial and sexual ambivalence.[28] But an erotic and violent white supremacy is ultimately attached to the very thing that produces white anxiety—the incomprehensibility of the Other's desire.[29] In this manner, racism is a form of obscene enjoyment. As Jared Sexton notes, "*[W]hite supremacy and antiblackness produce miscegenation* as a precious renewable resource, a necessary threat against which they are constructed, a loyal opposition, a double exposure. They rely upon miscegenation to reproduce their social relations; their relations are, in fact, this very reproduction."[30] Displacing white guilt, miscegenation discourse restages a primal scene to avoid acknowledgment and culpability for the sexual and racist violence of colonialism and slavery. The identification of white women and men of color with lack shields white men from the knowledge of their own symbolic pre-Oedipal castration. Kaja Silverman reminds us that the primal scene is uncanny because castration (a function of the signifier) occurs prior to knowledge of sexual difference.[31] The scene, then, must be restaged because racial and sexual difference not only threaten a secondary castration, but also the knowledge of white men's *a priori* castration upon entering the symbolic.[32] Rather than admit their own lack, white masculinity is constituted through a disavowal of castration by its projection onto racial and sexual Others.

Racist tirades simulate the rhetorical process of disavowal that is orchestrated to close the gap between hearing and understanding the primal scene of miscegenation. Here, the signifiers of racism are "taken hostage by fantasy" insofar as those signifiers are an articulation or rationalization for the trauma and incomprehensibility of witnessing something that one should not have to witness or experience.[33] By projecting lack onto women and people of color, racism offers a vicarious encounter with lack but in a form that shields white male subjects from knowledge of both their own castration as well as their culpability for the origins of racism. After all, the postracial fantasy is of racial transcendence without addressing the legacy of white supremacy. Thus, these tapes exist in a social context in which racist irruptions shield white audiences from the traumatic knowledge of their racist complicity. Rather than unmask and indict overt racism, the wide circulation of such outbursts does the work of postracial culture by staging an encounter with lack but with significant distance between *hearing* and *understanding*. Put differently, white audiences might hear the sexual and racial violation in Gibson's perverse growl, but understanding of the event is ultimately *screened* by the tropes of postracial culture—a culture in which race itself is a signifier that stands in the place of racism. Because racism is too evocative of a charge for most white subjects to acknowledge (knowledge of both primary and secondary castration), race takes its place as a "phantasmic screen enabling us to avoid confrontation with social antagonism."[34] Gibson, Richards, and Hogan's transgressions are all reminders of a primal scene that must be repressed or understood retroactively from the vantage point of postracial fantasy.

When a Stranger Calls

Mel Gibson's tirade presents the stock tropes of anti-miscegenation melodramas: the fallen women, the dark-skinned rapist, and the aggrieved yet virtuous white man.[35] These characters are the inverse of the original scene: the colonial agent assumes the position of victim-hero, while the subjugated takes on the role of villain or perpetrator. These neocolonial character types are ubiquitous throughout the white racial imaginary, populating political address, novels, music, television, and films.[36] An ambiguous interplay of sex and violence, Gibson's long breathy pauses, hyperventilating, heavy panting, lewd growling, and snarling are all eerily reminiscent of the perverted prank caller in horror films such as *When a Stranger Calls* (1979) and *Black Christmas* (1974). In this real-life drama, Gibson cast Grigorieva as the fallen women: immoral, dishonest, duplicitous, sexually promiscuous, and money-grubbing. It is important to consider the mythos of this character type—a gender role that bears the responsibility for the Black and indigenous men's lust as well as the white hero's controlled and discrete use of defensive violence.[37] Gibson ruminates on her immodest appearance, the spectacle of her body, and how she makes it visible for others to enjoy. In their first conversation, Gibson declares that her "fake tits" make her look like "some Vegas bitch" and "Vegas whore." He seethes, "You go around sashaying around in your tight clothes, and stuff. I won't stand for that anymore." The fallen women is fraudulent, a deceitful imitation of beauty that offends white men's sense of decorum while fomenting the savage man's lust. Much like the aesthetics of Las Vegas, Gibson presents her visage as a tantalizing yet artificial simulation of genuine attractiveness that stirs lurid impulses. She represents a kind of honeytrap—a dangerous yet irresistible form of bait that lures in morally inferior men.

Gibson declared his intellectual and moral superiority by his unwillingness to withstand her bodily excess as an enticing visual spectacle. He retraced the well-worn pathways of the dark-skinned rapist trope and the indigenous captivity narrative by making clear that there will be physical and spiritual punishment for her transgressions.[38] He exclaimed, and it bears repeating, "You look like a fucking bitch in heat, and if you get raped by a pack of [expletive], it'll be your fault. All right? Because you provoked it. You are provocatively dressed all the time, with your fake boobs, you feel you have to show off in tight outfits and tight pants (*garbled*) you can see your pussy from behind." Gibson coupled his violent racism with a dehumanizing vivisection of women into sexualized body parts. Both figures are not only reduced to their body but are also pornotroped into *flesh* that only obeys impulses. At many points in their conversations, Gibson also refers to her by a number of vulgar insults that orchestrate containment of femininity by way of a violent reduction and relegation of women to their body.[39] At the same time, both are more animalistic than human. She is "a bitch in heat," likened to a female dog whose excessive and cacophonous sexuality attracts the "pack" of wild or tribal creatures who only obey the primal laws of nature. The violent scene of interracial sexuality calls forth the white male civilizer to bring order and civilization to the violence, chaos, and amorality of nature. Gibson's racism is phobic yet also erotically charged—pontificating on the violent sexual potency of dark-skinned men and sexual receptivity of fallen white women.

At the same time, the fallen women is not simply a body, character, or object but rather a visual spectacle that is made to bear the white man's lack. Note how he suggests that she commands the gaze: she *shows off* her body, invites spectators to *look*, and *provokes* their desire. She is objectified by Gibson but only in as much as her command of the gaze brings about an encounter with sexual difference—her castration inferred by his ad nauseam repetition of misogynistic insults. In his ruminations on Grigorieva's appearance, Gibson brushes up against the gaze but without controlling it. In early feminist theories of the gaze, the cinematic apparatus was thought to offer visual pleasures to the spectator who was invited to take up a sadistic and controlling male gaze.[40] Beyond the screen and in a more Foucauldian sense of the word, the gaze also names the privilege to look, the power relations entailed by different-looking relationships, and institutional positionality alongside the disciplinary practices entailed by demands for visibility.[41] And while the audience here is auditory eavesdroppers rather than visual spectators, there is certainly a parallel auditory regime that specularizes women by another means. But in Gibson's caricature, the fallen women lacks precisely because she attempts to command the gaze. Silverman notes that men have long dissociated from the visual, instead opting to project their lack onto images of women so that they might vicariously recover the *jouissance* they renounced in the process. Even though we cannot see Grigorieva, Gibson's lexicon is vivid and visually evocative enough to conjure pornified images of women's sexual difference. For Lacan, however, the gaze is neither something the subject can control nor does the subject even seek mastery in such an encounter. Silverman's more thoroughly Lacanian approach to the cinematic apparatus takes the specularization of the womanly object as an indirect route to encounter the male subject's own lack. Gibson's words no more command the gaze than the object of the visual spectacle. His hapless indignation—along with his grunts and garbled screams—speaks to a loss of control, or the enjoyment experienced when the subject understands themself to be the object of the gaze. Eavesdroppers, then, are confronted with an auditory experience of white masculinity *out of control*, perverted and unrestrained by norms and conventions.

In more concrete terms, Gibson's tirade evinces how white masculinity projects lack onto women and men of color so that it can enjoyed in a guised and bearable form. The fact that Gibson constructs Grigorieva's lack as sexual receptivity illustrates the psychical functions of white masculine ambivalence about miscegenation; that is, the sudden appearance of sexually aggressive dark-skinned perpetrators constructs them as an object of both disgust and desire. In this erotic drama, the fallen women serves as a fetish to shield white men from their own desires for racial Others. At the same time, the interracial sexual encounter also strips white femininity of its metonymic association with purity and innocence. As such, Grigorieva comes to represent a monstrous femininity that is both lacking and castrating. Gibson repeats his belief that she is a "gold digger" with an insatiable lust for sex and material goods. For instance, he yells, "You could be a woman that supports instead of a woman that sucked off of me. And just fucking sucks me dry. And wants, and wants, *get out of this relationship if you're a good woman and you love me. I don't believe you anymore* [italics added]!" He further excoriates her:

> I need a woman! Not a fucking little girl with a fucking dysfunctional cunt. I need a fucking woman. (*panting*) I don't need medication. You need a fucking bat in the side of the head. All right? How 'bout that? You need a fucking doctor. You need a fucking brain transplant. You need a fucking, you need a fucking soul. I need medication? I need someone who treats me like a man, like a human being. With kindness, who understands what gratitude is, because I fucking bend over backwards with my balls in a knot to do it all for her and she gives me shit, like a fucking sour look or says I'm mean.

These passages illustrate how white masculinity casts its own deficiencies and absences onto the fallen woman. In turn, her lack transforms into an exigence for white men to experience "regeneration through violence," a process exemplified by his thought that a "bat in the side of the head" or a "brain transplant" would rightly punish and unburden him of her monstrous and "dysfunctional" sexuality.[42] She is an obstacle to be overcome, a test that strengthens white male fortitude, spirit, and moral resolve.

It is this foil that not only bears responsibility for his violent disposition but also protects white male subjects from awareness of their own lack. Note Gibson's violent insults are coupled with references to his humanity— something only attained through the support of a "good woman" who "supports" instead of "sucking" and "draining" his essence. White male lack is thinly disguised by his references to female castration ("dysfunctional") and mangled genitalia ("balls in a knot"). His construction of the good woman compensates for lack through a demand for feminine deference, "kindness," and "gratitude." At the same time, the fallen women's refusal of white male authority constitutes receptivity or implicit invitation to rape and defensive white masculine violence. Gibson's rape fantasy therefore serves a number of psychical needs: to be protected from knowledge of primary castration and align white men with a spirit of self-mastery and control over the primal scene.

Although Gibson's personal psychology is beyond the scope of rhetorical analysis, we can take his lewd words as an illustration of how whiteness restages the primal scene of miscegenation, but in an inverse form to facilitate a seamless disavowal of sexual and racial violence. Put another way, miscegenation discourse represses the primal scene and its mixture of eroticism and violence by constructing white women and men of color as the perpetrators of and accomplices to rape. But my broader inquiry here concerns the act of revealing such a traumatic scene and how it intervenes in the psychical structures that shape how eavesdroppers are invited to engage racism, misogyny, and discourses of miscegenation in a postracial context. That is to say, what happens when audiences are invited to reexperience the primal scene but with the power dynamics of colonialism and slavery reversed? It is doubtful that many who listened to Gibson's tirade would identify with him and take up racial and sexual violence in a spirit of regeneration. But, if we understand the primal scene as something experienced (or believed by the subject to have been experienced) twice—first, prior to knowledge of sexual difference and, second, after secondary castration—then it is in the scene's restaging within the Symbolic that generates racial consciousness in white subjects. Such understanding is filtered through postracial culture to conceal the original trauma of the primal scene.

The miscegenation threat, however, is not an aberration of the white imaginary even though it is most commonly voiced by unashamed white supremacists. If raced subjects are the barrier to a postracial future, then Gibson's rape fantasy is merely an intensification of underlying anxieties concerning the sexual impurity and racial contamination of white stock. His tirade and others like it are mechanisms by which postracial culture aligns and conflates signifiers of race and racism. In other words, the enjoyment of racism is predicated in compulsively overcoming the threat of race— returning over and over again to the scene, a perpetual game of *fort/da*.[43] Miscegenation constitutes the conditions of possibility for postracialism by enabling whites to overcome the threat of interracial sexuality. That is to say that in the process of repudiating Gibson's diatribe, we expel his racism as an aberration (the return of the repressed) at the same time as we repress the historical knowledge of eroticized racism.

Postracialism *must* conceal the primal scene of colonialism to maintain its core fiction that racial Otherness threatens to eradicate whiteness rather than the reverse. In this way, postracial culture scurries to repress its own legacy of racist sexual violence. Since understanding of the primal scene is always retroactive, postracial discourse prefigures the racist irruption as an unhomely encounter with the origins of race. Although one might genuinely repute Gibson's violent racism, they might also take up the postracial invitation to disavow the very threat of race itself. Since miscegenation is conceptualized as the very means by which race contaminates the raceless social imaginary, interracial sexuality is abject and must therefore be expelled to resolidify the borders of postracial culture. Gibson's obscenity positions race to be expelled alongside his racism in redrawing the boundaries of the normal. Understood as that which threatens the feigned association between whiteness and colorless humanity, race is rendered *abject*.[44] What this leaked audio reveals is the degree to which race incites phobic reactions (repulsion and fascination) that compel subjects to expel and disown any element or object that reminds them of their radical incoherence, mortality, or debt to the nature.[45]

The Banality of Racism

Gibson's tirade is emblematic of how white masculinity relies on racism to control and manipulate white women. Racism is also a source of enjoyment, which is to say that compulsively returning to the traumatic origins of race has become the means by which racial difference can be domesticated or cast out. Within the structures of whiteness, enjoyment is underwritten by the tropological conflation of white selfhood with universal humanness. Thus, hate speech positions whiteness as a stand-in for unicity whose rhetorical labor anchors white subjects to the Symbolic and Imaginary. Such racism underwrites the protection rackets that extort adherence to white patriarchy by evoking the racist terror of racialized masculinity run amok. The fact that his statements were uttered in the context of intimate partner violence does not limit the scope of their traumatizing effect. The consequences of racist speech are seldom isolated to persons or groups directly victimized, for it is in every utterance that an epithet summons a history of usage, rehearses through-lines, cements racial tropology, and creates precedent for future usage.[46] George Jerry Sefa Dei et al. explain that in a subject's encounters with the banality of everyday racism, "[W]e must remind ourselves that the violations of such moments speak to far more than the words being uttered; they speak also to the context, histories and positionings that they have on our bodies and minds."[47] They maintain that traumatic racist events constitute figurative erasures that organize everyday race relations even if such outbursts are uncommon. In fact, it is the "frequent and unpredictable nature of racism's traumatic intrusions" that reminds the oppressed that they are "being watched at all times" and "should always be careful—because the moment can recur at any time and in any place."[48] Thus, in the aftermath of a racist outburst, the offender may be reprimanded and forced to apologize for their transgressions (neither of which apply in Gibson's case), yet racism persists nonetheless because erratic behavior is crucial to the smooth operation of its more structural predictability. The mere potential for white fragility to be triggered spontaneously and without warning reinforces the postracial mandate to curb provocative race talk.[49] Although outbursts are often constructed as exceptions, anachronisms, or aberrations, in a postracial culture the threat of white rage, and the silence and discipline it extorts, replace the tedium of everyday overt racism as a more powerful coefficient of white supremacy. But it would be mistaken to characterize white rage as irrational or confounding; rather, it is a complement to structural racism that mobilizes the threat of racial difference, in turn, organizing collective investments in white supremacy.

White rage, then, is a rhetorical form; a violent script whose coherence is belied by its sudden appearance as erratic, improvised, and unintelligible discourse. The function of white rage is to conceal the structured organization of the white racial unconscious. White rage is directed at indigenous people and people of color because it is their very presence, their very being, that evokes the terror of being inundated and overwhelmed by what Mark Lawrence McPhail calls "negative difference."[50] White rage organizes and channels racial phobia into a discourse that can contain and disavow the origins of race—a biological and ontological terror created to give whiteness its coherence.[51] In this sense, white rage is a necessary step in disavowing the primal scene, or knowledge of how the origins of race are sutured to the birth of the sexual threat to white purity.[52]

Here, I take the case of Michael Richards as emblematic of the rhetoric of white rage and the problematic entailments of its heavy media circulation. In November 2006, former *Seinfeld* star Richards was filmed by an audience member at *The Laugh Factory* during a performance in which he verbally accosted two Black men (Kelly Doss and Frank McBride) for purportedly interrupting his comedy act. In the grainy footage, Richards appears to frenetically traverse the stage while screaming racial obscenities and violently gesticulating toward a group of unseen club patrons. The tape begins with the altercation already in progress as Richard berates a group of Black audience members for talking during the performance. In his frenzied rage, he reminds the group that the punishment for Black incivility has been, and remains, violence. As Richards stated, "That's what happens when you interrupt a white man, don't you know?" It is no coincidence that his spontaneous rage instantly conjured images of *the flesh*, which is to say that in the white racial unconscious the threat of racial difference has always been contained by force so as to reduce people of color to non-beings. Despite his improvisational excess, the encounter was already scripted for Richards: Black masculine impudence has historically been met with white redemptive and compensatory violence. Richards himself acknowledged that the hecklers had summoned a strangely familiar racism from the depths of the white racial imaginary: "Alright, you see, this shocks you, it shocks you to see what's *buried beneath* [italics added], you stupid motherfucker!" Like Gibson, Richards rehearsed the Black rape fantasy, but this time the hypersexual and arrogant *Buck* is contained through the act of lynching.[53] The primal scene of miscegenation is restaged; however, in this fantasy, it is the white subject who penetrates the Buck—now a corpse hanging "upside down with a fork up [his] ass!" References to such a lynching offer various forms of proof: proof of white supremacy's dispersal and dominance throughout the body politic[54]; proof of Black men's lesser manhood[55]; proof of white men's virility[56]; and proof that racialized masculinity is reducible to flesh.

Unlike Gibson, Richards offered an apology in which he framed his outburst as misplaced rage rather than deep-seated prejudice. Following the incident in an interview on *Late Night with David Letterman*, a sullen and disheveled Richards offered the following explanation for his behavior:

> You know, I'm a performer. I push the envelope, I work in a very uncontrolled manner onstage. I do a lot of free association, it's spontaneous, I go into character. I don't know, in view of the situation and the act going where it was going, I don't know, the rage did go all over the place. It went to everybody in the room. But you can't you know it's, I don't I know people could, blacks could feel I'm not a racist, that's what so insane about this, and yet it's

said, it comes through, it fires out of me and even now in the passion that's here as I confront myself.[57]

As many whiteness scholars have observed of racist apologia, deflection, disavowal, and minimization are all stock tropes available to deny the existence of racism and maintain the central fictions of postracialism.[58] As Richards's response illustrates, racist offenders frequently turn their violations into personal object lessons in tolerance and self-improvement. Richards never characterizes his actions as racist, preferring instead a litany of colorblind euphemisms such as "I lost my temper," "went into a rage," and said "nasty things," and engaged in "a lot of trash talk." At times, he praised a future version of himself to "get to the force field of this hostility." At other times, he spoke in the passive voice of a rage without a body, "why the rage is in any of us, why the trash takes place, whether or not it's between me and a couple of hecklers in the audience or between this country and another nation, the rage." Such tactics are part of a well-worn genre of racist apologia. As Michele Holling et al. argue, "[W]hite public figures who commit racist violations generally reproduce the harm already done in their apologetic rhetoric."[59]

Indeed, Richards's apology attempted to minimize his culpability by framing his offense as a performative misfiring of an agentless affective economy of rage, but he is incidentally accurate in characterizing himself as a conduit for racist ideology, regardless of intent. If language translates ineffable felt intensities into the Symbolic,[60] then white rage is given form by assembling arbitrary racial signifiers into patterns that anchor white subjects overwhelmed by negative difference. Richards is, of course, wrong about his own culpability for his behavior; yet, his deflections are nonetheless illustrative of how racism is embedded in the white racial unconscious. An essentialist and arbitrary conception of negative difference is entrenched in language itself, where it lurks and lies in wait. As Fanon explains, "[E]very time there is delusional conviction there is a reproduction of the self," which is to say that the sudden appearance of negative difference simultaneously gives the white subject coherence even in its most fractured and hysterical state.[61] The white subject, confused by their own sudden racist tirade, nonetheless purchases for themself a sense of selfhood in that moment, even where that imago is, to a certain extent, terrifying. Richards's phobic reaction illustrates that racist language is a standing reserve or repository of symbolic material to bolster whiteness; when confronted, it is confronted with racism difference. As such, I read Richards's tirade and its circulation as part of the shifting, spontaneous, and improvisational nature of racism that appears *precisely* so it can be disavowed as simply a defensive rage. Such outbursts are certainly precipitous, impulsive, and sudden. They are spectacular and yet, at the same time, easy to minimize even as they point to larger systems of oppression, racist epistemologies and ideologies that enforce negative difference.

What happens when psychical investments in racism suddenly breach the surface and avail themselves through public discourse? In one sense, the circulation of racist rants exposes the latent racism that resides within the white imaginary. In another sense, the irruption conceals the operation of racism from white audiences through the sheer denial of the victim's vulnerability. In other words, Richards's enactment of a symbolic lynching constitutes an imaginative restaging of the primal scene as an exigence in which to avenge *white* vulnerability. In the context of anti-Blackness, Tommy Curry explains, "[A]s with our notions of racism, and even in slavery, Black males are imagined only in terms of their confrontation with white male power, never in terms of their vulnerability to rape or sexual violence at the hands of white men and women."[62] Throughout Richards's tirade, there is no room for rage as a legitimate political response to racist violence—a fact that was perhaps not lost on the group that he verbally assaulted. A member of the group thus continually responds to his vile remarks with the direct yet understated mantra: "That's uncalled for!" and "That's not necessary!" At another point, one of the group calmly remarks, "It's not funny. That's why you're a reject, never had no shows, never had no movies, *Seinfeld*, that's it." Although the group responds with insults of its own, at one point calling him a "cracker ass motherfucker," the assaulted group never loses its control, maintaining a firm yet even tone. To Curry's point, the group's reasonable response to Richards nonetheless ossifies the social positioning of racialized masculinity as always already defined through its confrontation with whiteness. Richards characterizes the group's identity precisely in such terms when he states, "You're now brave motherfucker!" and asks, "That's how you get back at the man?"

At this point in the interaction, the group is caught between two impossible positions: to match his tone and appear to be defiant or to show civility and restraint that in a racist culture might be read as tacit subservience. In fact, Richards attempts to constrain the group's potential response by suggesting that people of color are vengeful and hold unnecessary resentment toward white people. To respond in anger to such a proposition would certainly be understandable and principled, yet this response would also align with Richards's racist caricature of the club patrons. Richards relies on racist tropology to both incite an angry response and circumscribe how other patrons might understand their response. Of course, there is no greater racist superlatives that can be summoned to bring to bear the stigmatizing and suffocating violence of white supremacy. Hate speech aims to circumscribe the target's response with the threat of punishment and by imposing a racial framework wherein back talk putatively represents the victim's inherent proclivity for violence and savagery. Speaking back might be perceived as a direct threat, therefore exposing the victim to the risk of escalatory violence. According to Richard Delgado and Jean Stefancic, bystanders also "learn and internalize these messages," thus reinforcing both conscious and unconscious racism.[63] Richards evokes racist tropes that construct an insolent form of racial difference; a defiant, aggressive, and subhuman form that does not recognize its place in the white racial hierarchy. Even as the hecklers refuse the hail, Richards's words imply the theoretical existence of abject difference in the white imaginary, even if the audience members do not typify the image.

To greater or lesser effect, Richards also prefigures racializing others as inherently predatory even as he pornotropes bodies into lifeless emasculated corpses. His references to historic lynching imaginatively restage the psychosexual dynamics of a national primal fantasy. As Ersula Ore reminds us, lynching is a violent form of symbolic action that constitutes white civic identity by making an emphatic statement about race and national belong. Lynching also acts out the primal scene of white sovereignty and racial difference.[64] As Doreen Fowler observes of lynching, "[T]he white lynch mob assumes the role of father or law, who forbids merging; the black community, who watch, terrified, in hiding, represent the observing child-witnesses; and the lynched black man performs the mother's role—like the female other, he is the racial other whose alienation and presumed castration function as the fictive grounds on which racial difference depends."[65] The rhetoric of lynching makes racial Others bear the burden of castration while it aligns white men with the paternal function of prohibition that constitutes the Symbolic. Richards takes up the position of father in this regard, dolling out punishment for the threat of miscegenation and the prospect of Blackness run amok. However, Richards also appears not simply as the father of *prohibition* but instead as *father-jouissance*, which is to say that he represents not the law but rather the transgression of cultural prohibitions against violence.

He is instead *whiteness run amok*. More importantly, Richards is a conduit for the structures of whiteness and the unconscious that exceed his figural manifestation. He is a channel for a transgressive or surplus form of racist *jouissance*.

The tape concludes with audience members leaving the performance in disgust and Richards exiting the stage. While the crowd expressed disapproval of Richards's remarks, the video suggests that the accosted group were tacitly charged with leading the confrontation. This encounter mirrors Delgado and Stefancic's observation that neoliberal proponents of tolerance and the marketplace of ideas often put the burden of anti-racist confrontation directly onto the shoulders of hate speech victims. The video's low quality and limited perspective offer few clues as to how white audience members interacted with or responded to the hecklers; however, the tape is also the only textual artifact of the event. My goal is not to reconstruct the event but instead to understand the tape as an aperture into the scene of a racist encounter, much like any other. Thus, what do we make of the widespread circulation and secondhand witnessing of this scene? The broader audience for the tape is also indirectly addressed in that they are enlisted as bystanders to a strangely familiar rhetorical situation. It is not simply the viewing of the tape that makes viewers complicit, but rather that the tape offers roles for different characters in a public racist event.

The event rehearses the banality of everyday racism and the ever-present threat of white rage that polices the body politic. Yet, the tape also conceals this banality by representing racism as spectacular and erratic, thus eliding the less visible yet profoundly structural ways in which white supremacy functions. By restaging the primal scene as an origin of white fragility, the tape obscures the degree to which whiteness depends on the threat of race and miscegenation for its underlying coherence. There is a confrontation with racism, but one in which the victims put themselves at risk as white spectators remain paralyzed and dumbfounded. In this way, the tape scripts a racist encounter where the responsibility for de-escalation resides with the victim. It is the victim who must take the brunt of racial insults in order to protect neoliberal regimes of tolerance and civic temperament. This sacrifice shields white audiences from the knowledge of their own complicity. Witnessing white masculinity out of control—the traumatic scene of lynching—camouflages how it is the rigid organization of structural racism that benefits white audiences. As Stephen L. Esquith contends, "[W]hat makes everyday bystanders complicit, more than their failure to change their behavior toward severe violence, is the benefit they derive after the fact from severe violence."[66] In this case, there is nothing in the tape to prompt the crucial question of racial culpability. Instead, the compulsive return to the scene of vicarious racial trauma transforms racism into an experience of painful and ruinous *jouissance*.

Miscegenation and the Big Other

Miscegenation is a stock trope of white supremacy. Fear (and fascination) with interracial sexuality cultivate white investments in the purity of their racial stock. Miscegenation discourse projects onto people of color an essential biological and genetic predisposition toward hypersexuality, marked by extraordinary fertility and drive along with a lack of impulse control. Sexton calls miscegenation discourse a "precious renewable resource" because it offers a moral and biological threat to white existence that, in turn, calls for legal and extralegal forms of violence to control the Other's desires.[67] But this preoccupation with bodies and sexuality also evinces a tropological economy of white sexual desire. For instance, bell hooks has argued that in the white social imaginary, the primal scene of miscegenation represents a desire "not to dominate the Other, but rather so that they can be acted upon, so that they can be changed utterly."[68] In other words, an apparently benign yearning to be seduced by the Other is part of the colonizer's journey to assuage their guilt and deflect culpability for the world of "lack and loss" wrought by colonial domination. Instead, sexual desire for the "primitive" projects onto the Other "a sense of plenty, bounty, a field of dreams."[69] The tropology of interracial sexuality is thus overflowing with colonial desires that subordinate and fix the Other in structural asymmetry.

The Lacanian concept of the Big Other offers a productive supplement to colonial and postcolonial theory, particularly Fanon's critique of the white imaginary's relegation of colonized subjects to non-beings.[70] Lacan situates the unconscious external to the subject wherein whiteness can be understood as a structural and transindividual phenomenon. Racist and colonialist tropes repeat because the Symbolic is filled with the Other's desire. As Peter Hudson puts it, "this Big Other is white" meaning that "whiteness is the master signifier" in a Symbolic order underwritten by coloniality.[71] The language that subjects inherit does not alienate equally, where whites subjects identify with and are able to feign unicity in relation to the master signifier: "[T]he colonial symbolic is so constructed as to give the black subject nothing to hold onto—no orthopaedic support for an identity just a whiteness forever eluding him and a blackness that doesn't 'exist' in any case."[72] Tropes that merge the threat of race and sexuality render colonized subjects as imaginative spaces for white colonial desire and sexual violence. Miscegenation tropes also make whiteness durable as both a threatened object in need of preservation and the only pure and coherent form of selfhood with which all subjects can and must identify.

The primal scene of miscegenation repeats incessantly as an inversion of colonialism by representing people of color as the consummate threat to the master signifier of white. It is vital to recall that for Freud, the primal scene was found at the moment a child witnesses parental coitus, something believed to be experienced but only reconstructed through fantasies.[73] Laplanche and Pontalis add that the primal scene is one of "sexual intercourse between the parents which the child observes, or infers on the basis of certain indications and phantasies. It is generally interpreted by the child as an act of violence on the part of the father."[74] The child at the door in this fantasy stands in for an imagined state of unmediated gratification prior to the subject's entry into language.[75] The imagined violence against the mother represents the inevitable separation that the child must experience when they submit to the paternal "no."[76] In this scenario, the child at the door witnesses something they were not supposed to and, lacking the signifier, have no capacity in the moment to make sense of such a traumatic event. The primal scene must be reconstructed through the language of fantasy.

In this final example, I wish to position the spectator of erotic racism as the child at the door in a primal fantasy. My purpose is to illustrate the gap between witnessing and understanding of the primal scene, and to make sense of the origins story of whiteness and how it is perpetually restaged for spectators of racial and sexual scandal. I turn to one of the most taboo yet now quotidian forms of amateur media: the sex tape. Access to affordable recording devices along with the birth of the Internet led to exponential growth in the exhibition and consumption of homemade pornography. Of course, leaked celebrity sex tapes have commanded the public's attention, garnering views from unlikely audiences when they become national news. In some instances, sex tapes function as paratexts that attract audiences to celebrities, particularly those who star on reality TV.[77] Sex tapes are both quotidian and spectacular, a tension that makes them meaningful apertures into challenges of spectatorship in a democratic culture.

How much private disclosure is required to achieve total transparency and authenticity? Sex tapes are both mediated gossip, news, and pornography all at once. As such, they are vexing texts that call into question the boundaries of privacy and publicity. As Clarissa Smith, Feona Attwood, and Brian McNair contend, "[T]he rhetoric of the celebrity sex tape and its transformation into a pornographic text builds on the contradictions between the ordinary/extraordinary, public/private, inauthentic/authentic dynamics of sexual activity and revelation."[78] Though there are a number of ways to theorize the role of sex tapes in the construction of public intimacy, here I want to provisionally frame such texts as the staging and documentation of public sexual desire. *Mediated* sex in public is encoded with the raced, classed, and gendered ideological investments that exist in culture which regulates or disinhibits certain forms of sexual expression. Even in their salaciousness, the disclosure of white heterosexual sex acts constitutes an enunciative act of white heteronormativity that organizes fantasies of acceptable forms of public intimacy. Sex tapes peel back the layers of polished self-presentation, revealing not just sex acts but relations of intimacy that recur and are deeply historical.

Hence, I turn to a piece of mediate gossip that discloses the racial investments of white sexuality: the Hulk Hogan sex tape. I argue that Hogan's candid expressions of racism on a leaked sex tape evince the structures of enjoyment that organize spectators' encounter with interracial sexuality. In 2015, Hogan sued the gossip website Gawker for leaking a video that featured himself having sex with Heather Clem, the wife of shock jock Bubba the Love Sponge. The lawsuit attracted the attention of billionaire and PayPal founder Peter Thiel, who helped fund Hogan's legal action as revenge for Gawker outing him as gay in 2007. The lawsuit focused primarily on issues of celebrity privacy and whether or not Terry Bollea (Hogan's real name) deserved to remain outside of the public spotlight. Hogan was awarded damages of $115 million, receiving $31 million in payments that ultimately bankrupted Gawker.[79] The salacious sexual details of the case and the subsequent tale of revenge have come to overshadow the tape's troubling racist content.

Following the sexual encounter, Hogan can be heard making casual racist remarks about his daughter Brooke's professional friendship with SoBe Entertainment founder Cecile Barker and a possible sexual relationship between Brooke and Barker's son Yannique (whose stage name is Stacks). Although portions of the conversation are inaudible or otherwise incoherent, Hogan seems to complain about financially supporting

Brooke's music career and that he had hoped Barker might pick up the bill. He expressed disapproval of their relationship but found a silver lining in that Brooke might enrich her family's fortune by sleeping with a wealthy Black man. Hogan asserted, "'I don't give a fuck if she [inaudible] an eight-foot-tall basketball player. If we're gonna fuck with [expletive], let's get a rich one!" In his remarks, Hogan attempted to distinguish between who he considered to be "nice people" and people who conform to racist stereotypes. Hogan confessed that he was "racist to a point, ya know [expletive deleted], but then when it comes to nice people and [redacted]." Clem agreed, "We are all that way." Hearing her support of his general premise, Hogan continued, "Yeah, cool, when it comes to nice people, you gotta . . . you can't, you can't say the [inaudible]." Hogan's casual racism conveys a kind of ease and familiarity with using such terms as if they were innocent colloquial forms of address. Later, in his apology, Hogan confirmed as much by explaining that "I'm not a racist but I never should have said what I said. It was wrong. I'm embarrassed by it. People need to realize that you inherit things from your environment. And where I grew up was south Tampa, Port Tampa, and it was a really rough neighborhood, very low income. And all my friends, we greeted each other saying that word."[80] His comments and apology both engender the ideology of commonsense racism, which is not conveyed through an overtly hateful attitude, but instead a naturalization and acceptance of racial difference as an interpretive scheme for social reality. As such, his comments about class are a further clarification of the differences between nice, affluent people of color and the menacing thugs he grew up with in the ghetto. Presumably, the Barker family belonged to the former category and was therefore exempt from such racist derision.

Hogan's comments illustrate a white person's presumed ability to categorize, define, and determine schemas of racial difference. Like Richards's rant, even if the targets of his racist remarks do not fit the stereotype he conjured, racism functions precisely through the parsing of distinctions between acceptable and unacceptable forms of difference. His suggestion that he is "racist, up to a point" merely distinguishes his commonsense racism from more violent examples of overt hatred. The threshold for this facile distinction hinges on the respectability that comes with an abundance of wealth and natural talent. When Blackness becomes useful, Hogan suggests he can overlook its most monstrous visage—the "eight-foot-tall basketball player" who escaped poverty. All of this is to say that Hogan disavows his more unseemly racism with a corollary expression of *desire for* the Other—be it derived from wealth or monstrously gifted physical ability.

Praise and desire are essential counterparts of the more violent and brutal legacy of white supremacy. Structural racism maintains hegemony precisely by offering a highly visible and select few opportunities for upward mobility to promulgate the fiction of class permeability and racial transcendence.[81] The distinction between acceptable and unacceptable forms of racial difference spells out the conditions for success within racial capitalism that are outlined in the next chapter. One should embrace their positive difference to fulfill the mandates of diversity and inclusion while remaining ostensibly colorless and deferential to white authority. Hogan's statements make the terms and conditions of racial capitalism clear: "Let's get a rich one." For Hogan, racial difference is unseemly and abject, but not if the price is right. Hogan's conditional acceptance of and praise for Barker complements the more explicit and violent racism heard on Gibson's and Richards's tapes.

Whereas Gibson and Richards enact symbolic racial violence, Hogan supplants the violent legacy of lynching with a scene of desire where the Other's difference is imagined as plentitude. Hogan's fantasy whisks away eavesdroppers from the primal scene where the lack projected onto the Other becomes bearable and nonthreatening. Desirable difference is an alibi for the crimes committed, and subsequently omitted, from the primal scene: a white racial origin story that celebrates the abundance of the Other, the very thing colonialism and slavery destroyed. Ultimately, this fantasy domesticates and converts racial difference into a fungible commodity. It is only such a wealthy and affable form of racial difference that is worthy of their erotic gaze. Hogan's remarks approach the primal scene of miscegenation as a kind of joint investment in which all parties may prosper without threatening white authority. Similar to Gibson and Richards, the Hogan tape further obscures investments in white as a master signifier. In this case, racism masquerades as desire that attributes to the Other a plentitude awaiting to be colonized.

Hogan's tirade is particularly illustrative in light of his redemption years after his public exile. Temporary embarrassment aside, Hogan has ultimately evaded substantial long-term consequences for his racist transgressions.[82] In fact, Hogan successfully resurrected his image by playing into the conventions of racial melodrama—not unlike the moral polarities and heroic victimhood laid bare in Gibson's tirade. Although the WWE (World Wrestling Entertainment) immediately suspended Hogan's contract and removed him from the organization's Hall of Fame, they ultimately reinstated him in 2018. The WWE stated that "this second chance follows Hogan's numerous public apologies and volunteering to work with young people, where he is helping them learn from his mistake. . . . These efforts led to a recent induction into the Boys & Girls Clubs of America Alumni Hall of Fame."[83] Despite his expressions of contrition, Hogan and his fans reconstructed him as a victim of political correctness. Shortly after the tape became public, Hogan retweeted to his 1.35 million Twitter followers: "Bi-racial President Obama uses N word, is applauded and keeps his job. @HulkHogan uses N word, is vilified and loses his job."[84] Brooke Hogan defended her father by composing an effusive poem about his "tender heart," writing, "If you knew the dad I knew/ you'd know his tender heart./ He'd never want to hurt his fans,/ or family from the start."[85] With poetic cadence, the narrative of Hogan's fall and redemption mimicked the conventions of racial melodrama in which Hogan was cast as a martyred hero-victim whose return signifies an overcoming of dark and malevolent forces. Obscuring the conditions of Hogan's original sin, this melodrama constructs an innocent and fragile form of whiteness.

Hogan also ultimately benefited from a media and political culture that had turned politics into a spectator sport, not unlike professional wrestling. Not only was Hogan reportedly a longtime friend of Donald Trump, but Trump himself was also a fan of professional wrestling. Trump not only hosted pay-per-view wrestling events at his Atlantic City casinos but even made an appearance on WrestleMania 23 ("The Battle of the Billionaires"), in which he body-slammed WWE CEO Vince McMahon.[86] As evidenced in Chapter 4, Trump's persona shares much in common with the "heel" archetype from professional wrestling, performing the role of rule-breaking villain who antagonizes the "faces" or heroic protagonist. Hogan tweeted his support of Trump by thanking God for his victory over Hillary Clinton. I note this odd connection between these two individuals to illustrate how a media culture organized around celebrity enabled both figures to evade accountability by tapping into the melodramatic frameworks that have come to dominate political culture. As "heels," Trump and Hogan transgress the rules that govern the "faces." Hogan was welcomed back into the fold by Trump's supporters who cited his "cancellation" as PC culture run amok.

Hogan's struggles illustrate how embattlement (and vulnerability) represent the very condition of possibility for whiteness.[87] The white "spirit" must undergo trials by dark forces to purify and solidify mythic whiteness; a journey in which the terror of racial impurity must be overcome.[88] Hogan's references to Obama's biracialism evoke the threat of miscegenation and emphasize the risks to the purity of white stock.[89] The offense of the biracial body displaced Hogan's racism to perform the vital function of postracialism—to foreground the threat of *race* over the threat of *racism*.[90] This journey is sexual in as much as feminized dark forces threaten to corrupt the vulnerable white body. In this case, it is worth noting that prior to Hogan's racist comments, the tape captured Hogan's muscular white body in the performance of a sex act. As Eric King Watts writes, "[M]aster narratives that pursue mythic whiteness often pit white men against feminized dark forces from within and without the white body as tests of immanent manhood."[91] In the moral polarities that define melodrama, darkness represents decay and corruption, with whiteness standing as pure, transcendent, and heroic. The redemption of Hogan's "tender heart" elides the psychical and bodily damage inflicted by racist hate speech by foregrounding white precarity, or the fantasy of its own racial injury. His racist transgression becomes a tale of trial and triumph, a racial trope that fortifies the white spirit against the threat of race.

Fantasies of Transcendence

These three high-profile racist events illustrate how tirades, outbursts, and irruptions function to obscure the structural and psychical scaffolding of white supremacy. They are part of an archive of hate that misrepresents racism as disruptive of the normal functioning of a healthy public sphere. But the outburst is a necessary accompaniment to tense and pregnant pauses in between that silently terrorize people of color. The tirade is not a hiccup but instead an organizing part of a more diffuse system of white supremacy that need not speak its dictates into the air for them to be known. Gibson, Richards, and Hogan are not points of origin but instead points of articulation in a vast affective economy of racism that often operates without a subject's knowledge or understanding. The racist tirade conceals how racism operates not merely as an event but as an omnipresent material condition and psychical structure.

Postracial culture prefigures racist transgressions as *racial* ones, meaning that such events serve as trials for the redemption of mythic whiteness more so than they indict the ongoing legacy of racism. In this regard, each tirade temporalizes racism as something that happen*ed* to people of color in the past, but race as something still happen*ing* to white subjects in the here in now. Each, then, speak to the fantasies of transcendence that are mobilized to contain the traumatic intrusion of the Real—that the nation's original sin is not, in fact, slavery but rather the seemingly sudden and agentless invention of race. Rather than face the primal scene as it occurred, postracial discourse shields white subjects from traumatic knowledge of their complicity in racist and misogynistic violence. In place of the original scene, postracial culture installs the fiction that race threatens to eviscerate white as a master signifier. This fiction depends on the myth that miscegenation portends an invasion of insurrectional racial difference that threatens to overwhelm vulnerable white subjects. This reimagined scene inverts the power dynamics of the original where the sexual threat emanated from white men. In this new scene, whiteness is either innocent or redeemable through a mythic journey of the hero-victim. Gibson, Richards, and Hogan all present themselves as aggrieved subjects whose vulnerability elides their status as racist perpetrators.

Finally, each case study illustrates how white masculinity is predicated on a disavowal of both primary and secondary castration. The primal scene of miscegenation and the terrifying tableaux of lynching make white women and men of color bear this burden for white men. Racism is a form of ob-scene enjoyment that enables white perpetrators to stage an encounter with *objet petit a*. Although in a symbolic lynching, the white perpetrator places themselves in the position of the father of prohibition, they ultimate occupy the space of the ruinous father-*jouissance*, or the seemingly impossible un-castrated or nonlacking father unbound by the rule of the Symbolic. Yet, this fraught encounter with lack is terrifying and induces fantasies to shield them from knowledge of primary castration so that racism can be enjoyed. For instance, each figure's preoccupation with miscegenation threatens to un-leash knowledge of their own castration through a breach of latent sexual desire. Saidiya V. Hartman speaks of "the figurative capacities of blackness,"[92] in which "blackness provided the occasion for self-reflection as well as for an exploration of terror, desire, fear, loathing, and longing."[93] Though at times the white imaginary constructs racial difference as the incarnation of lack, at other times this overwhelming lack is tempered by a corollary representation of difference as completeness in relation to its proximity to *objet petit a*. That is to say that this enjoying Other appears as a subject of desire but without the accompaniment of lack. Todd McGowan argues that such fantasies are the source material for racial violence that are repetitively "directed toward the other who appears as a barrier to the subject's enjoyment."[94] The primal scene of miscegenation must be restaged in response to the "exigence of the death drive."[95] Put another way, whiteness desires miscegenation, it *needs* misceg-enation in fact, for its own feigned coherence. Lack may appear in either a positive or negative form; either way, castration is projected onto the Other so as to purchase a temporary and futile reprieve from such knowledge. The outburst is a ruinous, self-destructive, and futile gesture to conceal the void on which white masculinity is built.

2

Anxiety, Racial Capitalism, and
the Donald Sterling Tapes

Yeah, it bothers me a lot you want
to broadcast that you're associating
with Black people. Do you have to?

—Donald Sterling

I love the Black people.

—Donald Sterling

On April 25, 2014, TMZ Sports released a nine-minute audio recording of a phone conversation between Los Angeles Clippers owner Donald Sterling and his girlfriend V. Stiviano. In this conversation, Sterling chastised Stiviano for posting pictures to Instagram of her with Earvin (Magic) Johnson and, in his words, "broadcasting" her association with Black people at NBA games. Stiviano, who identifies as Black and Latina, responded to his racist remarks with astonishment. She repeatedly asked Sterling to explain how he could, on the one hand, love a mixed-race person and associate with Black NBA players and, on the other, demand that she conceal her relationships with Black people to avoid his embarrassment. At one point, Stiviano pleads, "I'm sorry that you still have people around you that are full of racism and hate in their heart. I'm sorry that you're still racist in your heart." Emphatic that he was *not* a racist, Sterling explained that Stiviano misunderstood his concern—it was not that he hated or resented Black people, but rather that the elite white world he inhabited did not permit interracial fraternizing in public. For him, "there's a culture. People feel certain things. Hispanics feel certain things towards Blacks. Blacks feel certain things toward other groups. It's been that way historically, and it will always be that way." Sterling then carefully parsed a distinction between what the heart may privately desire

Caught on Tape. Casey Ryan Kelly, Oxford University Press. © Oxford University Press 2023.
DOI: 10.1093/oso/9780197677865.003.0003

and what the mind knows is publicly unacceptable. When Stiviano declared, "I can't be racist in my heart," Sterling lamented "And that's good. I'm living in a culture, and I have to live within the culture. So, that's the way it is. That's all I got it. I got the whole message. You live with your heart. I don't. You can't be flexible. You can't." Or, to put it differently, whiteness accepts the inevitability of interracial sex and sociality but must keep such promiscuous indiscretions hidden from public view.

Sterling failed to elaborate further on the rules of racial etiquette that governed his rarified social world; however, his remarks do illustrate the entailments of the *plantation culture* that pervades the world of professional sports ownership—a lucrative political economy that trades in predominantly athletes of color and from which arises a host of social arrangements, attitudes, ideologies, and material practices that reproduce racial stratification and white supremacy.[1] Professional sports extend the racial logics and tropes of plantation slavery, where people of color are constructed, classified, measured, and evaluating according to racialized conceptions of innate athletic ability. For instance, Thomas P. Oates contends the NFL draft mirrors that same erotic gaze of slave auctions, where wealthy white team owners trade in racist fantasies of the extraordinary, primitive athleticism of players of color.[2] Professional sports owners, who are by and large white, often engage in material and symbolic practices that commodify, exploit, surveil, and control the way players of color behave, speak, and even dress.[3] Of course, Sterling is not the first professional sports team owner caught making racist remarks. Cincinnati Red's team owner Marge Schott openly used anti-Black, anti-Asian, anti-Semitic slurs and in 1996 praised Adolf Hitler, an act that compelled Major League Baseball to force her to sell the team in 1998.[4] Similarly, former Cleveland Cavalier's owner Ted Stepien, who is often remembered as being one of the worst owners in NBA history, suggested that teams should be required to have a roster that was half-white because white fans did not want to see a league dominated by Black players.[5] Recently, an investigation of the NBA's Phoenix Suns alleged that owner Robert Sarver routinely made racist and misogynistic statements to his employees.[6] These incidents are just a small cross-section of the racist mentality and behaviors that pervades the culture of professional sports ownership.

The political and symbolic economy of professional sports is a fitting representation of *racial capitalism* in the United States. As Cedric J. Robinson argues, racial capitalism embeds the economic relations of production and extraction of value from difference into the cultural superstructure it underwrites.[7] From a market economy founded on the racial exploitation of labor arose governance structures, political cultures, and relational norms organized around the preservation of white authority. The practice of slavery and the exclusion of women, people of color, and indigenous people from social and economic relations helped fuse white masculinity with property rights, thus constituting a political and economic system dominated by white men. Sterling simply articulated those racial and sexual norms that are a byproduct of racialized economic exploitation: the codes and etiquette of a modern plantation system that commodifies and exploits athletes of color for profit.[8] By plantation culture, I am referring to specific critiques leveled against billionaire franchise owners such as Sterling who commodify and extract extraordinary surplus value from the labor of athletes of color. But plantation culture also names how professional sports remain governed by modes of social and economic relations similar to those between slave owners and enslaved persons. A plantation mentality typically denotes relations of extraction as well as white paternalistic control over the social habits and behaviors of workers of color, exemplified by codes that demand deference and regulate speech, manner of dress, drug use, diet, contracts, and public behavior—all out of an expressed concern for their welfare.[9]

Above all, the plantation is a fantasy zone of racial exception to the paternal rules of cultural prohibition. Plantation culture promulgates an array of fantasies of white invulnerability and self-mastery over the very racial threats that sprung from the white imaginary. But as a zone of exception, the plantation offers a reprieve from the taboos of race mixing and miscegenation so long as such indulgences do not threaten the racial order. The plantation permits both cruelty and compassion—opposites unified insofar as they both organize white enjoyment. Note that Sterling uses stock racist tropes to counter Stiviano's accusations: white benevolence. Sterling exclaims: "I support them and give them food, and clothes, and cars, and houses. Who gives it to them? Does someone else give it to them? Do I know that I have— Who makes the game? Do I make the game, or do they make the game? Is there 30 owners, that created the league?" As such remarks epitomize, the benevolence of plantation culture is an effort to compensate for its brutality with concern for the well-being of those whom it exploits. Of course, it is also about defending billions in profits from public scrutiny. In this case, Sterling's benevolence occludes the modes of racial exploitation and extraction entailed by capitalism. Although professional sports are populated with rich and famous athletes of color, that number is relatively small compared to the number of athletes who struggle to make it to the elite class of professional stardom. Meanwhile, the owner and management ranks of professional sports are by and large white and male. To quote comedian Chris Rock, "Shaq [O'Neal] is *rich*, the white man who signs his check is *wealthy*."[10]

Sterling's remarks also highlight how a plantation culture organizes the subjectivity of the owning class in relation to race, albeit to protect their own enjoyment. How do figures like Sterling, both within and outside of professional sports, enable themselves to inhabit a profession and culture dominated by people of color without relinquishing the benefits of white supremacy? The Sterling–Stiviano tapes announced an unstated racial doctrine that permits the white bourgeois class to enter into sexual relationships, friendships, and business associations with people of color but without losing their position in the racial hierarchy and the privileges of whiteness. But as bell hooks observes, "[T]o makes one's self vulnerable to the seduction of difference, to seek an encounter with the Other, does not require that one relinquish forever one's mainstream positionality."[11] He can be benevolent and even loving toward people of color without forfeiting the benefits of white supremacy so long as the strict boundaries of racial capitalism are maintained. Consistent with the evolution of postracialism, Sterling allowed himself to acknowledge the existence of race and racism without a corresponding obligation to change.[12] Market goods and philanthropy obviate any need to address racial inequality at the point of production: "cars," "food," "homes," and "clothes" are sufficient rewards for respecting such boundaries. Whiteness, synonymous with wholeness, is in a position to bestow these goods, to distribute them throughout the economy of racial difference it created and maintains. How do such figures negotiate their enjoyment in exigencies that provoke a simultaneous repulsion and attraction to athletes of color? Indeed, the Sterling tapes illustrate the phobic reaction, or the anxiety provoked, when racialized bodies trespass into white territory. In this case, the moment of racial anxiety occurs when persons of color violate the boundaries between ownership and labor mandated by racial capitalism. For Sterling, persons of color do have a place in his world; it is simply not in the luxury box or the various leisure spaces of the white owning class, superstar Magic Johnson included.

But what happens when the doctrines of racial capitalism are explicitly announced in such a fashion? Does exposure make such secret doctrines wither under public scrutiny? What happens when a racist "secret" is folded into the dynamics of celebrity and spectatorship that underwrite U.S. media culture? In this chapter, I reframe the Sterling–Stiviano tapes as *public* texts that mediates white rage and anxiety over the advancement of people of color. Although Sterling never foresaw his private conversations being made into a public spectacle, his racism was already a public secret. Within the NBA and the city of Los Angeles, Sterling wore his racist investments more or less in the open but was rarely, if ever, held accountable. The exposure of this private conversation announced what was *already known* (not to be known) about Sterling in particular and white supremacy in general: that racial capitalists attempt to preserve the "property of whiteness" by claiming the right to exclude.[13] This double exposure of Sterling's racism is also underwritten by white anxiety: the idea that racial capitalism is somehow a well-kept secret belies that its hypervisibility is precisely what enables it to function.

I suggest that the exposure of the tape prefigured its contents as "secret" racism; yet, racial capitalism does more to disclose and perform its logics through public spectacles of race.

Building on the previous chapter's exploration of *pornotroping*, this chapter illustrates how the biopolitical governance structures that support racial capitalism depend precisely on the public marking of racial and sexual difference.[14] The discovery of "secret" racism, then, obscures how Sterling's racism already exists comfortably in the open, particularly when practiced within the flesh factory that is professional sports. The secret, then, is that racial capitalism has no secrets. Yet, such a revelation suggests the opposite: that private racism and the hidden machinations of white networks are more fundamental to white supremacy than the spectacle of people of color seemingly performing contentment for white audiences. Yet, racial capitalism already always operates in full view: the star system of professional sports eroticizes and exoticizes people of color and presents them for public consumption.[15] Racialized competitors are valorized for their spectacular athletic abilities and also discarded when they break down or become unruly (consider, e.g., the fate of Colin Kaepernick). NBA players such as Blake Griffin and Christopher Paul recount stories of Sterling making impromptu visits to the Clippers' locker room to touch and gawk at his "beautiful black bodies." At the same time, those athletes of color are unwelcome in his spaces of white leisure.

In this case, the source of the secret revelation is vitally important because it establishes the disposition audiences are invited to adopt. Unlike traditional journalistic outlets, TMZ is a known purchaser of lucrative celebrity gossip. When they release a scandalous tape, they do so to direct massive flows of Web traffic to their online content and televisual programming. Since 2014, TMZ.com has had an entire tab completely devoted to Sterling gossip, including the tawdry details of his divorce, sexual relationships, continuing legal battles, and lashing out against the press and the NBA. Although the tape brought attention to significant racial concerns, by virtue of TMZ's ethos and branding strategies, his racist credos have become equivocated with other forms of celebrity gossip and, ironically, valued precisely because his statements shock and offend. The same can be said for TMZ's release of footage of NFL player Ray Rice knocking unconscious his then fiancée Janay Palmer in an Atlantic City casino. While the tape compelled the NFL to extend its punishment of Rice to an indefinite suspension, TMZ ultimately profited by turning an incident of domestic violence into shocking entertainment. In a similar manner, the Sterling–Stiviano tapes represent racism as a tawdry secret that can monetized and promoted as part of a tabloid brand. TMZ directs Web traffic to the racist and misogynistic spectacle that Sterling has come to embody. In the spirit of democratic scopophilia, TMZ and its shocking revelations conflate spectatorship with civics. The tabloidization of racism monetizes social problems while making profitability a precondition for racist incidents to make their way into the public record.

Sterling's very public racism and participation in a system of open racist exploitation come to constitute the public secret, or in Michael Taussig's words, "knowing what not to know."[16] Ironically, it is this open dynamic of racial capitalism that is concealed by the revelation—a dynamics that is precisely what sustains spectatorial desire. As Jack Bratich writes, "[O]ur obsession with secrecy as a box to be opened is itself part of the spectacle."[17] Thus, the challenge posed by exposing Sterling's "private" views is that they are folded in the spectacle of racial capitalism. Spectators are supposed to continue *not knowing* that his racism was very much at home in the world of professional (white) sports ownership. After Sterling's exile, sponsors such as State Farm Insurance were more than happy to return their lucrative advertising dollars to an industry still plagued by racist ownership structures. The exposure of Sterling's racial credo threatened to interrupt white spectator's enjoyment of sports and, in doing so, reinscribed the very anxiety the tapes purported to expose. Working from Lacan's concept of anxiety, this chapter examines the publicization of private conversations between Sterling and Stiviano as an anxious and ambivalent text, one that illustrates how white subjects preserve *and* evade race so that it can be enjoyed in an ostensibly raceless world. Thus, I attend to not only Sterling's anxiety but also how the tapes constitute a kind of organized "knowing what not to know" about racial capitalism. I conclude that the Sterling–Stiviano tapes are part and parcel of the public spectacle that sustains racial capitalism.

Whiteness and Anxiety

Racial capitalism is a system for managing white anxiety, which is to say that it entails tacit codes, rules, and hierarchies that help craft economic arrangements and social interactions to insulate whiteness from its own self-created and terrorizing image of negative difference. Sterling's "racial lens" preserves and shields white space, as well as the white self-image, from racial contamination.[18] Both whiteness and racial Otherness can therefore be enjoyed but with a type of discretion that helps disavow the historicity and symbolicity of whiteness. The Other's consent to this relational dynamic, or the appearance thereof, sustains the fantasy that the Other's enjoyment compensates for or even nullifies their subjugation. In this regard, Sterling actually expressed a principle that transcends the culture of white billionaires, one that negotiates a series of ambivalent tensions at the core of white identity. Hence, the tape's revelation reflected the very system designed to distance white spectators from people of color but also to shield them from knowledge of their own participation in racial capitalism. Within white identity, there is an equal pull of two mutually opposed forces: a desire to not be seen as racist and at the same time a desire to be seen as economically and racially superior.[19] Both of these forces are further imperiled by the demands of postracialism, which ostensibly prohibits public race talk—portending the condition of anxiety where the white subject suffers a *lack of lack*. This tension crafts a public culture that seeks to evacuate racial signifiers from public life but without making any substantive changes that might threaten white privilege, in essence preserving an economy of difference in which lack is projected onto the Other.

As I argued elsewhere, *white ambivalence* produces "a condition that entails that white identity, history, and culture be respected as morally superior but, at the same time, not be characterized as white supremacy."[20] Ambivalence demands love and appreciation for people of color absent a structural commitment and sacrifice to anti-racism. Whiteness seeks both recognition of its superiority but without being named as such so that it can maintain its unspoken metonymic connection to universal humanness.[21] Whiteness desires

Otherness but needs boundary conditions to also keep actual persons and communities of color at a safe distance. From the vantage point of psychoanalysis, E. Chebrolu contends that white ambivalence also names the peculiar form of *anxiety* stemming from a conflation of whiteness and being, or universal humanness.[22] That is to say that whiteness is a purely symbolic conception, a floating signifier, but one that appears to white subjects as the very object foreclosed by the Symbolic. As *objet petit a*, whiteness presents the subject with a *lack of lack*, or an impossible absence of desire in an image of completeness. Anxiety overwhelms the subject through proximity to the fulfillment of fantasy that spells the end of desire.[23] The subject comes to the horrifying knowledge that white is simply a signifier like any other, one that forecloses rather than affords access to the Real. Spectators come to this knowledge when their enjoyment is interrupted by the suffocating proximity to an object of desire. Anxiety, the lack of lack, arises from the interruption of enjoyment; an enjoyment sustained by the subject's necessary failure to obtain *objet petit a*. Lacan argues that anxiety concerns uncertainty about the desire of the Other; therefore, proximity interrupts the fantasy by availing subjects that the Other's desire is incomprehensible and beyond their control. He writes that it "is the sudden appearance of lack in a positive form that is the source of anxiety."[24] It is anxiety that causes fantasies to break down and the enclosure of the enjoying other produces the conditions that underwrite the reassertion of white sovereignty. The Sterling–Stiviano tapes constitute precisely this kind of interruption.

Sterling's fretting over what he considers to be fundamental racial realities reflects the rhetorical entailments of white anxiety: of being overwhelmed by the possibility that race is simply a construct and the intricately defined rules of racial capitalism are arbitrary. Sterling names the source of anxiety: of being contaminated by racialized bodies, of being confronted by the knowledge that white is merely a signifier, of being aware that one necessarily benefits from and enjoys white supremacy, and of learning the exclusion of white subjectivity from play of racial difference that organizes the Symbolic. As Chebrolu explains, "[R]acial anxiety emerges with those uncanny reminders that whiteness is not a universal given, but rather a specific identity, when subjects are caught within a net of signifiers that block disavowal of the fact that whiteness is an object—an aspect of themselves, their community, their way of life—that they enjoy."[25] In "configuring signifiers of the flesh" to anchor whiteness, racial capitalism maintains its "naturalness and inevitability" through symbolic and material violence.[26]

White subjectivity is therefore organized around series of structural tensions that are fraught with uncertainty. As Homi K. Bhabha observed of colonial discourse, the character of Otherness "is at once an object of desire and derision, an articulation of difference contained within the fantasy of origin and identity."[27] Colonial discourse splits the colonized subject into two mutually untenable projections of lack: a subject whose difference must be overcome through assimilation and another whose singularity must be denied to maintain the symbolic economy of racial difference. Similarly, whiteness is fraught by its own exile from the very system of racial difference it constructs. If whiteness is invisible, ineffable, and unrepresentable, and if the invention of whiteness is the very means by which difference *is* rendered visible, then whiteness is ostensibly excluded from the Symbolic. As Kalpana Seshardi-Crooks puts it, "[T]he master signifier makes difference possible, but it is also excluded from the play of signification that is supports."[28] In positing an impossible connection between whiteness (a wholly historical and symbolic concept) and being (the Real foreclosed by the signifier), the logic of race produces *anxiety*, or the lack of lack. Thus, the secret of racial difference is that there is no secret, no thing obscured by the signifier.[29]

To contain its phobic reactions to racial difference, bourgeois white culture organizes itself into private enclaves where "backstage racism" is permissible, and whiteness can be celebrated at a safe proximity from racial Others.[30] The sudden presence of backstage racism in public is arresting not only because it obscures postracial mythology but also because it interrupt white enjoyment of the labor of people of color that depends on racism remaining a public secret. Knowledge of racism must remain at a safe distance to sustain postracial fantasies.

Donald Sterling's entire career and social world revolved around insulating himself from the threat of race. As a Los Angeles real estate developer, Sterling has a reputation as a racist slumlord, known for harassing and refusing to rent to Black and Latinx tenants. Sterling stated that he did like to rent to Black tenants because they "smell and attract vermin."[31] In 2009, Sterling settled a Department of Justice housing discrimination lawsuit for $2.73 million.[32] A lawsuit filed by Clippers General Manager Elgin Baylor revealed both the depths of Sterling's ineptitude as a team owner and his "vision of a Southern plantation-type structure."[33] His private conversations corroborate his financial and symbolic investments in segregating the racial geography of Los Angeles. Sterling's social world revolved around private white enclaves: country clubs, resorts, luxury boxes, fraternities, gated communities, and so forth. The tapes availed shocked spectators of a type of racism that structures white political, social, and economic relations with people of color, yet can only be articulated in hushed tones within private white enclaves.[34] Yet, this revelation is hardly surprising to nearly anyone who is familiar with Sterling's business dealings. What happens in private, then, is neither irrational nor pathological; rather, it is where white interest-based politics are crafted and refined. In public sphere theory, Nancy Fraser characterizes enclaves as "spaces of withdrawal and regroupment" where groups can train and craft their responses to public discourse.[35] Karma R. Chávez also defines enclaves as spaces where activists "interpret external rhetorical messages that are created about them, the constituencies they represent, or both."[36] Of course, these conceptions of enclaves foreground their potentiality for radical and marginalized social movements to craft their resistance to structures of power without prying eyes. Whiteness, however, also benefits from its self-imposed sequester. Enclaves are spaces in which white people are free to craft rhetorical frameworks that domesticate the threat of race.[37] But in isolating race talk to private spaces, whiteness also produces the conditions of its own fragility in relation to encounters with racial difference. The tapes, then, illustrate how white racism operates but in ways that are not as obvious as they might seem. In condemning Sterling's racism, spectators might miss that although these views were expressed in private, they were actually put into practice in plain sight.

Of course, there is a vital relation between these kinds of backstage talk and postracialism. Namely, Sterling wished to express racist views without being called a racist, something to which he takes great offense. But, the preoccupation with "secret" racism misses the central symptoms of anxiety that structure his discourse—a condition that implicates all white spectators. As Joe R. Feagin argues, "[W]hites often speak and act differently in the all-white backstage and the often more diverse frontstage. There is an interesting rationalizing phenomenon: If whites do not articulate racist ideas in public, if they keep them to themselves or just express them in the backstage, then they or their white friends and relatives frequently do not see them as seriously 'racist.'"[38] Indeed, because Sterling made his remarks in private, he expressed resentment that Stiviano would characterize them as racist. As Feagin contends, if backstage racism happens out of earshot of its victims, it simply does not register as racism. This is also the case because postracial culture has so narrowly defined racism that anything short of explicit racial slurs or fighting words spoken in face-to-face encounters can be dismissed as relatively harmless. Hence, even as he lays out the basic philosophy of racial capitalism he put into practice in his real estate empire, he seems apoplectic that such a philosophy could be characterized as racist.[39]

The Sterling–Stiviano tapes make explicit the unspoken rules of racial capitalism that work to stabilize white supremacy. Although his remarks are fitting examples of covert racism, they also serve as a source of taboo and abject knowledge of race—namely, its threat to whiteness as master signifier of universal humanness. The public circulation of Sterling's credo serves to amplify white anxiety, structurally speaking, as its territories and boundaries are increasingly contested. His diatribe assembles a net of signifiers and tropes that constitute the logic and epistemology underpinning racial capitalism; a vast signifying system that stabilizes and mediates white identity in relation to racial difference. Of course, Sterling is not the originator of such discourse, but rather an articulator of racial logics embedded in white culture. Even as his comments drew a strong rebuke from the league, players, and the public, they nonetheless reproduce and amplify the white racial frame. Feagin observes that the white racial frame is "a comprehensive orienting structure, a 'tool kit' that whites and others have long used to understand, interpret, and act in social settings."[40] In the frame, racism operates according to commonsense logics in statements that, on their surface, seem more descriptive than normative. Sterling insisted that his words were not indicative of inherent hatred or malice but were simply a realistic account of the way the world works: white people and people of color inhabit a stratified social order that is predicated on people of color understanding their role in spaces of white community and leisure. Presumably, this was the "culture" to which he was referring. For Sterling, stratification and segregation were fundamental to the social world he inhabited. Stiviano's public friendships with Black players and anti-racist attitudes would be admirable if it were not for the fact that she threatens to upend an intricately constructed racial order. The Sterling–Stiviano tapes evince how white supremacy reconstitutes and purifies itself by conjuring an unruly apparition of negative difference that threatens to undo the highly structured universe of racial capitalism. As public texts, their content names what *should not be known*, thus maintaining the public secret of racial capitalism.

Broadcasting

Who am I disrespecting (*raises voice*)?

—V. Stiviano

The world before you.

—Donald Sterling

Donald Sterling inhabited a social world that would be unfathomable to most people. Even after the Sterling Trust was forced by the NBA to sell the Clippers to Steve Ballmer, Sterling still boasted a net worth of $3.8 billion[41] and his real estate empire included 162 properties throughout Los Angeles.[42] Prior to this incident, Sterling's views on race had already been loudly and clearly telegraphed in a series of high-profile housing discrimination and tenant harassment lawsuits. These incidents illustrated that though Sterling's business dealings required him to interact with a diversity of tenants, he did not see himself as part of Los Angeles' multicultural society. It is important to keep in mind that Sterling articulated his views on race relations from a particular standpoint within the class system. He lived in a world of obscene white affluence—reaching the absolute stratosphere of private wealth accumulation and doing so through the exploitation of people of color. In the same way that the "wages of whiteness" pay the white working class in petty privileges so as to garner their investment in racialized class identity, so, too, does whiteness garner surplus value and pay symbolic and psychic dividends for the white owning class.[43] Class lines thus become racial lines. Sterling's position within racial capitalism afforded him intangible benefits not available to even most white people; namely, economic power over the lives of others. In other words, the white bourgeois class has always sustained a racialized investment in their class standing. To say that Sterling embodied a plantation mentality does not simply speak to his attitude as an NBA owner, but instead his broader investment in a racialized system of economic extraction and the cultural superstructure it dictated. It is a system that necessarily entails white social and economic relationships with persons of color, but also a world in which contracts, geographic boundaries, discretion, and private enclaves functioned as guard rails that protect whiteness from contamination.

Throughout their conversations, Sterling performs a rhetorical high-wire act in his attempt to distinguish the norms and codes of white affluence from more prototypical examples of individual racial prejudice. Thus, the central antagonism between Sterling and Stiviano does not concern her friendships or intimate relationships with Black men, but instead the visibility of Black men in white space as equals. Sterling referred to her behavior as "broadcasting," by which he meant that Stiviano flaunted her relationships with Black men in public ways that negatively reflected on him. An antonymic term might therefore be *discretion,* as in both a sense of careful regard for private affairs as well as the agency to choose how and when, if ever, to make private affairs known. The fact that Stiviano seemed baffled by his explanations, or that she somehow did not understand his careful mincing of words, speaks more to the incoherence of Sterling's perspective on race than her failure to appreciate his elegant disavowals. Listeners are introduced to their conversation when Stiviano, perhaps facetiously, apologized to Sterling for the putative offense of her melanin: "I wish I could change the color of my skin." This prompted Sterling to emphatically assert that she had misread his statements about broadcasting as racism. "That isn't the issue. You've missed the issue," he explained. She persists, asking, "What's wrong with minorities? What's wrong with Black people?" Sterling grew more upset, "Nothing. Nothing." Frustrated, he continued, "It's like talking to an enemy. There's nothing wrong with minorities. They're fabulous. Because you're an enemy to me. . . . Because you don't understand." Stiviano, then, named the issue: "That racism is still alive?" "No," he insisted, "but there's a culture." In this exchange, Sterling located racism within broader cultural attitudes but in no way implicated his own views. His concern, he suggests, was that Stiviano did not understand how the world works and her multicultural idealism violated an unstated racial contract.[44]

Sterling's racism could be characterized as bigotry, prejudice, and hate—it is all of these things to be sure—but it's more apt to characterize his speech as *racist realism,* an epistemology designed to protect white subjects from radical alterity. "There is a culture," he explained, a racial caste system that superseded his personal sentiments toward people of color, whom he referred to during the conversation as "fabulous." While much of the public scrutiny concerned his personal racism, many missed what was hiding in plain sight: he disclosed the structural dynamics of racism that govern professional sports (what he explicitly named as "a culture"), not simply his individual racism. He insisted that "it isn't a question—we don't evaluate what's right and wrong, we live in a society. We live in a culture. We have to live within that culture." But the rationale for its laws and dictates are not for any of us to know. Sterling's use of the passive voice is instructive: race and racism simply exist, there is nothing anyone can do about it, and there are immutable laws that govern both social and intimate relations between races. No one is malevolent, but no one is accountable either. Sterling's words reflect what Robert Terrill calls "post-postracial" or "post-ethical" racial discourse, a manifestation of contemporary racism that acknowledges the existence of racism but without any accompanying sense that this knowledge obligates audiences to do anything about it.[45] Hence, Sterling asserted that the only reasonable response he could muster to this cultural condition is to simply acquiesce and adapt. When confronted with Sterling's cynicism, Stiviano stated "but it's not that way in my heart and in my mind." Sterling flatly replied, "But maybe you want to adjust to the world." In short, it is perfectly acceptable to privately hold such idealism, but the external world will likely be unsympathetic if not hostile and suspicious toward racial promiscuity. According to Sterling, he cannot "live with [his] heart" because the culture of racial realism is not "flexible."

Stiviano's offense was that she broke the unspoken and unbending rules of propriety that govern Sterling's social world. Sterling suggested that because Stiviano is a person of color, that perhaps she did not understand how the world works from his standpoint. "Maybe you're stupid," he averred, "Maybe you don't know what people think of you. It does matter, yeah (*raises voice*). It matters." In this sense, Sterling offered Stiviano insight into the rules of the game so that she could appreciate the difficulty of his position while allaying his anxiety concerning the prying eyes of others. But the culture Sterling describes mirrors Eduardo Bonilla-Silva's conception of "racism with racists," an invisible and systemic racism that does not comport with the popular impression of racism as deliberate and overt acts of violence.[46] Sterling disowned his racism but by describing the very function of racism in our present age: an invisible system of codes, norms, and behaviors that systematically thwart the advancement and livelihood of people of color within the class system. For Sterling, there is nothing inherently wrong or inferior about people of color; instead, the issue concerns incommensurate cultural differences and racial hierarchies. He read Stiviano's disrespect as an affront to "the world before [her]," by which he means a social and economic system designed to manage racial difference. Focusing on Sterling's personal racism misses the ways in which he overtly names the broader structural dimensions of racial capitalism—a point that might implicate all those who participate in its operations, spectators included.

Yet, who is the Other that determines these rules? Despite his vagueness, Sterling's remarks sketch a white cultural landscape that is anxiously preoccupied with perceptions and visibility. But his statements about external perceptions of race refer not to his own line of sight but something more akin to Lacan's conception of the gaze, or an anxious self-awareness that one is being looked at. Recall that for Lacan, the gaze names the point at which the subject comes to realize itself as an object of the gaze and disallowed from looking at safe distance. In the following selection of dialogue, I suggest that Sterling situates the white imaginary's relationship with racial difference within the purview of the objective gaze (an Other inscribed into the Symbolic whose desires are incomprehensible and unassimilable).

V.S.:   Do you know that I'm mixed?

D.S.:   No, I don't know that (*sarcastically*). You told me you were going to remove those. You said, "Yes, I understand you." I mean you change from day to day. Wow. So painful. Wow.

V.S.:   People call you and tell you that I have Black people on my Instagram. And it bothers you.

D.S.:   Yeah, it bothers me a lot you want to . . . broadcast that you're associating with Black people. Do you have to?

V.S.:   You associate with Black people.

D.S.:   I'm not you, and you're not me. You're supposed to be a delicate white or delicate Latina girl.

V.S.:   I'm a mixed girl.

D.S.:   Ok, well . . .

V.S.:   And you're in love with me. And I'm Black and Mexican. Whether you like it or not. Whether the world accepts it or not. And you're asking me to remove something that's part of my bloodstream. Because the world thinks different of me and you're afraid of what they're going to think because of your upbringing. You want me to have hate towards Black people.

D.S.:   I don't want you to have hate. That's what people—they turn things around. I want you to love them—privately. In your whole life, every day, you can be with them. Every single day of your life.

In this exchange, Sterling's concern with "broadcasting" is that Stiviano invites the gaze of the Other, that indeterminate "they" that constitutes the law of the Symbolic. Anxiety encloses upon him as he registers his awareness that her actions might also make him the object of the gaze. The informal racial rules that govern Sterling's world dictate that a "delicate" white or Latina girl must conceal her relationships with people of color. The Other dictates as much but does not make the underwriting logics of its desires known or apparent.

It is noteworthy that Sterling is at a loss to explain why public associations with people of color are forbidden or precisely who issues such rigid edicts. Sterling clarified that these rules are inflexible and must be obeyed. His understanding of these conventions is what enabled him to have business and sexual relationships with people of color without putting his whiteness in jeopardy. Thus, he responded to her charges of hypocrisy by plainly stating, "I'm not you, and you're not me," a statement that can be taken to mean that he cannot abide her risk-taking behavior. Sterling's consternation with Stiviano was her refusal to obey the law of the Symbolic and her transgressions risk the Other's sanction. Sterling argued that the issue was neither hate nor inherent inferiority. His remarks nonetheless convey an underlying anxiety about the status of whiteness in relation to the gaze and the threat of racial difference. In other words, race "mixing" may be unavoidable if not desirable, but its visibility threatens the status of white as a master signifier. It is fitting that Sterling framed such interracial relations in terms of cost–benefit analysis: "Is there a benefit to you?" This question is perhaps facetious but suggests that white people only associate with other races publicly if it is in their private interest.

Here, Sterling's remarks illustrate how the logics of anti-miscegenation anchor white identity in what is otherwise a chaotic discursive field of radical alterity. Stiviano's "delicateness," even if merely a matter of perception, speaks to how Sterling constructs whiteness as imperiled by the visibility of its own particularity, its constructed-ness, its impurities. Unseated by its own improprieties and promiscuity, whiteness might then appear as simply an object like any other. This is precisely the moment at which anxiety closes in on the subject and the object-cause of desire comes into question. Much like the white eavesdropper, Sterling was caught in an objective gaze where whiteness can no longer sustain fantasies of universal humanness, completeness, and control. People of color in white spaces threaten to envelope whiteness where a fundamental and essentialist sense of negative difference can no longer be sustained. For Sterling, one must maintain and invest in the world of appearances to sustain the fantasy structure of whiteness. Subjects obey these vexing rules of whiteness because they help organize and direct their desire. When whiteness appears to the white subject as an object—as it appears to both Sterling as well as the potential white eavesdropper— whiteness can no longer sustain desire because it cannot enable the subject to stage an encounter with *objet petit a*. The subject is then overcome by a lack of lack. Sterling's remarks named this anxious investment in whiteness. He sutured this investment to a system of racial capitalism that simultaneously fetishizes and despises the identities of the racialized bodies it exploits. In a fitting conclusion to this banter, Sterling concludes, "How about your whole life, every day, you could do whatever you want. You can sleep with them. You can bring them in, you can do whatever you want. The little I ask you is not to promote it on that and not to bring them to my games." No other statement could provide a more fitting summation of precisely how whiteness manages its racial anxiety. Yet, exposure of his supposedly "secret" racism draws attention from the material fact of his open participation in racial capitalism.

Refusing Particularity

And are the black Jews less than the white Jews?

—V. Stiviano

A hundred percent, fifty, a hundred percent.

—Donald Sterling

Stiviano's line of questioning seems designed to illustrate the contradictions of Sterling's racial lens: that he does not want to be seen consorting with persons of color, yet he also maintains an intimate relationship with a Black Latina woman and owns a sports franchise in a predominantly Black league. He attempts to evade allegations of hypocrisy by taking up the same position as a plantation owner within the institution of slavery. From this position, whites may enjoy the plentitude of racial difference while shielding their indiscretions from the view of other whites who might think less of them for doing so. For Sterling, what is consistent is that people of color do not belong in spaces of white leisure unless race and class distinctions are clear to the outside world. It would be perfectly appropriate, then, for Magic Johnson to be seen at a Clippers game because he is both a basketball icon and a part owner in several Los Angeles sports franchises. What needs to be clear, however, is that Johnson does not attend these games as Sterling's equal. Thus,

Sterling's rhetoric is a forceful example of how whiteness functions as property and capital within racial capitalism.[47] Put another way, whiteness loses its market value where it no longer occupies the position of universal humanness.[48] As anxiety closes in, Sterling retreated to a racialized class position that is fortified by ontological distinctions between whiteness and its Others.

There is also a sense in which Sterling refused to take up any racialized particularity even when confronted with his Jewish identity. In other words, he defines neither whiteness nor Jewishness as distinct identities among others that might constitute him as a part of a multicultural discursive field. This diverges from contemporary white supremacy, which seeks to particularize whiteness and tether it to European ancestry so that it might be enjoyed as an aggrieved identity.[49] Stiviano appealed to his Jewish heritage so he could step outside his whiteness to appreciate the harm of his racist attitude. Although one might expect Sterling to reference the persistence of anti-Semitism to refute his racial privilege and attest to an understanding of racism, he refused to do so. After all, Stiviano offers him that opportunity when she asked, "Isn't it wrong? Wasn't it wrong then? With the Holocaust? And you're Jewish, you understand discrimination." Instead, Sterling turned the tables on Stiviano by rearticulating the centrality of Black–white dichotomies to certain racialized conceptions of Jewish identity. Appealing to an immutable conception of race, he notes, "It's the world! You go to Israel, the blacks are just treated like dogs!" Disabusing her of the notion that his Jewishness somehow racializes his identity or provides a standpoint from which to reflect about the harms of discrimination and persecution, he insisted that "there's white Jews and black Jews, do you understand?"

Sterling's deployment of Black–white binaries speaks to how whiteness has offered some Jewish American communities the ability to insulate themselves from persecution and ascend through the class system by adhering to the ideologies of race that structured U.S. culture.

Historian Eric L. Goldstein observed "the tremendous pressures Jews and similar groups were under to conform to the dominant racial paradigm, and the significant constraints that were placed on expressions of group difference by a world intent on seeing itself in terms of black and white."[50] For this reason, some Jews were "pushed toward whiteness" in the pursuit of performing Americanness.[51] Anti-Semitism notwithstanding, for Jewish immigrants from Europe, whiteness unlocked some racial and class privileges.

Formerly named Donald Tokowitz, Sterling and his family fled Eastern Europe to escape persecution and settled in Chicago. Several community newspapers rebuked Sterling's comments and noted that he has not maintained a strong connection with the Jewish community, Los Angeles, or anywhere for that matter, since his youth.[52] In shedding his ethnic and religious identity, Sterling crafted for himself a colorless persona along with a colorless name, synonymous with success: "Sterling." He reportedly told one colleague, "You have to name yourself after something that's really good, that people have confidence in. People want to know that you're the best."[53] As Sterling suggests, his colorlessness is more salient to him than his Jewish identity. Here, the Black–white dichotomy also insulated his whiteness from contamination from his Jewish ancestry. To the extent he cannot outrun history, he made it clear that white Jews are at the top of the racial hierarchy.

Furthermore, Sterling balked at the notion that his ancestry necessitates that he take up an anti-racist stance. Racism is simply the reality in which we live, neither a question of "what's right and wrong" nor something we should feel compelled to change. More importantly, to adopt an anti-racist stance based on his own identity, or Stiviano's for that matter, would be to acknowledge that whiteness is constructed and therefore does not share a taken-for-granted and ontological relationship with humanness. It would be to acknowledge that there is an aspect of his ancestry that aligns him with a historic identity category that has experienced persecution.

Stiviano asked, "But shouldn't we take a stand for what's wrong? And be the change and the difference?" Sterling responded, "I don't want to change the culture, because I can't. It's too big." Although Sterling conflated desirability with efficacy, he ultimately refused to acknowledge a scenario in which he might experience anti-Semitism; scenarios that might in some way darken his complexion by racializing his identity. Sterling's remarks illustrate the rhetorical entailments of anxiety once again, but this time in a refusal of empathy that might otherwise admit that whiteness is neither pure nor static. Sterling's racial realism dictates that the Black–white dichotomy be understood as inescapable, normative, and ontological. His repudiation of interracial or interethnic solidarity refused an understanding of whiteness as an arbitrary, promiscuous, and impure category that would exclude Jews from its privileges.

As their conversation came to a close, Sterling refused Stiviano's efforts to contextualize his racial lens as part of a history of racial hatred:

D.S.:   I don't want to change. If my girl can't do what I want, I don't want the girl. I'll find a girl that will do what I want! Believe me. I thought you were that girl—because I tried to do what you want. But you're not that girl.

V.S.:   It's like saying, "Let's just persecute and kill all of the Jews."

D.S.:   Oh, it's the same thing, right?

V.S.:   Isn't it wrong? Wasn't it wrong then? With the Holocaust? And you're Jewish, you understand discrimination.

D.S.:   You're a mental case, you're really a mental case. The Holocaust, we're comparing with—

V.S.:   Racism! Discrimination.

D.S.:   There's no racism here. If you don't want to be . . . walking . . . into a basketball game with a certain . . . person, is that racism?

Though her comparison of anti-Blackness to Nazism lacks sophistication and elides important historical differences in racist violence, Sterling's objection to this characterization of his racial lens advanced a willful ignorance of the continuities in racism across comparative contexts. This exchange illustrates several strategies of white denialism. First, Sterling personalized Stiviano's remarks as harmful to their relationship, even calling her remarks "painful." Second, he pathologized her remarks as the delusions of someone with a diminished mental capacity, calling her a "mental case" for comparing the Holocaust with other forms of racism. Finally, he minimized her concern by framing his perspective as simply a question of free association. Here, only something as significant and incomparable as the Holocaust can be characterized as racism. Everyday racism, then, is banal or otherwise reducible to an apolitical notion of personal choice. Here, Sterling both protected his whiteness by refusing racist violence as a possible point of identification with Stiviano and by minimizing racism as mundane, apolitical, and inevitable.

Racist Apologia and Ritual Purification

Donald Sterling expressed a racist doctrine that is rarely voiced publicly by prominent figures or celebrities. Of course, his comments were never meant for public consumption. Although virtually no one came to his defense, figures such as NBA team owner Mark Cuban and comedian Bill Maher both expressed apprehension about private conversations becoming fodder for public controversies.[54] Others questioned Stiviano's motives for recording the conversation and entrusting the tape to a friend who allegedly released it to TMZ. Many in the tabloid press have speculated that Stiviano recorded their conversation as retaliation for Rochelle Sterling's $1.8 million lawsuit against her for millions in gifts she received from Donald.[55] Questions of privacy and ill motive aside, the publication of their conversations transformed Sterling's backstage racism into a highly visible manifestation of white anxiety over people of color trespassing into spaces of white leisure. At the same time, the tapes obscure the fact that Sterling had already always practiced racism in the open with little to no sanction from the NBA and other team owners. The tapes are artifacts of racial capitalism that illustrate how white bourgeois subjects cultivate investments in whiteness to insulate white identity from contamination by the interracial relationships that their social and economic systems entail. The rhetorical work on whiteness happens as much in public as it does within the enclaves where racial difference is not permitted to enter, though typically in a more opaque form. Anxiety is provoked at precisely the moment that people of color enter white enclaves and threaten to destabilize the assumed yet arbitrary connection between whiteness and universal humanness.

As a matter of rhetorical concern, the publication of these tapes also threatened to expose and destabilize the white power structures of professional sports, particularly in a league that can only muster three Black-majority owners.[56] Hence, the Sterling tapes exist within a symbolic economy that demands safe distance between privately held interests and publicly expressed commitments. The recordings did not merely index or portray Sterling's personal experience of racial anxiety, but instead publicized a collective yet unacknowledged bourgeois investments in white as a master signifier. At the highest echelons of professional sports ownership, whiteness is prime real estate. Sterling's words are illustrative of broader white phobic reactions to abject conceptions of negative difference, particularly where the meaning of white space is transformed by the presence of people of color. In this case, inclusion threatened to undo the structures of racial capitalism that protected whiteness from the threat of negative difference.

At the same time, whiteness is ambivalent as to how to manage the fear of difference. White ambivalence names a conflicted desire to maintain racial stratification but asks that such a system not be characterized as racist. American novelist James Baldwin presciently observed that white ambivalence of this kind was the central dynamic precluding racial equality in America. He wrote in 1962 that "a vast amount of the energy that goes into what we call the Negro problem is produced by the white man's profound desire not to be judged by those who are not white, not to be seen as he is, and at the same time a vast amount of the white anguish is rooted in the white man's equally profound need to be seen as he is, to be released from the tyranny of his mirror."[57] Sterling is a fitting embodiment of Baldwin's portrait—a man who can demand that his girlfriend not broadcast her association with Black men and, in the same breath, say that such Black men are "fabulous." He expressed racists attitudes but was also offended by Stiviano's accusation that such attitudes be branded as racism. Thus, we might say that his rhetoric mediates a crisis of whiteness that is induced by the visibility of upwardly mobile people of color.

Similar to the racist tirades examined in the previous chapter, Sterling's remarks help maintain the public secret of racial capitalism. Distracted by the desire to continually reveal the secret nature of "real racism," eavesdroppers are diverted from an encounter with the open operation of racial capitalism that hides in plain sight. Sterling had practiced racial discrimination and harassment publicly without even a reprimand from the league until the leaked tapes became public. The spectacular promise of the big reveal overshadows that racism was never hidden in the first place. This is the case because his comments are only *rhetorically* divergent from the public brand of the NBA, not its actual ownership practices. Although other owners may not share his racist views, the ownership structure of the NBA is by and large white. That means the ownership ranks are seldom permeable and that the elite social world erected around those ownership structures does not reflect the diversity of its laborers. Moreover, this white ownership structure profits from a trade in athletes of color. Sterling named this reality when he noted that Black men are fabulous but that they also have no place in his social world. Yet, even without the publication of his remarks, Clipper's players understood that this was Sterling's credo. In both the 2020 documentary *Blackballed* and the EPSN *30-for-30* podcast series "The Sterling Affairs," Clippers players Chris Paul and Blake Griffin recalled disturbing incidents in which Sterling would make surprise visits with his friends to the locker room before games.[58] In these visits, Sterling would show off and "pet" the player's "beautiful black bodies." ESPN Sports commentator Stephen A. Smith surmised that Sterling "viewed NBA players as cattle."[59] Similar practices were documented in Elgin Baylor's

2009 discrimination lawsuit but did not draw sanction from the league.[60] It took a scandal over explicitly racist speech and the protests of Clipper's players and coaches to hold him accountable for years of racist practices.[61] In this way, the big reveal concealed what was already known.

Although NBA commissioner Adam Silver issued Sterling a lifetime ban from the league, he framed his decision in terms of the league's commitment to multiculturalism rather than his systematically racist ownership practices, including his sexual harassment of players and insistence on building all-Black teams from the "ghetto" with white coaches and managers.[62] Silver responded to Sterling's remarks with a series of vague postracial platitudes, declaring that "the views expressed by Mr. Sterling are deeply offensive and harmful; that they came from an NBA owner only heightens the damage and my personal outrage. Sentiments of this kind are contrary to the principles of inclusion and respect that form the foundation of our diverse, multicultural and multiethnic league."[63] Although Silver is correct that the league is diverse, its ownership structure is not. The tapes, then, represent the return of the repressed—racist discourses and practices thought to have been banished to the private enclave suddenly reappearing to explicitly mark an underlying investment in whiteness. Although the investments expressed by Sterling ultimately structure racial capitalism, Silver did not connect these individual expressions of racism to the larger structures that do not conceal their operations.

Though perhaps well intentioned, Silver's banishment inadvertently preserved the league's racial stratification by simply removing an individual perpetrator. Much like other racist tirades, the Sterling–Stiviano tapes initiated a public ritual of scapegoating that functioned to relegate such racial sentiments back to the private enclave—to perhaps be "discovered" again when the next racist incident comes to light. While Sterling's comments constitute a phobic reaction to racial difference, his rhetoric did initiate an uncomfortable public discussion about racism in professional sports. As several scholars have noted, however, Silver and the popular press responded to Sterling with a myriad of postracial tropes, which include, among others, that Sterling's racism is aberrant in our present multicultural world.[64] As Katherine L. Lavelle writes: "[T]he league simultaneously celebrates Black culture, while attempting to regulate any potential consequences from the 'messiness' of its identity."[65] Indeed, postracial culture quickly absorbed Sterling's remarks and transformed them into an occasion to celebrate diversity without acknowledging the ongoing structural racism in professional sports and beyond. Silver's statement ultimately allayed the very white racial anxiety entailed in Sterling's remarks.

Sterling's "apology" not only contributed to Silver's postracial framing but also resurrected the very racism he wished to disown. In a CNN interview, Sterling explained, "I love my league, I love my partners. Am I entitled to one mistake? It's a terrible mistake, and I'll never do it again. . . . I'm here to apologize."[66] Of course, the suggestion that his remarks were a mistake is refuted by decades of well-documented racist behavior. It is fitting that Sterling referred to the league as a personal possession, much in the same manner as he treated *his* Black players. Throughout the interview, Sterling vacillated between gestures of contrition and diversionary attacks on both Stiviano and Magic Johnson. In one sense, he evaded responsibility by blaming Stiviano for baiting him into expressing beliefs that were supposedly not his own. Sterling argued: "When I listen to that tape, I don't even know how I can say words like that. . . . I don't know why the girl had me say those things. . . . Yes, I was baited. I mean, that's not the way I talk. I don't talk about people for one thing, ever. I talk about ideas and other things. I don't talk about people." Here, Sterling constructs a split subjectivity: a present self who disowns the statements of his other, less recognizable version of himself. This other self was an easily deceived dotard, "an 80-year-old man" who is "kind of foolish." Thus, Sterling cast Stiviano in the role of a conniving femme fatale who tricked him into making false and incriminating statements. "I just wish I could ask her why, and if she was just setting me up." He cast himself as a dupe who bore no responsibility for his careless remarks. If anything, Sterling would have us believe that *he* was the real victim of this tragedy.

Despite his contention that his does not talk negatively about other people, Sterling proceeded to make more demeaning and racist statements about Johnson's HIV status. Sterling constructed Johnson as a disease pariah: a hypersexual, AIDS-infected monster who is undeserving of white respect. Sterling suggested that "if I said anything wrong I'm sorry. He's a good person. . . . I mean, what am I going to say? Has he done everything he can do to help minorities? I don't think so. But I'll say it, he's great. But I don't think he's a good example for the children of Los Angeles." When asked to clarify what his cryptic remarks meant, Sterling accused Johnson of being a hypersexual and disease-spreading buck. Sterling boldly declared that "he acts so holy. He made love to every girl in every city in America, and he got AIDS. . . . I didn't criticize him. I could have. Is he an example to those children?" Incredulously, he asked Anderson Cooper, "What has he done?" As

Cooper began to respond, Sterling interrupted: "He's got AIDS. . . . I think he should be ashamed of himself. I think he should go in the background." Here, Sterling's use of paralipsis centers attention on the subject he professes he wished to avoid: Johnson's moral (sexual and racial) character. Of course, this is precisely the issue for Sterling: Johnson, he believes, is not someone worth defending. Sterling's remarks also reflect how the rhetoric of HIV/AIDS impose what Chávez refers to as "alienizing logics" that excise and exclude communities associated with contagion.[67] In addition to exclusion, Jeffrey A. Bennett observes that rhetorics of contagion enable "normal" citizens "to articulate their identities with the culturally sanitized images of the nation-state that circulated in popular discourse of nationalism."[68] In the same vein, Sterling constructed Johnson as a shameful and dangerous contagion to not only discredit his public image but also to sanitize and sanctify his own.

At this point, Sterling's apology unraveled and merely served to clarify his concerns about Stiviano appearing with Johnson in public. Sterling's anxiety concerned not only racial but also sexual contamination by association. For Sterling, Johnson was a hypersexual disease pariah, and any hint of an intimate relationship between him and Stiviano threatened both physical and symbolic pollution. Sterling mobilized the affective economies of anti-Blackness and contagion that shaped the cold and indifferent responses at the beginning of the HIV/AIDS crisis. Sterling uses Johnson's HIV-positive status to impugn Black masculinity for its excessive sexuality and to punish its transgression. In this way, he also intimates that Johnson shares much in common with the gay men who were blamed for the HIV/AIDS crisis, particularly the notion that becoming infected was punishment for sin.

In other ways, his "apology" simply fleshed out the racist inferences left unexplained in his previous conversations with Stiviano. Like the racist melodrama explored in Chapter 1, Sterling resurrects stock characters who embattle and threaten white masculinity: the fallen woman (Stiviano), the buck (Johnson), and the victimized white hero (himself). Although Sterling's own sexual affairs undoubtedly showcase the hypocrisy of his moralizing, Sterling relies on his whiteness to protect him from such scrutiny. That is to say that tropes of hypersexuality and disease pariahs tend to locate the excesses of white masculinity exclusively in people of color.[69] He relied on the poor character attributed to men and women of color to protect his own reputation and evade responsibility for his racist beliefs and practices.

The ritual purification that took place after the release of the Sterling tapes functioned to contain both Sterling and the threat of racial difference. It is fitting the Sterling invoked abject representations of Johnson and Stiviano to expel them and resecure the borders of whiteness. Of course, Sterling's comments were threatening not simply because they were racist, but because they spelled out the informal and often opaque norms that underwrite the structures of contemporary racial capitalism. His legal and rhetorical banishment ultimately bolstered the myth that professional sports is a paragon of structural racial equality. Sterling himself becomes abject in the process: a racist monster who must be expelled for a sense of normalcy to return. Although the NBA has a far better track record on race than other professional sports organizations, Sterling's comments pointed directly to the structural mechanisms that foreclose the possibility that its ownership structures might actually match its lofty ideals.

These articulations of containment also make sense of how Sterling rhetorically delimited charges of racism through tropes long associated with stigmatizing and dehumanizing victims of marginalization and discrimination. His words discredit the very people wounded by his racist attitudes and shifted the conversation toward questions of the other's moral character. In short, he attempted to silence their right to speak or, at the very least, minimize their concerns by constructing himself as a victim of their treachery. He constructs Stiviano as the *fallen women*: a gold-digger, a master manipulator, and a liar. Johnson—the target of Sterling's racism—was rendered unworthy of Sterling's apology on account of his morally dubious character and physical contagion. He cast Johnson as a hypersexual buck whose lack of sexual restraint made him unworthy of breathing the same rarified air as Sterling. Sterling, too, cast them out of his social world much in the same way he evicted tenants from his Los Angeles rental properties—people he also systematically abused and dehumanized through the tropes of contagion. The difference is that he committed these acts in full public view; something more worthy of our attention than the fruitless pursuit of perpetually outing the secret racist beliefs of people who participate in larger systems of oppression. Sterling's double exposure was simply to be folded back into the spectacle of racial capitalism. The crime is that it took white people this long to notice.

3

YouRacist.com

The Libidinal Economy of Public Freak Out Videos

On his YouTube channel "Roland Martin Unfiltered," journalist Roland S. Martin features a recurring segment entitled "Crazy Ass White People." In this segment, Martin presents and comments on the latest viral videos of racist outbursts "caught on tape." The segment is introduced with a montage of grainy amateur smartphone footage of white people harassing people of color, using racial epithets, and generally displaying aggressive and out-of-control behaviors. Martin and his guests offer commentary and analysis of the events depicted for viewers—ranging from apoplectic criticism to satirical mockery. Martin even provides his Black viewers with tips about how to use smartphones to capture the best-quality video when they encounter a volatile white person caught up in the throes of a racist panic.[1] Martin explained that the instructions are "how to identify and capture crazy-ass white people . . . when they doing and saying crazy ass shit." Joking tones aside, his advice offers practical self-protection for people of color who face the threat of systemic harassment and violence when they leave their homes. Documenting racist behavior in public can help identify racist assailants, exonerate victims from blame, and potentially deter further escalation. Smartphone technology has made it remarkably easier for witnesses to provide concrete evidence of racist violence and police brutality—as was the case with the successful prosecution of Derek Chauvin for the murder of George Floyd.

Martin's "Crazy Ass White People" segment curates an ever-growing collection of amateur videos that document everyday racists incidents. As the tongue-in-cheek title suggests, there is a great deal that does not make sense in videos that present white people lashing out at people of color for inexplicable reasons. One key insight of psychoanalysis is that subjects often do and say things for motives they do not consciously understand. This does not absolve racist perpetrators, but simply acknowledges that racism speaks in the voice of the Other. The Other's irruptions bespeak a language and culture

Caught on Tape. Casey Ryan Kelly, Oxford University Press. © Oxford University Press 2023.
DOI: 10.1093/oso/9780197677865.003.0004

organized around the libidinal economy of chattel slavery and its attendant delusions, fantasies, and anxieties. A structural approach explains how the mere presence of racial difference in presumptively white spaces seems to rouse these white subjects into what at first blush appears to be an irrational and uncontrollable rage.

Yet, to call the subject's featured in this genre "crazy" belies both the banality and underwriting logics of racist violence—which is to say that there *is* a logical and historical coherence to white rage. Ersula Ore's scholarship on lynching rhetoric illustrates how seemingly spontaneous acts of racist violence have always operated according to perverse yet lucid doctrines derived from a racist common sense concerning the threat of "black debauchery."[2] Echoing Ida B. Wells, Ore writes that "antiblack violence was not aberrant to America's ways but a constitutive practice of them and its people."[3] A pathological framing of racist outbursts, then, partitions the ecstatic rage of white supremacy from the general operation of whiteness. It locates racism within individual subjects—sick or toxic individuals—as opposed to an immanent presence embedded within the social structures that govern everyday life.[4] As Derek Hook argues, "[R]acist *jouissance* . . . is never simply a spontaneous individual psychological reaction. It is, by contrast, conditioned by precise historical and symbolic conditions . . . the threat that the racial order is thought to pose is invariably defined relative to the ego-ideals of a given society, to those symbolic values for which members of the society are willing to live and die for."[5] Here, obscene enjoyment is difficult to pin down as a structural dynamic because it appears to audiences in such an arresting and spectacular form. To the extent that racist *jouissance* terrorizes people of color and buttresses white sovereignty, it constitutes white supremacy taken to its ultimate conclusion in symbolic and physical violence. Noting how racism is frequently reduced to an individual pathology, Nathan Stormer implores critics to "learn from Black pain, not to stare at its spectacle."[6] Much like spectators of lynching, it is the excessive spectacle of racist *jouissance* that mediates against white subjects seeing parts of themselves in the violence captured on their smartphones.

My purpose is not to critique Martin's advice to people of color, but rather to use his recurring segment as an aperture into the drama of racist *jouissance* that spills out recklessly into our social networks and to explore the implications of consuming an emerging genre of amateur video: the "racist freak out." The ubiquity of cameras and recording technology virtually guarantees that no excessive transgression or public outburst will go undocumented. The diffusion of new media technologies arms ordinary citizens with the capacity to make news and notoriety out of the everyday events that occur in their proximity. In convergence culture, a video or sound recording can transform into an object of intense collective scrutiny and outrageous investment—from the ordinary citizen lurking in the comment section of YouTube to the cadre of talking heads paraded throughout broadcast media. Platforms that depend on user-generated content for advertising revenue entice users to plug such transgressive and shocking moments into a vast technological and cultural infrastructure in the hopes that what would have otherwise been an ephemeral event will "go viral" and command our collective attention economies. A thirty-second racist outburst at a local fast-food restaurant or convenience store can be memorialized, circulated, and shared instantly across multiple social media platforms, and later remediated on the local or national television news.[7] A perverse mixture of outrage and voyeuristic curiosity guides spectators as algorithms ferry them across a media ecosphere that privileges and affords controversy, taboo, and excess.[8] A shared link from a friend or colleague, for instance, can propel one down a virtual rabbit hole of extreme amateur content. Viewing a video labeled "INSANE Racist Freak-Out at Walmart" might lead a user into a maze of other viral indexes: "Most Ridiculous Racist Rants of 2017," "Racist Karen has MELTDOWN Over Black Lives Matter," or "Man Goes on Racist Rant at Mexican Restaurant." Each view might be accompanied by an explicit call to "like" and "subscribe," or an implicit invitation to (re)watch, comment, react, or share. Social media networks also implore spectators to transform themselves into content producers—to film reality as it unfolds at the same time as contemporary media culture turns to unscripted programming to generate low-budget entertainment.[9] The point is to not merely anticipate and capture volatile situations in our everyday lives but perhaps to even seek out and provoke uncomfortable encounters with the racism bubbling beneath the surface.

Transformations in new and emerging media have also constructed a new scaffolding through which everyday people can achieve (or at the very least, consume) fame and notoriety. Celebrity is no longer the exclusive province of the "star system"[10] of corporately controlled media industries; rather, celebrity is the byproduct of a diffuse and localized collection of "self-presentation practices" that garner followers and sustain attention in a distracted and hype-mediated cultural milieu.[11] Marwick observes, on social networks "the highest value is given to mediation, visibility, and attention."[12]

As convergence culture depends on consumers for the relentless circulation and production of content, everyday life becomes both the terrain and the source material for entertaining content.[13] The predominance and convergence of reality television and social networking mean that virtually anyone, regardless of intent, can attain notoriety. Consider that reality television elevates ordinariness as the basis of celebrity (programming about unexceptional people and their travails) while also making stars into ordinary people (programming about celebrities in unexceptional circumstances). Both senses of celebrity operate by the logics of *exposure*: ordinary people are revealed to be spectacular and spectacular people are revealed to be ordinary. Social networking sites amplify the new dynamics of celebrity in reality television by revolutionizing public conceptions of privacy and affording both a greater degree of self-disclosure along with an impulse to also publicize other people's excessive behaviors. In both social networks and reality television, self-disclosure and raw emotion have currency insofar as they are seen as expressions of our authentic selves. Obscene behavior is more likely to circulate because it is both spectacular and "real" or "genuine." As Dubrofksy observes, these dynamics explain, in part, why Donald Trump was so successful in mobilizing his electorate.[14] As I will argue in Chapter 4, Trump embodied and tapped into the libidinal economies of social networking and reality television where authenticity and raw affect organize spectator's enjoyment. Hence, the more obscene and audacious the behavior, the more likely his content would circulate. Thus, in a convergence culture that traffics in both fame and notoriety, authenticity and raw affect, the ordinary media spectator is awash in other people's enjoyment.

Thus far, this book has been concerned with fraught modes of spectatorship relative to scandals involving powerful public figures caught up in ruinous forms of racist and misogynistic *jouissance*. This chapter, however, is concerned with the diffusion of obscene enjoyment into social networks and the kind of gratifications enjoined by the consumption and circulation of public transgression. As social networks scale down the concept of celebrity, they also scale up public scandal from the mundane to the spectacular. A well-timed or serendipitous YouTube video can both make an ordinary person famous overnight as much as it can bring them infamy, unwanted hostility, and public scrutiny. Among its many affordances, YouTube is a *scandal machine*: it invites users to document the terrible behaviors of ordinary people and upload them for the world to behold. The platform's repertoire of taboo content includes amateur footage of fist fights over toys at Walmart, violent road rage incidents, verbal assaults on service workers, profanity-laced tirades, and vile incidents of hate speech. Although YouTube prohibits racist and otherwise violent content, it permits some forms of hate speech but only if it is presented in documentary or educational contexts.[15] This exempts some footage posted or aggregated by individual users as well as clips from news broadcasts reporting about viral videos of hate speech incidents. As such, YouTube has evolved into a repository of racist *jouissance*, or the increasingly "illicit gratifications of racism" in a political and cultural environment "where racism is prohibited."[16] This chapter explores the documentation of everyday racist irruptions as they are then assembled into a social feed, circulated, and consumed—ostensibly for the educational benefit of the viewer. What kind of encounter with racism do such videos stage for the viewer? What is, to use Raymond Williams's words, the "structure of feeling" that organizes viewers relationship to ordinary people caught on tape?[17] What kind of social structures are made visible or, perhaps more importantly, concealed by exposure to everyday hate speech? How do such videos figure into the politics of white masculinity?

In addressing these questions, this chapter argues that the documentation of racist outbursts on YouTube and other user-generated content sites is governed by a libidinal economy that structurally (re)secures whiteness and white masculinity against the threat of race. By libidinal economy, I am referring to a system of exchange and valuation of fantasies, desires, enjoyment, and anxiety. I am concerned, then, with how psychical energies that govern investments in race and gender are mobilized, affected, directed, and exchanged. Libidinal economy denotes the balance of psychical costs and payoff of spectatorship, the organization of psychical impulses, and the satisfactions that are routed through and attached to specific objects (in Freud's words, *cathexis*).[18] Frank B. Wilderson observes that libidinal economy "is linked not only to forms of attraction, affection, and alliance, but also to aggression, destruction, and the violence of lethal consumption."[19] As Fanon reminds us, the libidinal economy of anti-black racism is organized around both fantasies of control, violence, and mass murder but also delusions of sexual consumption by Blackness.[20] In conversation with Wilderson, Jared Sexton notes that libidinal economy charts how "anti-black fantasies attain objective value in the political and economic life of society and in the psychic life of culture as well."[21] In this context, it is important to ask why it is that we must circulate the ritual dehumanization and humiliation of people of color to provide an object lesson on the ongoing power of white supremacy? In answering this question economically, this chapter approaches "racist freak out" videos as displacements of desire that shield the spectator from seeing themselves in the presentational regime of white supremacy. Videos under such categorization court affective investments in the experience of racist *jouissance* as that which putatively unlocks antiracist alternatives. Following Hartman, I attended to how the documentation of racism calls on white subjects to "participate in such scenes," but by disidentifying with the racist perpetrators and segregating their actions from progressive white identity. This disidentification takes place through two registers. First, racist freak out videos and YouTube compilations pathologize white supremacy by representing racism as violent excess rather than banal and routine practice. Second, racist freak out videos borrow from the pacing schemes also found in both pornographic films and reality television whereby the moment of racist revelation and punishment comes to represent racism in its "real" or authentic form. Both registers enable white spectators to disavow their relationship with racism and blame white supremacy on "bad apples" whose anachronistic bigotry precludes the fulfillment of a progressive postracial society. In the remainder of this chapter, then, I follow the algorithm that traffics users throughout YouTube's libidinal economy by beginning with a search for "racist freak outs," "racist rant," and "racist outburst" and following the algorithm-recommended videos to illustrate the patterns of racial disavowal that emerge in repetitive viewing practices in relation to racist *jouissance*.[22]

Platform Pathologies

YouTube is the platform of choice for amateur video. In 2021, YouTube had 2.6 billion active monthly users worldwide who cumulatively watched 1 billion hours of video, with 500 hours of video uploaded every minute. In the United States, approximately 81 percent of adults use YouTube. Thus, the platform is also extraordinarily lucrative. In 2021 alone, the site generated $8.6 billion in advertising revenue.[23] Although YouTube supports a wide variety of amateur and professional content, the platform's infrastructure, algorithms, and policies enable certain kinds of videos to circulate with ease. Despite having specific policies barring violence and hate speech, YouTube tends to approach regulating the platform in a manner consistent with Silicon Valley's libertarian and neoliberal ethos.[24] The site's algorithm, which helps customize content for particular viewers and recommends additional videos, tends to privilege and circulate controversial and polemical content. This accounts for the prevalence of racism and hate speech that traffics throughout the site, much of which is difficult to monitor and remove. As so much of online racism is dressed up in irony and satire, it makes it exceedingly difficult for content monitors to label content as inappropriate. Likewise, racist freak out videos (which circulate quite well) tend to evade censorship because they do not automatically register as endorsements of hate speech. The work they do on behalf of white supremacy takes an extraordinary amount of rhetorical acumen that one would not necessarily expect to find in those who manage the site. Ariadna Matamoros-Fernández uses the term "platform racism" to describe how this combination of laisse-faire policy, algorithmic bias, and amplification tools (likes, shares, and comments) helps traffic racism throughout YouTube.[25] She explains that platforms such as YouTube are "tools for amplifying and manufacturing racist discourse both by means of users' appropriations of their affordances and through their design and algorithmic shaping of sociability."[26] Platform racism characterizes how choices made by programmers and the algorithms they program build in affordances for racism to circulate, particularly when racist freak outs are assumed to be anti-racist and educational.[27] Permitting such videos to circulate suggests to spectators that their content is either neutral or disconnected from the libidinal economy of white supremacy. Yet, as this chapter suggests, these videos function as a kinder, gentler accompaniment to more graphic and extreme videos of police murders as well as videos that openly endorse hate speech and racist violence.

As Steve Martinot and Sexton observe, representations of excessive overt acts of white supremacy draw attention away from the banality of everyday racist violence.[28] In their critique of recordings of police brutality, they contend that "if the hegemony of white supremacy is already (and only) excessive, its acts of repetition are its access to unrepresentability; they dissolve its excessiveness into invisibility as simply daily occurrence."[29] The spectacular pathologizes white supremacy and obscures how everyday passive whiteness owes its existence to violence and terror. The informal networks of power and privilege that maintain structural racial inequality owe a debt to spectacular violence for both terrorizing people of color and distancing whites from their complicity with white supremacy. The portrait of racism that emerges from the spectacular is that white supremacy is primarily maintained by rogue white cops, rural and southern conservatives, mentally ill individuals, and poorly educated whites. Whiteness, however, is an ideology rather than a character defect in aberrant individuals. The privileges of whiteness are conferred to white subjects often without their awareness or consent. Yet, the structures of spectatorship would have viewers make sense of racist behaviors as pathologies—aberrations, deviancies, or diseases that corrupt the normal operation of innocent or progressive white identity. It is therefore possible that documenting racist outbursts can, at once, make white supremacy visible and occlude its more banal but nonetheless terrifying presence in everyday life.

This pathological frame does not simply suggest that racism is the byproduct of mental illness or stress, but that racism itself is an irrational belief structure held by whites with low IQs and poor moral character. Hence, portraits of overwrought, uncontrolled, and excessive racist *jouissance* belies the privileges conferred by white supremacy and the rational interests it serves—even if it is simply paying the *psychological* wage of whiteness.[30] The mysterious and ecstatic quality of *jouissance* should not occlude how racist irruptions figure into the logical and ideological consistency of white supremacy. As racism is structural and systemic, racism is not solely located in the corrupted minds of individuals who harass people of color, spew hate speech, and preach white supremacy. Yet, as Eduardo Bonilla-Silva argues, "hunting for 'racists' is the sport of choice of those who practice the 'clinical approach' to race relations—the careful separation of good and bad, tolerant and intolerant Americans."[31] Racist freak out videos can easily engender this "clinical approach" to racism by segmenting and quarantining racist offenders from the general population—gawking at and chastising their seemingly aberrant behavior. Indeed, whiteness escapes scrutiny where individual racism is what separates bad whites from good; irrational from rational.[32]

The titles of racist freak out videos bespeak this pathological frame: "INSANE Racist Freak-out at a Walmart,"[33] "Another Day, Another INSANE RACIST FREAKOUT at Walmart,"[34] "Racist Lunatic Harasses Gas Station Worker,"[35] "Crazy A$$ Racist Harasses Black Neighbor,"[36] and "WTH?!? Crazy Racist Man Hurls N-Word at a Black Woman During a Road-Rage Incident."[37] Advertising extreme and controversial content, such titles are primed to circulate according to YouTube's algorithms that provide viewers with additional video recommendations to keep them watching.[38] The videos show racism expressed in the form of rage where the perpetrator seems to lose control of their mental faculties and inhibitions. Some subjects appear to be mentally ill, inebriated, or under the influence of drugs. Their words are slurred and their statements are incoherent. They sometimes cackle inappropriately, express a wild swing of emotions, and even seem like they might be a danger to themselves. Sometimes they resort to physical violence. Ultimately, the perpetrator's state of mind can only be a matter of speculation; however, the videos and their creators help frame an encounter with racism in an ecstatic and seemingly uncontrolled form.

Naming is, to be sure, an important rhetorical act that has the power to define, frame, interpret, and construct reality. The above titles are designed to not only capture a viewer's attention, but also to circumscribe the meaning of the experience being documented for their consumption. Prior to viewing, such titles already articulate racist events as pathological excesses. Racism expressed in public is framed as insanity, lunacy, and out(rage)ousness—anything but the expression of an investment and interest in preserving white power, or at the very least, distancing good white people from the "bad apples."[39] But Carol Anderson observes that white rage *does* have a logical structure that is internally consistent. Simply put, "[T]he trigger for white rage, inevitably, is black advancement."[40] This is precisely the logical structure one can lose sight of when they descend into the racist outburst rabbit hole.

Before attending to the rhetorical and mediated structure of such videos, it is important to note that individual YouTube users and content creators frequently treat racist videos as educational resources and use them to dispel and demystify the nonsensical rantings of pathological racists. In this regard, racist outburst videos are a resource for left-of-center and progressive content creators to take up the clinical practice of distancing good whites from bad.

Many racist freak out videos feature both white men and white women publicly policing the behavior of people of color. Although it would be strictly speculative to conjecture about behavioral motives, the cultural assumptions about what constitutes an acceptable expression of public emotions can explain how spectators are positioned to interpret emotional excess. For white men, rage is often one of the only suitable emotions fit for public expression.[41] For white women, however, a host of gender norms circumscribe their ability to express anger, including longstanding beliefs that women are always already governed by emotion and sentiment rather than reason. Although white men's racist outbursts are still nonetheless arresting, white women's outbursts de-gender the assailants insofar as they are traditionally conceptualized under patriarchy as meek, demur, pious, passive, and servile. Yet, white women's racist outbursts nonetheless serve the interests of white masculine authority by policing people of color and protecting white men's dominion over public space.

Hence, I read white men and white women's racist tirades as supportive of a white masculine social and political order. To the degree that such videos enable spectators to distance themselves from racist excess, viewing such videos occludes the racialized and gendered complexity of white supremacy. Videos that feature white women's racist outbursts are often organized under the label of "racist Karen." By "Karen" posters refer to a popular caricature (and meme) of middle-aged white women who throw public tantrums when they are inconvenienced or call the police on persons of color based on their warped perception that they are somehow threatening or do not belong in public spaces.[42] In videos featuring so-called Karens, the violation is perhaps more extreme, given the degree to which white supremacy is assumed to be carried out primarily by men. Yet, white women have always played an important role in the maintenance of white supremacy—as both icons of innocence in anti-miscegenation rhetoric and as subjects afforded privileges by virtue of their proximity to white masculine power.[43] White women have played a vital role in hate groups such as the Ku Klux Klan, particularly its second iteration in the 1920s.[44] Despite his overt misogyny, a majority of white women voted for Trump in 2016. There is, then, an internally consistent logic between white femininity and masculinized white supremacy that is overlooked in videos about "mad" men and "crazy" Karens.

In both cases, race freak out videos present white supremacy as an individual pathology disconnected from broader ideological investments. There are countless videos to choose from; thus, I have selected videos that have been viewed hundreds of thousands, if not millions, of times, and that are indicative of a larger pattern of representation. For example, one user, Hasan Abi, who has approximately 758,000 subscribers, frequently posts videos with commentary related to public outburst, bigotry, and the perplexing public behavior of conservatives.[45] On August 6, 2021, Abi livestreamed his analysis of a viral video of a racist outburst by a Los Angeles firefighter ("INSANE Racist Freak Out at Walmart"). In this video, Abi replays portions of the viral video, occasionally pausing to satirize and refute the outrageous claims made by the assailant. His tactic was to point out the utter absurdity and stupidity of racism, often resorting to caricatures of racist statement mimicked in an exaggerated southern accent. At one point in the video, he mocked the perpetrator by speaking in character as an ignorant racist with a rural southern drawl: "He could have just said . . . yeah I don't give a fuck I'm just racist, I want to be racist, okay I'm gonna do racism, I was a firefighter and I want to do racism, okay." The punchline to this joke is that racism is a kind of social illiteracy practiced by backward, poorly educated, southern whites. This move exemplifies what Jeanne Theoharis has characterized as the broad misuse of civil rights history to exonerate Jim Crow and white supremacy outside of the U.S. South.[46] The myth that white supremacy was and remains a regional phenomenon elides northern financial support for slavery, the second iteration of the Ku Klux Klan, widespread adherence to biological racism and eugenics, segregation, redlining, anti-immigrant nativism, and other forms of racism that thrived in the Midwest, North, and West.[47] As Brian J. Purnell and Theoharis suggest, "[I]f racism is only pictured in spitting and screaming, in torches and vigilante justice and an allegiance to the Confederacy, many Americans can rest easy, believing they share little responsibility in its perpetuation. But the truth is, Americans all over the country do bear responsibility for racial segregation and inequality."[48] Indeed, Abi's caricature of southern racism is not only misplaced—the incident took place in Nebraska and the alleged perpetrator was from California—but also exemplifies how progressives alleviate their responsibility for racism by casting white supremacy as a southern pathological attachment to the "Lost Cause" of the Confederacy.

Throughout the remainder of the video, Abi identifies the logical incoherence of racist statements, noting the various inconsistencies and fallacies embraced by white men in a fit of rage. When the white man in the video justifies his hatred toward foreigners by referencing the 9/11 attacks, Abi pauses the video and in a laughing and incredulous tone remarks: "What the fuck?! Wait I don't understand, he's says that, like, he gets to be racist and fucking attack like a random Muslim woman and then fucking tell her to learn English because like 9/11? What the fuck?!" Although it is easy to share his apoplectic attitude, Abi's critique misses the inner coherence of the man's naked embrace of nativism and white supremacy. Indeed, Abi is right that the man seems to conflate Islamic extremism with the perceived threat of Spanish-speaking immigrants. Yet, when seen as a "phobic reaction" to a dark-skinned Other, his tirade channels an affective state of racial panic, which for Fanon argued that "there is an organization that been given form"; a form "endowed with evil intentions and with all the attributes of a malefic power."[49] As E. Chebrolu puts it, the man deployed a "racial lens" to read a "hieroglyphics of flesh," a network of racial signifiers inherited from the history of slavery, imperialism, and colonialism.[50] That his discourse is a pastiche of different racial stereotypes and delusion is beside the point—the man is engaged in a racist bricolage all underwritten by a consistent and contiguous set of white anxieties. But Abi continues to mock the man's racist contradictions, noting, "Bro, I'm like confused, like dude get your racist ducks in order . . . figure it out, do the right kind of racism, if you're going to do racism, like make us understand! . . . firefighters in another part of the country died 20 years ago so now I can yell racial slurs at whoever I want, is the incredible argument he is making, to be honest." Indeed, Abi is correct that racists are disturbingly comfortable with their own logical and ideological contradictions. But by focusing on rationality, his critique misses the overall affective economy that governs the confrontation.

Furthermore, the trouble with his analysis (and countless others like it) returns to Copjec's notion of "realist imbecility," or the liberal delusion that pointing out lies, fact-checking, and transparency can overcome deep psychic investments and desires.[51] In other words, pointing out that racism is rife with logical fallacies does not dislodge from the white imaginary the axiomatic conflation of whiteness and universal humanness. At best, reality referencing white supremacists woefully underestimates the affective gravity of racism. At worst, mocking caricatures can be pointed to as evidence of white men's aggrievement and further solidify the in-group identity of white supremacists.[52] Ultimately, the user's commentary reinforces the myth that racism is both regional and irrational.

While some individual users take advantage of livestream formats to dissect and analyze racist viral videos, other YouTube channels produce more professionally polished content. For instance, the channel for the popular culture blog *What's Trending* produces television-quality entertainment news segments about viral trends that mirror the production values and style of the E! network. The channel features several segments about racist freak out videos that remix widely viewed clips with host commentary. A segment entitled "Most Ridiculous Racist Rants of 2017" features a countdown of the most viewed and circulated videos from the year. The host Ava Gordy adopts a lighthearted and somewhat satirical tone as she laments the absurdity of each recorded incident. Although the tenor of Gordy's commentary is fitting for a website that features stories about social media trends, gaming, celebrities, fashion and makeup trends, it is at odds with the seriousness of the subject matter. Gordy introduces the compilation by announcing, "If 2017 has shown us anything, it's [that] American racism didn't end when Obama was president. I mean why would it? Why did we think it would? Truly?

Nope. Intolerance is still alive, like, Trump's Muslim ban and like that Nazi protest where literal white supremacists were marching in Charlottesville. What . . . the . . . fuck?!" Gordy's entertainment news cadence positions the viewer to relish the vile content but under a protective layer of dissociative humor. Her comic surprise that white supremacy has grown more comfortable in the open might prompt us ask: Is there anything especially astonishing about the ubiquity of overt racism?

What's Trending treats the subjects featured in these infamous videos as belonging to a class of poor and disreputable whites. First, after presenting each video, the host points out the assailant's poor logic. After a white man's anti-Spanish language rant, she laughingly chides the man, remarking, "American isn't a language" and jesting, "Don't throw your McDonald's! Oh! He threw his McDonald's at him." After several videos filmed in the same chain stores, Gordy observes, "All of these racist rants take place in just the top-notch places of the world. Walmart and McDonald's everybody." By noting, and quite sarcastically so, that these encounters happen in places that cater to low-income communities, Gordy also associates racism with poverty and ignorance. Looking down on such establishments as "low-class," there is a sense that one is more likely to encounter racism in places frequented by poor and uneducated whites. The poverty and ignorance frame is cemented by the fact that she refutes each assailant's undereducated claims: Obama is not a Muslim, one victim was in fact a U.S. citizen, and American is not a language. The portrait of racism assembled in this compilation is emblematic of the host of strategies by which racism is pathologized and good whites are separated from bad ones. These incidents are reframed as radical divergences from respectable progressive white identity. The perpetrators are segregated from this innocent white identity by virtue of their poor intellects, moral character, and irrational behavior. Their anachronistic attachment to racist thinking is a sign of pathology. Within this libidinal economy, the spectator is invited to see their desires as fundamentally different than those of the perverts depicted on screen.

The Money Shot

In her pioneering work on "body genres," film scholar Linda Williams contends that texts with a "low" cultural status such as pornography and horror tend to be maligned because they address the spectator's body and seek to elicit an involuntary mimicry of sensations—excesses we typically wish to exclude from public life.[53] Amateur videos of racist encounters traffic in similar sensations and affects as they court and tease out audience desire. Perverse as it may seem, the pleasure of such texts is the anticipation of the moment of rupture and release triggered by the instant when a fairly unremarkable public confrontation transforms into a potentially violent racist event. Each video builds intensity to an affective crescendo when the racist antagonist finally reveals their hidden fantasies and phobias—exposing their supposedly *true* and *authentic* self. Like pornography, there is a substitution of visceral for visual pleasure insofar as the spectator can only participate vicariously in a scene of racist *jouissance*. Such amateur productions borrow an important pacing device from pornography: *the money shot*. In pornographic films, that label is a euphemism for the moment at which a male actor visibly ejaculates and in doing so provides proof that pleasure, male pleasure that is, has been experienced and that the scene has concluded.[54] From a psychoanalytical perspective, the money shot exemplifies the sacrifice of enjoyment that takes place when the subject takes up the signifier. That is to say that the money shot offers an ersatz substitution for unmediated enjoyment and, consequently, organizes the spectator's affective experience of the text. Joshua Gunn makes sense of the money shot as a kind of pacing device that is not the exclusive province of pornography.[55] He observes that body genres organize the spectators encounter with *jouissance* by cultivating and satisfying appetites similar to the compulsive act of repetition. He writes that "a Lacanian understanding describes the 'pleasure' of repetition as a substitute satisfaction, for to realize the motor behind repetition itself is quite painful or beyond the symbolic registers of named emotions."[56] In terms of libidinal economy, racist freak out videos invite spectators to repeat the same experience: to stage an encounter with the irruption of racist *jouissance* into public life where such expressions are ostensibly prohibited. It is the fact that such obscenity is barred from public expression that organizes the spectator's enjoyment. Of course, this is not to say that repetitive viewing is pleasurable in a colloquial sense of the word as viewing such videos can be quite painful and even traumatizing.

What, then, is the psychical payoff for subjects embedded in this libidinal economy? This conceptualization of body genres explains how racist freak out videos curate a particular encounter with what comes to signify "real" racism. Drawing from the logics of reality television, Laura Grindstaff argues that the money shot is read as a sign of authenticity in contemporary media culture, where frenzied emotional excess represents the appearance of an inner self that has been foreclosed by cultural prohibitions. As Grindstaff and Susan Murray surmise, "[S]uccess or failure hinges on the successful containment of the surprise and the perceived authenticity of the response prompted by the reveal."[57] Thought of this way, I read racist *jouissance* as an apparent disclosure of "real" or "authentic" racism; however, this encounter occludes the more cold, calculated, and structural operation of white supremacy. Repetitive viewing of racist outbursts stages a postracial fantasy of sleuthing out "genuine" racism—racism that is located somewhere, anywhere but in the mind of the audience. The spectator is positioned as an anti-racist detective whose ultimate payoff comes at the moment of the great reveal (the money shot) when the perpetrator outs themself in a moment of frenzied and uncontrolled racism. In order to sustain this fantasy, however, racism must be repetitively located in new individuals; hence, such videos exemplify a compulsion to document, aggregate, and (re)encounter the strange familiarity of racist excess. The fantasy shields the spectator from the uncanny knowledge of their own complicity. As Martinot and Sexton observe, racism is "considered to be either a real property of a person or an imaginary projection . . . not essential to the social structure, a system of social meanings and categorisations."[58] In short, the money shot enables the spectator to finally finger the culprit, whose backward ideology has continually thwarted the achievement of the postracial society. The spectator can simply skip to the end of the mystery story of white supremacy; a story that ends with the perpetrator being outed and shamed back into silence.

Racist freak out videos tend to be organized according to the following pattern: (1) a sudden introduction to a shocking altercation; (2) a steady escalation of conflict and intensity by the assailant; (3) the money shot, or a climactic revelation of racist motives by the perpetrator; and (4) a dénouement in which the perpetrator is punished, shamed, or removed from the scene. This pattern constitutes a form of compulsive repetition where the spectator is led through an encounter with obscene enjoyment that helps locate racism within the individual psyche of disturbed individuals. The encounter helps to domesticate the social displeasure of racism's uncanny irruption and to relegate racism back to the unconscious. Here, two viral videos (among countless others) are noteworthy for exemplifying this pattern. First, a YouTube video entitled "Racist Post Office Tantrum" rushes the audience to the scene of a verbal altercation in progress at a Dallas-area post office.[59] A bystander records footage without the apparent awareness of a white man berating a postal service employee. Other observers try to console the man, imploring him to calm down. The man yells, "I'm legitimately outraged!" and tells his patrons, "I don't care, shove it!" The man grows increasingly agitated, exclaiming, "Give me the form, you fool!" Given the title of the video, audiences can anticipate that the man's increasing frustration will eventually lead to an explosive racist outburst. He yells again, this time increasing the sharpness of his words: "Give me the form, you *asshole!*" This steady escalation teases the spectator, baiting them for the final moment of public release. Then, he delivers what was promised and yells two explicit racial epithets at the employee. The patrons audibly gasp in unison and agree that it is time to call the police. They recoil in horror at the man's extreme racist transgression. The perpetrator continues yelling racial insults as he exits the building while other customers express their disbelief and outrage at what has just occurred. Here, racism intrudes into daily life, only to be swept away from the prying eyes and ears of smartphone technology. The money shot makes racism visible but in a fashion that is sudden, uncontrolled, and disorienting.

In a second video entitled "Pennsylvania Woman Goes on Racist Rant in Walmart," a victim's shaky cell phone captures a white woman scolding her for getting in her way.[60] Her racist insults begin with the xenophobically tinged statements "Go back to Mexico" and "Go back to wherever you are from." The perpetrator reminds the Latinx woman, "You're in America!" Although these kinds of nativist sentiments have been somewhat mainstreamed by Trump-era populism, they certainly raise the stakes of the confrontation by revealing an underlying antipathy and phobic reaction to racial Others in ostensibly white spaces. The conflict escalates further when a woman out of the camera's view chastises the perpetrator for using "ignorant" language. The perpetrator blithely responds, "A <expletive> is calling me ignorant?" The harsh cadence of the racist term is belied by the casualness with which it is wielded. The women recording the altercation gasps, "Oh, my goodness!" A store clerk asks the woman to leave the store, stating, "This is inappropriate." The woman eventually storms off in incredulous anger, bringing a resolution to the scene. This pattern repeats across dozens, if not hundreds, of similar videos: conflict, escalation, racist public release, and the assailant fleeing the scene. These two examples show how a title that advertises a racist encounter pulls the spectator into a volatile scene that promises to locate inchoate racism in individual perpetrators, summon forth that racism with visual and auditory evidence, and, after the money shot, conclude the scene.

Other videos follow a similar pattern except that the perpetrator is punished either by violence or the immediate threat of it. In these videos, the unpleasant experience of hate speech and fighting words is compensated for by the vicarious enjoyment of justified violence.

For instance, one video entitled "Racist White Man Gets Beat Up After Calling Black Guy <Expletive> Outside the Cheesecake Factory" promises the reward of vigilante justice against a racist assailant.[61] After over a minute of a white man aggressively taunting a Black passerby, the perpetrator finally spews a racist insult. The woman recording the incident gasps in anticipation of the potential violence to follow, exclaiming, "Oh now, wait!" The man targeted by the insult immediately punches the man several times, knocking him to the ground. The shakiness of the camera at this climactic moment simulates a frenzied and disorienting experience of physical violence. The witness tells the man, "You should have never said <expletive>." This final summation retroactively narrates the encounter as a scene in which justice was appropriately dispensed. The dénouement then reestablishes the boundaries of postracial culture by expelling the racist perpetrator.

In another video viewed over 7 million times, a racist outburst by a patron in a convenience store provokes a Black customer to take matters into his own hands and strike the man with an alcoholic beverage. Posted on the YouTube channel "Desirable to Watch," the "Twisted Tea" video features a white assailant bombarding a store clerk with racist epithets as a bystander prepares for the possibility of violence by picking up a tall aluminum can.[62] The person recording the altercation observes that the patron is preparing for violence, noting, "He's gonna pop him." When the patron tells the assailant to stop using racial slurs, the assailant refuses and escalates his derision. The perpetrator observes the can in the other customer's hand and taunts him to "smack" him. Predictably, the customer obliges and strikes the man in the face. The can explodes and the perpetrator is knocked to the ground. A witness audibly observes, "Yeah, you got yours buddy!" The customer then tackles the stunned perpetrator and repeatedly punches him until he acknowledges his obscene behavior and agrees to stop. Following a predictable pattern, an act of defensive violence restores order and coerces the transgressor into compliance with public norms and conventions. The money shot features a spectacular release of libidinal energy—not to mention spurting liquid—discharged onto the body of the racist perpetrator.

In each video, the money shot is not the racist revelation per se but instead the retributive violence that punishes the racist transgression. The videos allow white spectators to *enjoy* racism—which is to say that staging and restaging encounters with white supremacy generate affective investments in an unbearable experience that nonetheless helps constitute one as part of a (post)racial public. As Christian Lundberg puts it, "[E]njoyment signals both an affectively charged state and a ritually repeated habit or compulsion that may as often be received as annoying or unpleasant as pleasurable."[63] In viewing these videos, a white spectator is invited to take up a specific relationship to white supremacy wherein racism's sudden and traumatic appearance becomes the condition of possibility within which a particular kind of postracial citizen-subject might constitute themself. As unpleasant as it is to witness, racism appears precisely so that it may be disavowed and contained. Thus, racism appear so that it may be overcome.

The introduction of justified violence helps sustain a series of fantasies that circulate within the libidinal economy of whiteness. One fantasy engendered by retribution videos is that racism can be managed through economies of shame and violence. In the previous two examples, the racist transgressor was put in their place with a judicious and legitimate use of force. The scene is reminiscent of Freud's "return of the repressed" where that which has been cast out from society or relegated to the margins of the unconscious nonetheless returns in a hideous and monstrous form.[64] Racism's sudden and arresting appearance is swiftly punished and removed from sight even though structural racism and the vast libidinal economy of whiteness are simply hidden from public consciousness.

At the same time, punishment of racism by individual acts of violence helps disavow the spectator's relationship to white supremacy by drawing from neoliberal and postracial ideologies that testify to the pastness of racism and the obsolescence of anti-racist policy. As Bonilla-Silva points out, whites generally view racism as individual prejudice, whereas people of color recognize racism as "systemic and institutionalized."[65] Thus, "racial neoliberalism" functions by individualizing racism—narrowing the range of redress to dispelling anachronistic viewpoints held largely by rural, uneducated, and aberrant whites.[66] These type of solutions rely on the laisse-faire marketplace of ideas to eliminate racist viewpoints in the absence of structural remedies.[67] From this perspective, if the civil rights movement already addressed racism at the level of policy, then large-scale projects to remedy historical and structural challenges are largely unnecessary and potentially counterproductive.[68] Although the videos offer no explicit viewpoints on how to address racism, they do invite spectator's affective investment in punishing individual acts of racism with cathartic acts of violence. In these videos, people of color and white bystanders address racism on their own, largely without the assistance of state or institutional authorities. Ultimately, such videos offer what amounts to a neoliberal theory of racial justice in which the individual citizen-subject of a surveillance society is responsible for documenting and/ or punishing racist transgressions without fundamental structural transformation. Although the money shot is indeed gratifying, without a racist assailant getting their comeuppance, it enacts white fantasies of racism dispelled without a costly interrogation of white supremacy and its historical continuity with chattel slavery and colonialism. Although these videos call out and punish individual acts of racism, they distance the spectator from their own complicity with larger structures of white supremacy.

Disidentification and Other Fantasies

YouTube users and content creators who post racist freak outs are supported by the core fantasies of democratic transparency and progressive postracialism. As the argument goes, documenting racism will expose the individual pathologies and secret prejudices that preclude the fulfillment of a postracial society. To the extent that racism still exists, exposure will trigger the mechanisms of accountability in a (self)surveillance society and offer other citizens with a civics lesson in tolerance. But it is ultimately up to the individual to police racism rather than governmental institutions. The fantasy that underwrites these videos is that sleuthing out hate speech will ultimately make it less dangerous, dispel its power, and shame racists into compliance with the norms of progressive white identity. This chapter is concerned with how obscene enjoyment traffics in our everyday social networks and what happens when racist *jouissance* is plugged into the technological and culture circuitry of shareability. YouTube algorithms privilege the most obscene and transgressive behavior. Racist freak out videos stage an encounter with feral whiteness—a whiteness that can be easily disavowed by spectators who believe themselves to be more progressive than the extreme and excessive racists who exist elsewhere in their social world. Ultimately, such spectatorship elides the mundane (which is hiding in plain sight in these videos), by helping viewers to *not* see themselves reflected in the videos.

Racist freak outs pique viewers' interest because they are organized around the emotional crescendos that are ubiquitous in contemporary media culture where a subject's raw emotion manifests. The money shot, then, explicates how these videos cultivated an authentic expression of emotional release. The reveal offers a climactic payoff: the laying bare of raw, real emotion for all to see. The YouTube racist rant features the white subject caught up in a system of excess, or the ecstatic performance of *jouissance*. Grindstaff and Murray suggest that media culture operates by "spotlighting the emotional expressiveness of ordinary people and branding this expressiveness as a signifier of both individuals and the genre as a whole."[69] Thus, the videos examined here trade in the "ordinariness of its nonactor participants and the production of 'authentic' emotion and affect as guarantors of realness."[70] These are portraits of "real" or "authentic" racism rearing its ugly head but as excess rather than banality.

Of course, hate circulates well in spaces like YouTube even when it is for the purpose of shame and punishment. As Sara Ahmed argues, "[H]ate is economic; it circulates between signifiers in relationships of difference and displacement. To understand such affective economies of hate, I will consider the way in which 'signs' of hate work, and their relations to bodies."[71] As I have argued, racism operates as a libidinal economy that routes, displaces, and distributes fantasies and desires. In André Brock's words, libidinal economies are "the combustion powering the engine—the visceral, powerful, and necessary component in any figuration. It is infrastructure, invisible to our perceptions just like the materials and processes we pass by or utilize every day—until a rupture occurs."[72] The libidinal economy of racist freak out videos operates by subjecting people of color to ritual humiliation for the refinement of white civic temperament. Spectators are supposed to be outraged at racism and violence, even as people of color appear to them in the form of diminished capacity, emasculation, and powerlessness. They add to the daily scroll of images of Black death and suffering that deprive people of color of their humanity.[73] All of this is to say that repeated viewing of people of color subjected to humiliation is ultimately for the benefit of the spectator, rather than the victims of hate speech. In the process, people of color transform into resilient and extraordinary subjects who must withstand racist *jouissance* as the price of achieving a progressive postracial society. The psychic payoff is measured by the spectators' relative enjoyment of racism where the banality of everyday white masculine authority ultimately evades scrutiny.

4

Access Hollywood and the Return of the Primal Father

On October 7, 2016, the *Washington Post* published a video of then presidential candidate Donald J. Trump engaging in a lurid conversation about women with *Access Hollywood* co-anchor Billy Bush. Taking place in 2005, a pair of "hot mics" captured audio of lewd banter between Trump and Bush during a behind-the-scenes interview on the "Access Across America" bus to Trump's guest appearance on the NBC soap opera *Days of Our Lives*. The video began with Trump describing his failed attempt to "fuck" former *Entertainment Tonight* host Nancy O'Dell. Trump recounted his effort to woo her by taking her furniture shopping, followed by his fledgling attempts to "move on her." To the amusement of Bush and other passengers, Trump recalled, "I moved on her like a bitch. But I couldn't get there. And she was married. Then all of a sudden I see her, she's now got the big phony tits and everything. She's totally changed her look." Bush enthusiastically interrupted this bawdy bit of gossip to point out that the actor (Adrianna Zucker) awaiting to escort Trump to the set was finally within their sights. He exclaimed, "Sheesh, your girl's hot as shit! In the purple." Trump emphatically agreed. Bush congratulated Trump. "Yes!" Bush excitedly declared, "The Donald has scored! Whoa, my man!" Trump prepared for his impending encounter with Zucker. "I better use some Tic Tacs in case I start kissing." He then further clarified his impulsive and illicit method of seduction: "You know, I'm automatically attracted to beautiful—I just start kissing them. It's like a magnet. Just kiss. I don't even wait." As if these vulgar comments were not illustrative of his brazen disregard for obtaining consent, Trump added, "When you're a star, they let you do it. You can do anything." Bush agreed flatly and restated Trump's point, "Whatever you want." By anything, he even meant, "grab 'em by the pussy. You can do anything." Thereafter, this exposé on the not-so-secret life of Trump's obscene desires ran on what seemed like a continual loop up until the November 2016 election.

Caught on Tape. Casey Ryan Kelly, Oxford University Press. © Oxford University Press 2023.
DOI: 10.1093/oso/9780197677865.003.0005

The now infamous *Access Hollywood* tape was a shocking revelation of misogynistic depravity. For Trump's critics, the disclosure of this scandalous footage would surely have spelled the end of his presidential campaign and restored the traditional political order. Even Republican National Committee Chair Reince Priebus and Speaker of the House Paul Ryan were certain that Trump would have no option but to step aside and be replaced on the national ticket. Of course, you already know how this story ends. Scoffing at calls to withdraw from the race, Trump went on the offensive and used the occasion to attack Bill Clinton for his history of harassment and sexual indiscretions. In his nationally televised "apology," Trump stated, "I've said some foolish things, but there's a big difference between the words and actions of other people. Bill Clinton has actually abused women, and Hillary has bullied, attacked, shamed and intimidated his victims."[1] He dismissed his lurid remarks as "locker-room banter, a private conversation that took place many years ago. Bill Clinton has said far worse to me on the golf course—not even close."[2] In an extraordinary act of audacity—characteristic of tabloid journalism and reality television—Trump's campaign chief executive Steve Bannon arranged for a joint press conference with three women who accused President Clinton of sexual misconduct. By Bannon's somewhat erotically charged account, he recalled telling Trump: "They're going to rub up on you and be crying. And you're going to be empathetic." As if he were recalling his council of Caligula, Bannon recollected that Trump closed his eyes, tilted his head back "like a Roman emperor," and declared, "I love it."[3] Within one news cycle, the *Access Hollywood* tape was buried underneath a deluge of other embarrassing disclosures, such as WikiLeaks' publication of hacked emails from Hillary Clinton's campaign chief John Podesta. Despite its nauseating content, the *Access Hollywood* tape barely registered as a blip in Trump's overall approval rating and in no way impeded his ascendance to the White House.

This final chapter turns to the *Access Hollywood* video for clues as to how its revelation failed to dissuade Trump's faithful electorate. I contend that the *Access Hollywood* video enacted a stultifying audience dynamic between Trump and his supporters that was largely consistent with the transgressive turn in white masculinity and the affective structures of new media spectatorship explored throughout this book. Specifically, Trump appeared to his followers as powerfully unencumbered by progressively coded social conventions and fulfilled in his enjoyment of illicit *jouissance*. For his opponents, Trump's obscene performance staged a traumatizing encounter with the Real and cast doubt on their ability to rein in his transgressions by appealing to the laws of prohibition. Although it is impossible to say with certainty that the video's revelation played a role in his electoral success, this chapter advances the argument that the tape presented Trump in a manner consistent with his overall theory of political power. That is to say that the video bolstered an illusion of Trump, known affectionately to some as The Donald, as a figure of exception: singularly powerful and beyond the law.[4] To build this claim, I begin by turning to Freud's parable of primal horde to explain how the decline of the paternal signifier and the erosion of cultural prohibitions paved the way for an autocratic form of white masculine politics that depends on a spectacle of depravity. In what follows, I engage in a close reading of the *Access Hollywood* video to illustrate how its revelation invited supportive audiences to invest in Trump's unrestrained white masculinity as a conduit to the nostalgic unicity exemplified by the slogan "Make America Great Again."

The Primal Horde

In *Totem and Taboo*, Freud recounts the myth of the primal horde, a parable about a band of brothers ruled by a cruel and jealous father.[5] This group existed in a primordial past, prior to the development of the incest taboo and the laws of exogamy that made society possible.[6] Hence, this "violent, jealous father . . . keeps all the females for himself and drives away the growing sons."[7] One day the "expelled brothers joined forces, slew and ate the father, and thus put an end to the father horde."[8] They accomplished their identification with him by devouring him and erected a totem in his place. The brothers were ambivalent about what they had done in as much as they desired to see him vanquished yet also envied his obscene *jouissance*. The totem of the father— the symbolic or *dead* father—put an end to his terrible enjoyment and the brothers foreswore the same pleasures thereafter in respect of the totem. This did not eliminate paternal authority; quite the contrary, the brother's sacrifice made paternal authority possible in the "Name-of-the-Father." Freud observed that the "dead now became stronger than the living had been, even as we observe it today in the destinies of men. What the fathers' presence had formerly prevented they themselves now prohibited in the psychic situation of 'subsequent obedience.'"[9] They declared that killing the totem, the father substitute, was prohibited and they renounced the fruits of their deed by denying themselves the pleasures of the father. The emergence of the surrogate father assuaged their guilt and brought reconciliation with the father, enabling paternal authority to properly function. As Lacan observed, this symbolic father of cultural prohibition is always the dead father: it is this dead father who oversees the norms and conventions of democratic societies and punishes transgressions.

This parable explains more than just the law of exogamy, but rather how the Symbolic functions according to paternal prohibition. If we substitute the primordial condition for the pre-Oedipal body, the father's unbridled enjoyment stands in for the subject's existence prior to the introduction of the signifier. The act of killing, then, performs the role of the signifier in that it blocks the subject's access to *jouissance*. As Lacan posits, "[T]he letter kills," meaning that it sacrifices the Real and overwrites the body with signifiers so that it can be brought into compliance with social and behavior norms.[10] The Name-of-the-Father, as a function of language, interdicts mother–child unity and compels the subject to take up language and submit to the conditions of the Symbolic that regulate norms and conventions. The totem, then, marks the illusory sacrifice of *objet petit a* for the Symbolic—the law which (necessarily so) stands in the way of retrieving it. At the same time, we can also conceptualize the Symbolic as a shield from the traumatic Real and that without the authority of the signifier the grounds for intersubjective communication become fragmented, destabilized, even horrifying. Furthermore, we can approach the parable as an explanation of how traditional lawful authority grounds itself within the Symbolic order: the authority of the signifier but also the authority of cultural prohibitions that coax the subject into compliance with taken-for-granted rules and principles.

The horror of our present political moment is indicative of a larger structural condition in which the traditional authority of the signifier—the dead father—has been devalued. In other words, Trump's election is not an aberration but a logical extension of the decline of the paternal signifier. Working from Lacan's three clinical structures, both Joshua Gunn and Calum Matheson have separately observed the emergence of cultural psychoses, a psychical structure characterized by a foreclosure or the refusal to integrate the Name-of-the- Father.[11] The mainstreaming of conspiracy theories and political paranoia are but two examples that illustrate how a psychotic clinical structure invests all signifiers with hidden meaning and therefore fails to abide the big Other. Sarah Stone Watt adds that in psychosis, the signifier is foreclosed to the subject, revealing a gap in the Symbolic that is filled with delusion. Watt writes that "the fact that delusional signifiers seem absurd does not necessarily indicate that they are inconsistent with the larger discursive system."[12] Watt's case study of Republican anti-abortion discourse reveals how so-called gaffes concerning rape and pregnancy reflect a delusional overinvestment in the paternal signifier to repair "ruptures in the signifying chain" where rape mythology defies consensus reality.[13]

Gunn's work on political perversion pinpoints the failure of the paternal signifier to enforce cultural prohibitions, a pathology brought about by rhetorical forms—social networks and reality television among them—that enable subjects to recognize yet subsequently disavow the authority of the signifier.[14] For some time now, Slavoj Žižek has written of the decline of so-called symbolic efficiency, a term he borrows from Claude Levi-Strauss to name postmodernity's fragmentation of metanarratives and skepticism toward the concepts of truth, knowledge, and authority. A culture of suspicion and incredulity has metastasized as paranoia in the body politic: every truth claim disguises a falsehood, every action in the name of the public good masks a hidden agenda, and every closed door conceals a crime. He writes that "the distrust of the big Other (the order of symbolic fictions), the subject's refusal to 'take it seriously', relies on the belief that there is an 'Other of the Other,' that a secret, invisible and all-powerful agent actually 'pulls the strings' and runs the show: behind the visible, public Power there is another obscene, invisible power structure."[15] In the face of psychosis and perversion, the neurotic is deprived of their ultimate weapon against disinformation, propaganda, and outright falsehoods: consensus reality.

The totem that installed the Symbolic order and regulates social life itself and shields the subject from the traumatic Real can no longer provide any such guarantee. As a result, expertise, truth claims, intersubjective communication, and all manner of traditional symbolic authority have been ostensibly nullified.[16] As Dana L. Cloud reminds us, a culture of fact-checking and moral hand-wringing over the eradication of political and social norms is no match for the power of affect and narrative.[17] The decline of symbolic efficiency and its attendant psychical structures is a harbinger that sets into motion the return of the primal father—the figure of obscene *jouissance*, unencumbered and uncastrated by the Symbolic.

The parable of the primal horde provides clues as to how the *Access Hollywood* tape exemplifies this broader dethroning of the big Other and supplants it with an intelligible authoritarian power structure. As Trump infamously declared: "When you are celebrity, *they let you do it* [italics added]."

I take this statement to be not merely descriptive of celebrity power but rather a projection of an audience dynamic characterized by masochism and self-objectification. In other words, the statement announces a form of political power grounded in the state of exception—a total abrogation of consent and the cultivation of an audience desire for subjugation. The subject who "lets you do it" transforms themself into the object of the Other's desire, actively constituting a body politic that molds itself to the capricious whims of unsublimated white masculinity, constantly seeking its own subjugation and debasement for his enjoyment. The *Access Hollywood* tape exhorts Trump's faithful electorate to continually ask themselves: What does Trump want of me? How can I better know and fulfill his wishes? In this mode of governance, basic reality-referencing, norms, and fact-checking are meaningless because they sidestep the central investment he cultivates in his supporters: to repudiate and renegotiate civic norms and prohibitions in pursuit of ultimate *jouissance.*

The *Access Hollywood* tape consolidated power among his base of supporters precisely by desecrating the totem of traditional symbolic authority (the Name-of-the-Father) and replacing it with the unbridled white masculinity found within most authoritarian power structures. Appearing as the jealous hoarder of enjoyment, Trump stood before his supporters as *un*lacking and therefore ultimately unconstrained by the Symbolic order that installs social reality. It is their duty to make the Other's desire intelligible and then act accordingly.

In turn, the incredulity expressed by those horrified and repelled by his grotesque behavior fall into what Joan Copjec calls the trap of "realist imbecility," or the assumption that the realistic function of the Symbolic (i.e., attacks on the transgression of Trump's statements) can outmaneuver desire; that is, the pursuit of *jouissance* for which he stood.[18] This transgressive and symbolically uncastrated iteration of Trump's public persona ("The Donald") remains extraordinarily powerful because it embodies a surplus residue of *jouissance,* appearing to his followers as something more than himself (*objet petit a*). The tape staged a form of white masculine authority that attains exception by desecrating symbolic prohibitions on *jouissance.* In fact, Trump's claim to authority is not grounded in a lawful social order insofar as the Symbolic is the realm where it is possible to punish such transgressions. He represented the return of Freud's *primal father,* who is less an individual figure than an emphatic pronouncement that the paternal signifier no longer governs and punishes transgressions. The audience is left to sort out the myriad ways they can please the primal father to avoid incurring his wrath—or, even better, to model or redirect his wrath toward those who would challenge his authority. For this reason, as Hal Foster surmised, "[T]here are legions of white guys who want to be his 'apprentices.'"[19] In fact, even the moral sanction of U.S. conservativism's coveted set of imaginary fathers (from George W. Bush to George Will) would prove no match for this form of unrestrained power. Trump as an imaginary father figure would have been incapable of sustaining the recognition demanded by a Symbolic order. But in operating from the traumatic Real, Trump as *primal* father registered as the incapacitating and horrifying return of a primordial authority that is unbeholden even to intelligibility itself.

The remainder of this chapter sketches how the *Access Hollywood* tape built on an audience dynamics already cultivated by the decline of symbolic efficiency and the virtualization of reality: an "uncanny satisfaction" of repetitive encounters with *jouissance* "at its purest."[20] Playing on a continual loop, Trump's transgressions exemplify the sheer inability of subjects to render *jouissance* intelligible. Rhetorically speaking, Trump addresses a public that is structurally powerless to meaningfully render judgment in that they are reified as passive objects. Indeed, his declaration that when you are a star, "you can do anything" and they "let you do it" bespeaks the subject position of transgressive white masculinity taken up by his administration; a strategy of governance that works by virtue of the fact the Other's desire is unintelligible. As a result, Trump's adherents often take up his dictates in ways that overidentify, literalize, and exceed his demands in a frantic effort to become the object of the Other's desire. The tape announced that the private interiors of white men's "locker rooms" now constituted a grotesque public exteriority—supplanting the joyless conceits and pretenses of postfeminist culture with an unapologetic indulgence in taboo behaviors without fear of repercussions. As Freud observed, within relations between the primal horde and the primal father, only a "passive-masochistic attitude is possible," particularly if that group "wishes to be governed by unrestricted force."[21] It is not "perception and reasoning" that governs the horde but instead "an erotic tie."[22] Indeed, the *Access Hollywood* tape cemented this erotic tie with his supporters and incapacitated those who could only appeal to democratic obligations or rhetorical prudence to summon accountability. In analyzing the *Access Hollywood* video, I attend to how its revelation helped organize a fantasy of transgressing cultural prohibitions on *jouissance*, thus structuring adherence to an authoritarian model of political sovereignty that is unencumbered by rules and conventions. Yet, the structural incapacity to evade prohibitions and model his behavior without consequence demanded that his idealized audience defer their agency to him within his political project.

The Decline of Paternal Authority and the Rise of The Donald

Since World War II, U.S. Republicans have by and large organized their vision of moral order around the white male-headed nuclear family. The dictates were clear, normative, and self-executing. This vision of the polity rested on the efficiency of benign heteronormative paternal authority, including the continual resurrection of a wistful vision of 1950s patriarchy, valorizations of imaginary (or ideal) father figures, and a policy agenda to promote conservative family values in everything from education and social services to foreign policy.[23] Jeffrey R. Dudas writes of Republican fondness for "households in which fathers exercised unstinting authority and mothers were supportive and nurturing but never overbearing, or smothering of, their (especially) male children. . . . [P]atriarchal family units were said to prepare the way for the mature, rights-bearing subjects who were needed for modern democratic practice."[24] This fondness was only outmatched by the tenor of moral opprobrium for bad fathers: deadbeat dads (Black dads in particular), philanderers, serial daters, and gay men among them. Lauren Berlant has detailed how the codification of a de facto national sexuality during the height of the Moral Majority movement entailed, among other things, the enactment of paternal governance in the name of protecting children and other infantile subjects from sexual deviance.[25] Though quick to shame others into compliance, the national heterosexual culture inaugurated by the New Right has always had a certain elasticity in relation to its own indiscretions. And though most may be comfortable living with contradictions, the conservative investment in traditional paternal authority has helped smooth out those contradictions by prefiguring indiscretions as personal moral failings rather than ideological incoherence. Fathers—real and imaginary—ultimately took a back seat to the Symbolic father, or the traditional authority of the norms and conventions to police sexual aberrations. Violators typically resigned in shame, demonstrated moral penitence, and accepted their exile from political office.[26]

The revelation of Trump's obscene behavior no doubt drew criticism from the political left and right. His refusal to resign, followed by his electoral victory, not only violated political wisdom and sexual decorum but also unseated the paternal authority engendered by the New Right's moral order. Up until that point, sex scandals were moments to recommit to cultural prohibitions and in some cases forge new ones. Trump's refusal to step aside revealed longstanding cultural prohibitions to be *mere* totems, or hollow threats standing in the way of our enjoyment. The trauma evoked by the *Access Hollywood* tape is manifold: the participant's unashamed ogling reducing women to body parts, Trump's proud admissions of philandering and sexual assault, and the sudden shift in tone when exiting the "locker room" into a public space, just to name a few. Underlying all these grotesque transgressions is a traumatic statement that cultural prohibitions and traditional paternal authority are null and the primal father has returned in the form of a terrible and ruinous *jouissance*. One can only hope to configure their desires to his dictates to avoid his wrath. Thus, the tape is a key artifact in the transformation of transgressive white masculinity and paternal authority. The tape illuminates a form of white masculinity that is ungoverned by shame and unburdened by norms that curtail the crass pursuit of self-interests, even self-destruction ones. This terrible *jouissance* is now ubiquitous throughout the culture—from white men openly marching for white supremacy without fear of consequences to their refusal to wear masks in public to protect the health and safety of others.

Before turning to the tape itself, it is important to contextualize this text as an artifact of an affectively and erotically charged environment that cemented the bonds between Trump and the primal horde. Prior to the publication of the tape, the 2016 campaign had already been a lurid and sexually charged affair. Those who study the "pornification" of U.S. electoral politics have observed that whereas women candidates are disadvantaged in a political and media ecology that objectifies, sexualizes, and degrades women, Trump and other candidates who embody the vulgarity and machismo of pornographic culture are more likely to be portrayed as authentic and therefore more authorized to violate taboos.[27] In this context, Trump made no effort to hide his base desires, often reveling in them for public consumption. For instance, when Republican primary candidate Marco Rubio mocked Trump for the size of his hands, he responded in the nationally televised debate: "And, he referred to my hands — 'if they're small, something else must be small.' I guarantee you there's no problem. I guarantee."[28] Although bragging about penis size is certainly beyond the pale of official presidential politics, the office is certainly gendered and past presidents have not shied away from projecting hypermasculine virility.[29] More pointedly, Trump's comments speak to the erotic investments sought out and reified by white masculinity elsewhere in the business world and U.S. media culture. Subsequent revelations and innuendo concerning the president's sex life figured Trump's unapologetic pursuit of sex, money, and power as part of his political appeal. Later revelations of an extramarital affair and hush money payments to pornographic film star Stormy Daniels, over two dozen allegations of sexual harassment and assault, along with gossip about a secret tape of lewd sex acts in a room in the Moscow Ritz-Carlton where Trump believed the Obama's had slept, only served to strengthen his supporter's investments.[30]

The Donald

The *Access Hollywood* tape distinguished Trump from the father of prohibition as the father of unbridled desire. This distinction begins with what is invisible to the audience: Trump himself. The scene opens with video footage of the Access Across America bus approaching its final destination synced with a "hot mic" recording of Trump's disembodied voice. As Amanda Nell Edgar notes, the vocal and sonic qualities of address create affective bonds between speakers and listeners—they can be read culturally for signs of authenticity, identity, and authority.[31] There is a "presidential sound" that is even-toned, reverent, measured, and sincere. That same sound is often interpreted by political outsiders as phony and condescending. For some, the high style of presidential oratory is the opposite of real talk or the plainspokenness that characterizes right-wing populism's impression of everyday people. Even prior to his presidential bid, Trump's voice has been frequently caricatured as bombastic, rude, indecorous, and frequently incoherent. His iconic catchphrase from *The Apprentice*, "You're fired!," has become synonymous with the cutthroat spirit of corporate America and reality television. On tape, Trump's tone is the opposite of presidential: his voice is glib, unfeeling, and detached. The voice is both unmistakably familiar yet unsettling. Since all the action happens offscreen, audiences are left to meditate on not simply his words but the sound of his voice; its irreverent tone and smirking malice. The braggadocious tone conveys an attitude in which the speaker is unencumbered and unashamed of his own perverse behaviors. In this regard, his tone and message are in sync.

Trump's voice also speaks from no particular place or body until he exits the bus and enters a public space ostensibly governed by norms and prohibitions. This form mimics the relationship between repression and the unconscious: it is not only *his* voice we hear, but another voice that speaks through him. This voice speaks as a disembodied voice-of-god narrator, an "I" we might mistake for the ego and whose agency and authority define and circumscribe the dramatic scene: "*I* moved on her," "*I* did try and fuck her," "*I* start kissing," "*I* don't even wait." The scene centers on the I's perilous desires and illicit pursuit of satisfaction. While one voice speaks as the specific ego of the flesh-and-blood Trump, the other speaks from the position of a cultural id ungoverned by the pleasure principle, neither ego nor superego, careening toward potential ruinous and (self)destructive fulfillment. Without discounting the cult of personality that defines Trump's brand, there is another voice that speaks through him or in his place: the Other. As Bruce Fink writes, language and the unconscious are "overflowing with other people's desires."[32] In other words, desires expressed in "ego mode" may nevertheless "be a foreign desire, the Other's desire" insofar as the language we inherit is not our own and structurally rules over our bodily desires.[33] What this means is that we understand this disembodied voice as part of a structural element of language and the unconscious. Trump's ego undoubtedly expresses its conscious fantasies, but the tape also concerns unconscious fantasies that register the libidinal investments of a patriarchal culture. Our inability to see Trump renders his voice a *cultural* one that speaks both the conscious and unconscious fantasies of the misogynistic imaginary. The tape concerns not Trump's desires alone, but rather a regime of cultural tropes that speak through him.

As a figural manifestation, the *Access Hollywood* Trump stands in for a kind of fulfillment that appears to his supporters as the enjoyment of *objet petit a*. It is this excess that cements the erotic bond with his supporters: it is that his manner of address is so unrestrained and that his enjoyment is so obscene that it becomes possible for him to appear to his supporters as something more. Recall that the horde not only feared but also *envied* the primal father. Copjec notes that envy is not about possessing what the Other has, but instead to be the Other in as much as they are fulfilled and complete in their enjoyment of an object.[34] Trump, as the father who *enjoys*, stands as this *un*lacking figure of completeness. Consider how the tape foregrounds

women as objects for Trump's exclusive enjoyment. After he recounts his
failed seduction of Nancy O'Dell, the conversation shifts to Adrianne Zucker
as she comes into their view. Bush exclaims, "*Your* girl's hot as shit. In the
purple." Offering resounding "whoas!," the group gleefully awaits their opportunity to witness Trump's notorious seduction methods. Bush then
declares, "Yes. The Donald has scored!" Bush and the camera crew frame the
impending encounter in terms of Trump's fulfillment. They convey his exclusive ownership over the encounter and its sexual potential. Note here that
Zucker is always addressed as a fetish, a kind of possession awaiting to be
acted upon and ruled over. Later in the conversation, Zucker is only referred
to by her outfit and her body parts ("the one in the gold," "the legs," "all I see is
legs," and "it looks good").

It is also significant that Bush also addresses Trump here figuratively as
"The Donald." While Zucker is reduced to the anonymity of her body parts,
Trump is abstracted into a cultural icon that is virtually synonymous with
power, dominance, and virility. Even a casual visit to the now-banned Reddit
page r/TheDonald (now hosted on its own separate site) illustrates how this
public persona has cultivated rabid fandom, violent investments, and deeply
problematic parasocial relationships. Participants invest Trump with mag-
ical omnipotence and create racist and misogynistic memes and related
content that portrays "The Donald" as a virile, muscular, and heroic action
figure.[35] Bush relates to Trump in a similar manner when he eagerly boasts
that it is *The Donald*, not only the flesh-and-blood Trump, who has "scored."
Bush and his compatriots express a sense of vicarious pleasure merely being
in the presence of this (omni)potent figure who embodies the most coarse
and hegemonic features of white manhood. They are invested in his fulfillment exclusively and thus assume roles as supplicants. Seeking confirmation
that he is pleased, Bush and the crew eagerly probe The Donald as to what
he likes about Zucker. The Donald admonishes someone in the group for
their non-participation, flatly stating, "Look at you. You are a pussy." Such a
statement enforces a powerful group dynamic that marks prohibitions and
morality as signs of weakness. Those who stand in the way of his enjoyment
are relegated to the absence that marks femininity in a patriarchal culture.
Extrapolated as an aspect of power, chastisement recenters Trump's political
project on The Donald's desires. It is a simple statement of authority, or a reminder to onlookers as to their role in his project.

This interaction suggests that adherence is a question of discerning The
Donald's desires. In this regard, we learn that his desire is insatiable and

unrestrained. There is a moment of confusion that follows: Is the long-legged bombshell in their sights the one who awaits Trump? Trump expresses some concern that she is not his prize, stating, "maybe it's a different one." Bush echoes his concern followed by certainty: "No, it's, it's her." Confident that Zucker is the object of his desire, Trump explains how he dispenses with the practice of consent. He states: "Yeah that's her with the gold. I better use some Tic Tacs just in case I start kissing her. You know I'm automatically attracted to beautiful—I just start kissing them. It's like a magnet. Just kiss. I don't even wait." This statement reiterates well-worn rape myths: men's sexual desires are beyond their conscious control, women can expect unwanted advances based on their dress and physical appearance, and women's consent is optional or irrelevant. The desires expressed here gesture at the forbidden enjoyment of those beyond the pleasure principle. The difference, however, is that when you are powerful, such violations are not considered to be sexual assault. What comes next, then, is illustrative: "And when you're a star, they let you do it. You can do anything." It is this qualification that renders his authority singular and unencumbered. What matters is not the fulfillment of another, but rather the notion that the Other wishes to please him. The Other "lets" not as a granting of permission but as the condition for his fulfillment. He is the one who "can," and the audience is the one who "lets."

In this sense, Trump's power and authority are underwritten by his dictation of the terms of desire: How can *we* please *him*? Indeed, this theory is later put into practice by how he addresses his followers. For example, his former tweets (and new ones to now come) and public statements may defy reality or stretch the bounds of credulity, but they work in a similar manner. Although his Twitter feed and rallies are filled with statements of untruths, we might better understand them as expressions of the conditions for fulfillment of his desire. Take, for instance, his refusal to accept the results of the 2020 presidential election. Prior to the election, Trump had emphatically stated that if he lost, it would only be the result of widespread voter fraud. Thus, as the results unfolded decidedly in favor of his opponent Joe Biden, he delivered a series of remarks that functioned to will this reality into existence. At a White House press conference, he stated: "If you count the legal votes, I easily win. If you count the illegal votes, they can try to steal the election from us. . . . I've already decisively won many critical states, including massive victories in Florida, Iowa, Indiana, Ohio, to name just a few. . . . As everybody saw, we won by historic numbers."[36] Pragmatically, these statements undermine public confidence in the election results to legitimize his effort to litigate the election in the courtroom rather than at the ballot box. In one sense, then, these statements ratify the reality he desires by suggesting that the audience has already observed this reality prior to his announcement. But in another sense, these statements are cues to his supporters as to how they can fulfill his desire.

The most committed members of his electorate, his allies in Congress, and the far right press often compete with each other to emphatically reflect this desired reality back to Trump, regardless of material constraints. Congressional Republicans and conservative news outlets refused to acknowledge Biden's victory while his supporters protested outside of ballot-counting facilities with contradictory messages. In Pennsylvania, they chanted, "Stop the Steal!" In Arizona, they cried, "Count the Votes!" The point is not that these messages are incoherent (to be sure, they are), but that they express a different kind of coherence because they aim, sometimes haphazardly, to fulfill Trump's desire. As the message shifted to suit his needs, Trump's supporters were left to guess or aim for what action they believed would make his wishes a reality.

This same structure of adherence is modeled in the *Access Hollywood* video. Members of his entourage aimed to deliver unto him what they imagined would please someone with a hypermasculine sex drive ("the legs," "the one in the gold"). His detractors were chastised for their admonishment ("you are a pussy"). They expressed joy at the prospect that they had pleased him ("Yes! The Donald has scored!"). In both cases, the onlookers' role is to join their wishes with his, even though the rewards are not mutual. Ideally, both audiences are subjects who either "let" or who facilitate his "can." No level of compromise or self-debasement need be spared. For instance, one man in Nevada interrupted a press conference given by the state registrar to theatrically reiterate Trump's claims, yelling to the brink of exhaustion, "The Biden crime family is stealing this election and the media is covering it up!"[37] In both cases, actions and adherence to beliefs that might otherwise seem embarrassing do rhetorical work to prove the subject's willingness to reflect back both a desired model of unwavering support and a reality that is pleasing to authority. His statements, then, function as tests of loyalty. Similar to the findings of Stanley Milgram's classic Stanford prison experiments on obedience to authority, the point is that onlookers might outdo each other to become the object of his desire—to even exceed the dictates of authority.[38] Trump often gives his supporters cues to follow. For instance, when a caravan of Texas Trump supporters nearly ran a Biden tour bus off the road, Trump responded with enthusiasm: "In my opinion, these patriots did nothing wrong."[39] Indeed, Trump does not explicitly demand that his supporters commit crimes or publicly embarrass themselves. He does not have to. His audience can read between the lines, or they believe they can. As PayPal co-founder and Trump supporter Peter Theil surmised, "A lot of voters who vote for Trump take Trump seriously but not literally."[40] Supporters, in other words, fill in the gap between what he says and what he means with actions and rhetoric that might render them part of his ideal audience. The point is that they are left to constantly interpret and help fulfill his desires and to go to extraordinary lengths to prove their allegiance.

"Grab 'em"

The most infamous and often repeated line from the video is delivered as Trump's final clarification of what he means by celebrity power: "Grab 'em by the pussy. You can do anything." This shocking statement was delivered with such casualness and candor that it perfectly conveyed the banality of sexual violence in U.S. culture. Such a proud admission is not necessarily surprising given Trump's public persona, but its utterance was nonetheless traumatic. The statement itself is both a representation and enactment of an intimate boundary violation. It conjures a portrait of feminine sexuality that is defined strictly in masculine terms. In Luce Irigaray's words, he presents a body reduced to passivity, as lacking in the sexual imaginary, "more or less [an] obliging prop for the enactment of male fantasies."[41] This feminine body is open, fecund, and awaiting subjugation. To "grab" this body is to rule over it as a kind of masculine *terra firma*. Such rule "revive[s] a very old relationship to the maternal" in that it stages a return to pre-Oedipal mother–child unity, but this time as an active agent who controls the enveloping and devouring mother.[42] If one imagines themself as uncastrated in this encounter, they stand in the place of the authoritarian and interdicting father, a harbinger of a ruinous *jouissance*. In somewhat simpler terms, the statement is both an expression of violent misogyny as well as a pronouncement of white masculine power over the feminine, not just bodies but all that is relegated to the status of feminine passivity. The phrase is an emphatic statement on white masculine agency; its capacities to hold another's body hostage, to subject it to one's own sadistic whims, to treat another as property.

The statement also names an audience dynamic in which spectators are passive, masochistic, and invested in their own subjugation. In *Apocalypse Man*, I called this dynamic "political sadomasochism," a relationship between Trump and his supporters based on the erotic tie of cruelty—the pleasure in both receiving and doling out pain. The primary evidence of this fraught relationship is found at his political rallies where Trump not only delights in the nation's capacity to inflict cruelty but also cultivates in his audience an investment in discovering their misery, failure, and humiliation. He continually regenerates the affective charge of anger by reminding his supporters that they are fools exploited by immigrants, feminists, deep state radicals, foreigners, liberals, and globalists alike.[43] He would have his audience know that the world is laughing at their weakness, taking advantage of their naiveté, and stealing their birthright. Indeed, "grab 'em by the pussy" conjures the kind of sexual humiliation one would find in the writings of the Marquis de Sade. But Trump's rhetoric as both presidential candidate and later as president has been consistently preoccupied with brute strength, violence, and humiliation.[44] For instance, at several of his rallies, Trump boasted of the brutality of Immigrations and Custom Enforcement (ICE) officers, claiming that "they grab them by the neck and they throw them the hell out of our country or they throw them into jail!"[45] Mere mention of "crooked Hillary" Clinton produces reflexive jeers and chants of "lock her up!" that, by any other name, might be characterized as a virtually explicit bondage fantasy of forcing a powerful woman into submission. These fantasies of violence are typically greeted with laughter and applause. Be it locking, grabbing, or throwing, such word choices convey hypermasculine aggression and strength. More importantly, they generate an affective bond between Trump and his audience through the erotics of violence. All of this is to say that the Trump persona featured in the *Access Hollywood* video is no different than the persona on stage in front of his supporters. In both contexts, Trump plays the role of a dominant and sexually aggressive strongman. It should come as no surprise, then, that the video did not upset the rhetorical dynamics that shape his relationship with his electorate. To the contrary, it reinforced this dynamic.

Of course, it is hard to deny that for some the pleasure—if we can call it that—of this obscene statement lies in its escalation of a group dynamic: he transforms the banter on tape from an exercise in girl-watching to the enactment of a vicarious rape fantasy. What is the role of the onlooker, the gawker, the bystander? If this is simply a crass joke or locker room banter, are we to take him seriously but not literally? Perhaps the point is that it is difficult for spectators to discern the difference. In this regard, the tape helped establish an audience dynamic that cultivates an investment in *his* enjoyment—*his* transgressions, *his* desires, and ultimately *his* freedom from the consequences and restraints imposed on others. Although many wish to be or emulate him, ultimately this dynamic primes his audiences to defer their agency to him, for only he is above the law. One might envy his ability to "grab 'em by the pussy" or the freedom to speak such cruelty, but as father-*jouissance* The Donald is the figure who hoards all the enjoyment.

An audience may domesticate the traumatic intrusion of the Real induced by such profane utterances by consuming them with the ironic detachment of viewing reality television. While he implicates all those who gawk at his obscenity, he also unburdens himself of responsibility with a kind of plausible deniability, a point persuasively argued by Gunn. Recall that we are to take him seriously but not literally. Such is the nature of his jokes and truthful hyperbole. Those who are entertained by his refusal of political correctness become his unwitting accomplices or enablers whose adoration eggs him on. Such is the spectacle of his showmanship: obscenity may be patently offensive. but it is more enjoyable than restrictive norms and prohibitions. Dubrofsky names this dynamic a "monstrous authenticity" to make sense of how the more extreme his statements become, the more his audiences attribute to him a kind of honesty found nowhere else in the culture.[46]

"How about a little hug?"

Although most viewers are familiar with the video's most iconic line, as the tape concludes, the interaction captured between Trump, Bush, and Zucker is particular instructive as to how the tape failed to bring about a grand reckoning. Part of the answer, I argue, is that Bush models the reverence, deference, and facilitation one is to adopt in relation to celebrity power. After the two exited the bus and exchanged pleasantries with Zucker, Bush made an uncomfortable request: "How about a little hug for The Donald, he's just off the bus?" Although his trip was hardly harrowing and the two have just met, Zucker responded positively to the request: "Would you like a little hug, darling?" Diverging from the lurid banter caught on the "hot mic," Trump assured everyone that the encounter was friendly and innocent: "Absolutely. Melania said this was okay." Performing his secondary role, Bush asked if he, too, could touch Zucker: "How about a little hug for the Bushy, I just got off the bus?" Zucker, again, granted the request. As the three moved toward the set of *Days of Our Lives*, Trump invited Bush to lock arms with Zucker: "Come on Billy, don't be shy. . . . Get over here, Billy." Sidling the two, Billy commanded, "Let the little guy in there. Come on." The three walked into the studio arm in arm. Bush then asked, "Now if you had to choose, honest, between one of us. Me or The Donald, who would it be? . . . Seriously, you had to take on of us as a date." As they reached the end of the corridor, Zucker laughed: "I'll take both." As the scene concluded, Bush informed Zucker and Trump that he must part ways and Zucker escorted Trump to his final destination.

Although this portion of the tape is fairly mundane when compared with Trump and Bush's candid backstage performances, this public exchange invites and models a particular kind of spectatorship in relation to Trump's obscene enjoyment. In one sense, the audience's role is to desire Trump's enjoyment, to facilitate his wishes, and most importantly, to keep his confidence. From the perspective of a supportive audience, the sudden shift in tone from male bonding over lurid and illicit fantasies to lighthearted and friendly banter is simply a reminder that what happens in men's private spaces is not only important to masculine identity, what happens in such spaces should not concern others. Trump's retroactive framing of this event as "locker room talk" emphasized the importance of men's private space in a so-called feminized culture—an idea that resonated with white men who claim to be suffocated by political correctness, misandry, and nanny state governance.[47] Men's rights activists, who were particularly vocal in their support of Trump, have long lamented the erosion of strong white masculine archetypes and spaces for male bonding that have been pried open by feminist demands for equality.[48] The sacred halls of white masculine power and comradery are important to Trump's brand: board rooms, golf resorts, private social clubs, auto garages, man caves, cigar clubs, gun ranges, fraternity houses, sports bars, strip clubs, and, of course, locker rooms.[49] The shift in tone, then, is not a sign of hypocrisy but instead a virtue so long as one reserves bawdy talk for private. The offense is not in what Trump said but rather in the fact that the news media chose to broadcast and capitalize on a conversation between men in which privacy was assumed. From this perspective, the tape's release was a violation of Trump's confidence and expectation of privacy. In some conservative circles, the tape's disclosure was a damning indictment of a crass and biased tabloid media—a caricature of peeping Toms and nightcrawlers chasing ambulances and digging through celebrity trash.[50] In other words, no one likes a tattletale. More importantly, for Trump's supporters, the tape evinced the waning respect for men's privacy and spaces for social bonding. Is any space sacred? The tape was only further evidence of cultural misandry and white men's victimization.

It is important to note that until the tape's publication, Bush kept Trump's confidence. After losing his job, Bush issued an apology for his behavior and denounced Trump's remarks.[51] Although he eventually turned on Trump, his behavior on tape models the behavior of an enabling audience. He remained silent concerning Trump's lewd utterances for perhaps a variety of reasons, including self-preservation. He may have found Trump's remarks to be offensive at the time but withheld his rebuke. Ultimately, his intentions do not matter to how we witness this encounter. What matters is that he did nothing to disrupt the group dynamic. In fact, he performed his role as expected, both on and off the bus. As Freud observed of group psychology, it is "a paramount and dangerous personality, towards whom only a passive-masochistic attitude is possible, to whom one's will has to be surrendered—while to be alone with him, 'to took him in fact', appears a hazardous enterprise. It is only in some such way as this that we can picture the relation of the individual member of the primal horde to the primal father."[52] In the presence of father-*jouissance*, the ruled acquiesce and submit their will to his alone. It is dangerous for the ruled to be in such close proximity to him because his will is destructive and shares no concern for the will or welfare of others. Indeed, only Bush suffered repercussions for his role in this event. Yet, Bush performed the role of the ideal spectator in this configuration of paternal power. This spectator risks being enveloped by father-*jouissance* in their facilitation of his ruinous desire. They are forced to take on the position of a masochistic subject, forsaking their own agency to stage an encounter with that which is forbidden. To see this process play out elsewhere during his administration, one need simply to note the carousel of figures who have served in Trump's cabinet or as his liaison and who subsequently suffered public humiliations in carrying out his mandates or explaining his confounding behavior.

Hence, we can observe how Bush discerns Trump's cues and plays the part of a loyal supplicant. He laughs at Trump's jokes, repeats his key phrases, and works to uphold a playful group dynamic. Even in the sudden shift from private to public, the role of the host is to be supportive. After all, *Access Hollywood* is a program that caters to and promotes celebrities by providing audiences with a glimpse of "authenticity" or what really goes on behind the screen. The program is part of a popular culture that cultivates parasocial relationships between fans and their favorite celebrities. *Access Hollywood* is also part of the reality television media ecology in which obscene transgressions receive top billing. But unlike programs such as *TMZ* where celebrities are degraded and humiliated by invasive paparazzi and salacious gossip, *Access Hollywood* offers largely positive and lighthearted portrayals of stars.[53] Where *TMZ* levels celebrity power by exposing the private lives of Hollywood stars, *Access Hollywood* helps celebrities build their brand and promote their projects. In short, *Access Hollywood* was not in the business of exposing celebrity secrets. Hence, there is a radical divergence between the private conservations on the bus and the stage performance thereafter. The difference between these two programs matters in terms of what relationship audiences might take up relative to larger-than-life figures. The publication of an unintentional "hot mic" moment exposed a different backstage, not the careful manicured backstage offered by *Access Hollywood*, but a lurid yet appealing backstage of pleasures reserved only for the rich and famous, or Hollywood's infamous "traffic in women."[54] But the tone of the program carries over into the candid and unscripted moments, compelling those around Trump throughout his visit to treat him with reverence, regardless of what he might say or do. Hence, the portrait of power that appears on tape is not disapproving and humiliating but tantalizing. Even in his public face, "the Bushy" is a supplicant requesting to take part, for a sparing moment, in Trump's world of the obscene. Although many were rightfully horrified, what he offered his supporters is freedom from moral sanctions and the vicarious enjoyment they themselves dare not partake. Bush's behavior at the tape's conclusion models a fraught and precarious relationship with father-*jouissance* that is, at its core, passive and masochistic. In this mode of enjoyment, there is no great reckoning, only collateral damage.

As a Father

The *Access Hollywood* tape is a confounding text because its revelation challenged the assumed relationship between transparency and accountability. The tape entered a media culture already organized around dramatic spectacles of depravity, cruelty, and misogyny; a media culture in which Trump developed his irreverent and transgressive brand of politics and business.

Although the tape depicted an extreme form of misogyny, Trump's grotesque hypermasculinity and debauched attitude toward women were hardly a public secret. Nor was it the case that his crass statements were at odds with the culture of tabloids, reality television, and social networking. Many of Trump's loyal supporters could simply dismiss the episode as just Trump being Trump, or even embrace the tape as yet another in a series of welcomed transgressions against the stuffy culture of feminism and political correctness. The *Access Hollywood* video amplified an audience dynamic burgeoning within U.S. political and media culture that embraced the dethroning of traditional authority and transgressing the parameters of acceptable political power. For his supporters, the video consummated white masculinist fantasies of unbridled political power unbeholden to democratic conventions such as the rule of law. Over the prior decade, white conservatives had increasingly characterized progressive policies that sought to correct historic and structural inequalities as oppressive and discriminatory. Embodied by Trump's open refusal to abide prohibitions against misogyny (and, elsewhere, racism), the tape signified a turning of the tables against feminists and progressive moralists. In this new political reality, conservatives could retain the right to exclusively govern the body politic in their interests by dispensing with democratic demands for inclusivity, equality, and shared political power.

Although some conservatives initially denounced Trump's statements, they ultimately attuned themselves with the new political reality. Returning to Freud's parable helps contextualize how and why Republican leaders were ultimately unable to accomplish what the brothers had achieved in killing and devouring the primal father. Their efforts to overthrow *father*-jouissance were half-hearted in their rebuke—they tentatively renounced Trump's specific statements and behaviors but not the theory of power the tape divulged. Nothing better exemplifies their subsequent deference to his authority than the GOP's unwillingness to acknowledge his 2020 electoral loss to Joe Biden. Recall that the brothers erected a totem not to glorify the act of killing per se, but rather to bear witness to what the sacrifice demanded of them. Many expressed moral outrage at his transgression yet nonetheless continued to back him for the presidency. Thus is the nature of envy: not to possess what the Other has but to be the Other insofar as they appear to be without lack. Hence, the important distinction to be made here is that the brothers renounced the primal father but, more importantly, they established a prohibition against his obscenity. They alleviated their ambivalence concerning what they had done by foreswearing his obscene enjoyment. As Kenneth Burke writes about the symbolism of the kill, it is the "'desire to kill' a certain person [that] is much more properly analyzable as a desire to *transform the principle* which that person *represents*."[55] Of course, Trump is not the primal father but rather a harbinger of a principle to which his authority and a theory of sovereignty are derived—an authority beyond prohibition. The primal father is not so much a person but a principle governing the Symbolic order that happens to find itself embodied in the figure of Trump.

The problem, I surmise, is that the GOP rejected Trump without rejecting Trump*ism*, something we might call a narcissistic and ruinous method of governance. Meanwhile, his electorate never wavered because he embodied the disposition of white masculinity in its ultimate refusal to abide democratic restrictions of its accumulation and enjoyment of power. Perhaps his opponent's biggest failure was their inability to recognize the cultural dissipation of the paternal signifier and the transformation in authority entailed by the decline of symbolic efficiency. Exposing Trump's faults and transgressions exemplifies Copjec's notion of "realist imbecility," that similar to President Ronald Reagan, denouncers across the politic spectrum failed to comprehend that supporters loved Trump *because of his faults*. In short, they love Trump precisely because he is Trump. As a cultural figure, "The Donald" stands in as something *more than* himself. Perhaps Trump was not being hyperbolic when he claimed that he could shoot someone on Fifth Avenue in Manhattan and not lose any voters.

In many ways, Reagan's presidency set the stage for this form of power. As a former Hollywood celebrity, Reagan's star power, stage presence, and charisma transformed U.S. political culture into a cult of personality. Like Trump, Reagan's mastery of dominant media forms (television) enabled him to translate political allegiance into rabid fandom. Both Reagan and Trump have been referred to as "Teflon" presidents, which is to say that no amount of bad press seemed to "stick" long enough to diminish their popular support. Both also benefited from the broader dethroning of traditional authority brought on by politicians and economists who embraced neoliberal economic policies and philosophies that emphasized the power of the market and individual over the state.[56] Both were renowned for bragging about their sexual prowess and affairs with women, and both were accused of sexual assault but faced no consequences.[57] Neither were particularly religious or pious but enjoyed the unflinching support of the evangelical community. The Donald and The Gipper promised to deliver their supporters back to a time when they were more complete, prosperous, and unified. Trump's transformation of political power is profound but not without precedent. His abrogation of traditional authority was set into motion nearly forty years prior with monumental shifts in media culture, technology, geopolitics, and philosophies of market governance.

This chapter has argued that the *Access Hollywood* tape represents the confluence of social forces that have transformed the operation of political sovereignty at this particular juncture. Thus, the GOP, having found its totemic ethos in rhetorics of benevolent paternalism, could not contain Trump's symbolic excess. Following the tape's release, most conservatives attempted to repudiate Trump by speaking about themselves as emissaries of the father of prohibition. For instance, Mike Pence stated: "As a husband and father, I was offended by the words and actions described by Donald Trump in the eleven-year-old video released yesterday."[58] Jeb Bush, whom Trump had humiliated and emasculated during the RNC primaries (calling him "low energy"), echoed the same sentiment by asserting that "as the grandfather of two precious girls, I find that no apology can excuse away Donald Trump's reprehensible comments degrading women."[59] Senate Majority Leader Mitch McConnell added to the chorus: "As the father of three daughters, I strongly believe that Trump needs to apologize directly to women and girls."[60] Others politicians also rebuked Trump by referencing their paternal relations with women in their families. For example, Ben Carson wrote, "In no way do I condone Trump's behavior—in fact I condemn any form of disrespect toward women. We should always honor and respect the dignity of our mothers, sisters and daughters."[61] Senator Ted Cruz remarked, "These comments are disturbing and inappropriate, there is simply no excuse for them. . . . Every wife, mother, daughter—every person—deserves to be treated with dignity and respect."[62] Senator Mitt Romney added: "Hitting on married women? Condoning assault? Such vile degradations demean our wives and daughters and corrupt America's face to the world."[63] Others repeated similar lines of rebuke. These patterned responses could be critiqued as empty platitudes, particularly since all of the men with the exception of Senator Romney ultimately endorsed Trump for president.

Beyond the hollowness of these denouncements, their ultimate failure is their misrecognition of the tape as an embarrassing exposure and that such revelations naturally galvanize and bring to bear norms of accountability. The tape announced that the prohibitions and taboos embraced by previous iterations of conservativism were actually an impediment to the raw exercise of power. Trump had already inoculated his supporters to such challenges by sowing resentment toward traditional conceptions of authority, the institutions underwritten by that authority, and the norms of political discourse that inhibit the crass pursuit of sadistic and autocratic impulses. He had cultivated an investment in his supporters to see him freed of constraints altogether, to defer their agency, and to simply let The Donald *be* The Donald.

These statements also failed to renounce the political economy of patriarchy in which women are reduced to a medium of exchange. Irigaray observed how in a competitive commercial marketplace, women take on the use and exchange value of commodities. She writes that "women are marked phallically by their fathers, husbands, procurers. And this branding determines their value in sexual commerce."[64] What conservatives seemed to protest was the threat of an illicit marketplace, cornered and manipulated by a cartel boss, where values are no longer determined by the laws of supply and demand. In other words, Trump is simply a market distortion or an externality that obstructed the free flow of commodities and hinders the ability of the market to set the price of goods and services. In this illicit marketplace, Trump is known for ranking women's bodies on an ordinal scale, commenting on the sexual attractiveness of underage women (including his own daughter), and declaring unruly women "nasty" or "pigs" among similar insults. Although Trump's valuation of women is more lurid and sexually explicit, this by no means suggests that the GOP's reverence for women escapes patriarchal culture's traffic in women. In these responses, women are still a medium of exchange in that their value is reduced to the subordinate social role (i.e., wives, mothers, daughters) they occupy in relation to men. These rebukes are an emphatic restatement of men's propertied relationship to women as commodities or the enforcement of a tacit sexual contract that subordinates women labor.[65]

From another perspective, the GOP's outrage might be characterized as benevolent patriarchy upheld through a masculinist protection impulse. In their responses, women are to be revered, protected, and honored as coveted and precious objects. Indeed, postfeminist culture operates as if malevolent patriarchy has been overcome or, at the very least, feminism is obsolete, unnecessary, and potentially harmful. In this sense, Trump's abhorrent behavior can be considered an aberration or a relic of the patriarchal past. But the evacuation of politics from feminism has emptied the term of meaning, thus carving out space for nearly any action that protects women from harm to be considered a feminist principle. The cultural amnesia required to advance this belief demands that we overlook the long history of protection as a rationale for the subjugation of women in the home and violence against Black men and racial others abroad. The gendered history of lynching and war evince, as Iris Marion Young writes, that "the role of the masculine protector puts those protected, paradigmatically women and children, in a subordinate position of dependence and obedience."[66] Like all protection rackets, masculinist protection of women's purity and virtue extorts from them subservience and silence as the price of security. Yet, postfeminist culture offers benign chivalry as an alternative masculinity to the self-conscious domineering and objectification of the old patriarchy. But in the repudiation of overt misogyny, the rhetoric of reverence and protection securitizes women and reestablishes the centrality of white patriarchy to the functioning of the social order. Facing this farcical reckoning with white masculinity, we are left to accept one of two unacceptable alternatives.

Epilogue

On Pointless Enjoyment

If you are reading this, it is too late. It is more than likely that we will be inundated with reports and raw footage of the latest celebrity or public figure "caught in the act." As I have argued, the return of racism and misogyny is virtually guaranteed by the overlapping structures of the rhetorical unconscious and contemporary modes of media spectatorship. This return, then, becomes the very condition for the spectator's enjoyment but only insofar as enjoyment is experienced as an assault from the outside, or a traumatic intrusion of enjoying others whose lack appears to be absent. Such enjoyment occasions fundamentalist calls for the return of traditional paternal authority, much like the GOP rebuking Trump by claiming the cultural mantle of traditional fatherhood or Adam Silver playing the lawful counterpart to Sterling's father-*jouissance*. In most cases, the same cycle will inevitably repeat: obscene violation followed by powerful rebukes, careful disavowals, and rituals of containment and order. These public rites will laud transparency and publicity as fundamental signs that democracy inevitably guarantees progress toward ending white supremacy and patriarchy. But, as I have argued throughout this book, it is not the perpetrator but the spectator who is caught on tape. It is the spectator's enjoyment that is predicated on continually and compulsively (re)discovering the very thing that produces their anxiety. In other words, these tapes play on a continual loop, and as the archive of hate grows larger, the democratic spectator is awash in obscene enjoyment. Our capacity to document every profane act of racism, misogyny, and violence creates a virtually infinite doom scroll from which there seems no respite. The realization of a (self)surveillance society, alas, will not save us.

In attending to obscene enjoyment, it is important to ask: How does this book avoid replicating the same audience dynamic it problematizes? Is the reader not put in the same position as the incredulous spectator? First, I take criticism to mean a kind of *repetition with a difference* that entails

Caught on Tape. Casey Ryan Kelly, Oxford University Press. © Oxford University Press 2023.
DOI: 10.1093/oso/9780197677865.003.0006

thoughtful and systematic attention to the structural dynamics that shape publics' encounter with obscene texts. By attending to moments when white masculinity's messy excessiveness irrupts into public life, each chapter has illustrated how white masculinity hides its psychical investments in plain sight. I suggest that adopting a critical orientation is not a matter of engaging or disengaging from obscene texts as much as it is about knowing how to look and acknowledging the role of enjoyment in the cultural production of white masculinity and white supremacy. My purpose was not therefore to expose the spectacular crimes of whiteness and white masculinity—such structures do an exemplary job of doing that on their own. Instead, my goal is to make sense of *what* white masculinity discloses about itself, and how such scandalous disclosures craft an audience dynamic that obscures precisely what it announces.

In a convergence culture, where all secrets will be laid bare, making a transgressive spectacle of oneself seemingly relieves one of the burdens, the Symbolic, and deprives a moralist of their ability to install and enforce the reality principle. The notion that cameras and secret recordings will reintroduce the law overlooks enjoyment as an ideological and "political factor."[1] In other words, "the idea that ideology works upon us not simply as a system of representation or a mode of discourse, but via the currency of enjoyment."[2] Media technologies entice audiences to compulsively stage and restage the white masculine spectacle as a route to experience *jouissance*. Thus, theorizing the role that convergence culture plays in transforming publics' relationship to white masculinity evinces how spectators' enjoyment has been organized and habituated by transformations in mediated forms. Although the death drive is an unavoidable aspect of psychical existence, it is possible to change our affective investment in fantastical ends that are attached to the repetition compulsion. Thus, this book has shown how careful attention to obscene enjoyment as a rhetorical phenomenon—one that hails spectators and organizes their desires—entails attention to the meaning subjects attach to repetition and what that process procures for their subjectivity. Hopefully, this invites readers to take up a healthier relationship to the death drive, no longer content to interminably deflect its psychical charge into public life. The ultimate goal of this project is to find ways that subjects might divest themselves of fantasies that keep them and us entangled in public scandals. Criticism, I submit, takes up a more ethical stance toward obscene enjoyment as it demands self-reflexive interrogation of one's own desires in relation to a text and traversing the fantasies it engenders. Criticism creates breathing room, or critical distance from the suffocating presence of other people's enjoyment.

Instead of arguing for critical distance, fundamentalists will likely call for the return of the law to shield subjects from this overwhelming encounter with the Other's enjoyment—which is, not incidentally, the very condition for the fundamentalist's own enjoyment. Yet, the politics of the death drive ensure that perpetual roadblocks will likely thwart this utopian realization of the good. Indeed, it is the death drive that makes the Other appear to the subject as a placeholder for the object-cause of desire. Ultimately, the fundamentalist seeks to desire again, something only possible with some measure of respite from the proximate object. As Todd McGowan observes, when authority appears "nonlacking and ubiquitous," it never allows "the subject the space to desire."[3] Part of what is traumatizing about transgressive white masculinity in this political moment is that it provides no space or distance from enjoyment. No longer content to be strong and silent, the mode of white masculinity I have explored here *demands* attention. It is loud, unapologetic, and unhinged from norms and conventions—even in a nominal or perfunctory sense. It is this genre of masculinity that bludgeons police officers with the American flag, puts its feet up on the desk belonging to the speaker of the House of Representatives, and smears feces on the hallowed halls of Congress. The white masculine figures that populate these pages do not appear to fear self-destruction—in fact, their expressions seem to welcome the cathartic release from the strictures of meaningfulness. Such power forecloses space for *indifference* to the Other's enjoyment. In making this claim, I do not mean to suggest that we should return to Victorian morality or sanitize public space—quite the contrary. Instead, I question how convergence culture demands that spectators pay heed to white masculine enjoyment as well as the concomitant fantasy that the next shocking revelation will realize the promise of democracy and bring back the benign father of prohibition. The compulsive repetition of the death drive is easily grafted onto an attention economy in which it is virtually impossible for spectators to ignore the cacophony of other people's desires. This structural dynamic takes hold of and organizes spectator's desire around the ruinous enjoyment of deeply flawed and problematic subjects.

The challenge of living in a surveillance (and self-surveillance) society is not simply that we *know* but that we are *invested* in the Other's enjoyment: Trump's sexual predilections, Mel Gibson's rape fantasies, Donald Sterling's enjoyment of Blackness, and the racist *jouissance* of ordinary white people. There is no ethical space for the subject to desire, yet the fundamentalist who seeks to restrict unhinged gratification inevitably *also* reintroduces anxiety through restrictions that merely intensify that enjoyment. What, if anything, is the alternative to this interminable repetition? I wish to close this examination of obscene enjoyment by reflecting on the ethics of enjoyment and desire, which is to say these cases prompt us to consider whether we are irrevocably ensnared in pathological fantasies—trapped in the liminality between secrecy and disclosure. How do we help people unplug from the technological and culture circuitry of obscene enjoyment?

As I have argued elsewhere, the affective charge of Trump's rhetoric never wavered from the kind of power he embraced on the Access America bus.[4] That is to say, he never wavered in his enjoyment of cruelty and ruinous desire run amok. The tape did not repel but rather pulled the spectator closer—even those who disapproved of his behavior. The same can be said of the racist tirades enacted by ordinary white people—their rhetoric enlisting spectators in white masculinity's fusion with the compulsions of the death drive in its pursuit of ultimate *jouissance*. Although as subjects we cannot help but engage in compulsive repetition, we can, however, change our relationship to this psychical aspect of our political and social existence.[5] White masculinity has come to embody a pathological politics of non-being and meaninglessness —illusory routes to ultimate *jouissance*. Caught in the spectacle of obscene enjoyment, the death drive compels us to call down the cruelty of the superego to punish us for our guilt. As objects rather than subjects of the gaze, it is this loss of control that predicates the spectator's enjoyment. Obscene enjoyment crafts an audience dynamic that is masochistic, where we are compelled to, in Terry Eagleton's words, "hug our chains."[6] A masochistic position does not entail self-violence as much as it positions the Other as the subject who enacts violence on the self. For instance, Trump's rhetoric of white masculine victimhood venerates the persecuted subject as the ideal citizen. In this regard, Trump's persecuted audience is caught up in an abusive relationship. At the same time, Trump's critics are no more free than his supporters. They, too, have attended to every new shocking revelation of his profanity, giddy that this time Trump will be held accountable. If not for fomenting a violent insurrection, what would it take for them to abandon him? Indeed, this audience dynamic goes far beyond party politics; it permeates the structure of U.S. media culture and will long outlast Trump.

But will resurrecting the totem of paternal authority precipitate the return of symbolic efficiency? Is Joe Biden's victory evidence that a structural transformation is on its way?

It is tempting to call for the law of prohibition to return (nostalgia), or normalcy for that matter, in response to this instantiation of white masculinity. Yet, the totem of authority that prohibits such obscene transgressions is the same authority that exempted white violence from sanction and molded white masculinity into the template of universal humanness. As Lisa Flores contends, "[W]hitened violence has a particular agency; it is victimless . . . justified, almost innocent." Such violence "orders society and ensures its civility."[7] Whereas Freud's primal totem established the laws of exogamy that made society possible, the prohibitive authority of U.S. colonialism and chattel slavery established the laws of race and anti-miscegenation that made a patriarchal white supremacist society possible. Racist, xenophobic, and sexual violence have historically escaped the norms of prohibition, particularly when carried out in the service of whiteness. Slavery and indigenous genocide were, at the time, legal practices and their effects are felt long past their formal prohibition. Indeed, we need a different orientation toward accountability that traverses the narcissism of liberal fantasy and the politics of demand.

Yet, proffering political alternatives to compulsion is difficult. Psychoanalysis offers neither a grand revolutionary political project nor a moral imperative to do good. Nor does it offer therapeutic solutions that help political subjects conform and adjust their psyche to social conventions.[8] "For psychoanalysis," McGowan writes, "the good is not just an unrealizable ideal but a deception incapable of orienting a coherent and sustainable politics."[9] This is the case because any conception of the good (the object-cause of desire) is only experienced by virtue of its prohibition—reproducing *objet a* so that it can be enjoyed. Without prohibition there is no sacrifice, no desire, no enjoyment. What if anything, then, constitutes an ethical relationship with obscene enjoyment? If violence, racism, and misogyny do not merely wish to destroy the Other's enjoyment, but to sustain it, then is this also the case for those who would demand moral accountability for its violent perpetrators?

Another challenge we face is that there is no respite from obscene enjoyment—it is too proximate and too overwhelming to envision new political fantasies. For instance, many experienced the Trump presidency as a repetitive assault on consensus reality. Trump, however, was also a symptom of a much larger destabilization of the Symbolic that some have characterized as a crisis of trust and confidence in neoliberal modes of subject formation.[10] As Jack Bratich and Sarah Banet-Weiser argue, perpetual economic crises have eroded the symbolic efficiency of neoliberal discourses because their entrepreneurial fantasies of self-mastery can never be fully realized.[11] But rather than traversing the fantasy, white men are diverted into networks of misogyny that invite them to blame women and people of color for their lack of confidence and success in the neoliberal marketplace. The uptick in racism and violent misogyny is, in part, the failure of neoliberal governmentality to produce subjects who continually reup their commitment to self-improvement despite their continual failure. Put another way, the failure of neoliberal subjectivization is experienced as a crisis of the enjoying Other's making. Seeking to sustain the conditions of desire, alienated white men turn to totalizing ideologies where desire is rerouted into fantasies of violence and subjugation. The same could be said of the rise of xenophobia and nativism and other racist ideologies that blame foreigners and people of color for the structural failures of neoliberalism. Neoliberal failure, then, engenders scapegoating (violence done to the Other) and fantasies of persecution (violence done to the self by the Other)—a disavowal of the death drive's self-inflicted violence. The crisis of neoliberal subject formation is not absence or lack, but a *lack of lack*—what is there left to desire when the fantasy unravels? Obscene enjoyment becomes a way to stage an encounter with *objet a* by reveling in the meaninglessness and loss of identity that stands behind the signifier. Yet, the pursuit of this ultimate satisfaction is not only structurally impossible but also counterproductive in that the barrier to our enjoyment is also the very source of such enjoyment. Like neoliberal fantasies, such fantasies mistake the eradication or transcendence of prohibitions for the achievement of ultimate satisfaction. The result is a perpetual deflection of the death drive into public life: scapegoating, victimhood, and violence.

Obscene enjoyment, however, represents a preoccupation with the ultimate satisfaction of the drives, rather than desire itself. An ethical position relative to the death drive would be to recognize that eradicating the barrier to our enjoyment does not and structurally cannot give us access to something we never had. Such a stance would represent not the moral dictates of a cruel superego but instead a subject avowing the desire installed by the signifier. As John Rajchman explained:

The aim of the analytic process is not to make moral agents or virtuous persons out of us, to make us obedient to the rules of some prescriptive code, or to impart to us the nature of "the good life." What one learns about oneself is neither a general knowledge of what is best for the species nor the acknowledgment of the rational character of the rules of mutual obligation. The ethic of psychoanalysis is thus not one of prudence or of duty. On the contrary, it leads to critical reflection about the essentializing assumptions on which prudential ethics have been built, and about the role of unconscious guilt in moralities of abstract duty or conscience.[12]

Instead, such critical reflection would illustrate that the (divided) subject is not the center of the moral universe and that such a subject might avow that the lost object is something imagined by oneself to repossess the *jouissance* blocked by the signifier. Such an ethic would stand in direct opposition to the self-annihilating pursuit of ultimate satisfaction.

To conclude, I do not propose a grand political project guided by a sense of the good but instead a defense of accountability that starts with the subject's avowal of desire. The politics of the death drive elude accountability through a constant deferral of enjoyment to some external and ultimate end. Rather than accounting for the subject's desire, we fixate instead on the barriers to enjoyment. Accountability for obscene transgressions risks being derailed into a search for monsters we must vanquish or guilt-ridden demands for the superego's punishment.[13] We might instead seek a form of accountability that decouples the drive of white masculinity from the death drive, thus refusing to ennoble sacrifice, scapegoating, and violence. We might also come to terms with the perpetual return of obscene enjoyment as a structural dynamic of a culture built on the very things it wishes to disavow.

What Is Accountability?

The perpetrators of racist and misogynist outbursts sometimes offer perplexing explanations for their transgressions. On March 14, 2021, a hot mic incident went viral involving Matt Rowan, a local announcer for an Oklahoma girl's high school basketball game. In the clip, the enraged announcer can be heard swearing at one of the players kneeling during the U.S. national anthem.[14] The announcer referred to the Black player by a common and dehumanizing racial epithet. In doing so, he channeled the reactionary culture of white rage in response to the Black Lives Matter movement and its amplification by professional athletes such as Colin Kaepernick.[15] Yet, Rowan offered an explanation for his hate speech that stretches the bounds of credulity: *high blood sugar*. In his apology, Rowan rehearsed many of the tropes of racist apologia spotlighted throughout this book that attempt to diminish white culpability for offensive speech and behavior. Thus, after boasting his credentials as a father and pious Christian—traits that putatively speak to his non-racist ethos—Rowan explained, "I have not only embarrassed and disappointed myself, I have embarrassed and disappointed my family and my friends. During the game my sugar was spiking. While not excusing my remarks, it is not unusual when my sugar spikes that I become disoriented and often say things that are not appropriate as well as hurtful."[16] He continued to insist that he did not consider himself a racist person and that absent diabetes he did not "believe that [he] would have made such horrible statements."[17] In offering an apology similar to other high-profile racist ones, Rowan evaded responsibility by appealing to mitigating factors that might lessen his responsibility and minimize the structural and systematic nature of racism. Moreover, he centered himself, his friends, and his family as the victims of his remarks, rather than the young woman and people of color he insulted.

In his statement, Rowan constructed such racism as an accident or mishap, rather than a conscious act of speech articulated within a purposeful system of racist dehumanization. In other words, he refused to admit that his speech was a product of white masculine and white supremacy. His statements opened space for him to be considered a tertiary victim of his own comments (and the Other's violence) insofar as racism is understood to be an involuntary somatic response to stressful situations, not an unacknowledged set of affective and ideological investments. While racism is not a side effect of diabetes, appeals to diminished capacity in the context of racism illustrate the workings of an informal culture of impunity in which bigoted speech acts are uttered. Tirades and outbursts are more easily discounted when racism and misogyny are considered to be both physical and cultural aberrations.

I pause on Rowan's comments to consider what amounts to accountability in the context of postracial and postfeminist culture. What is the relationship between whiteness, masculinity, and accountability in this cultural environment? What factors should publics take into account when adjudicating racist and/or misogynistic incidents? How might we understand the intersection of race and gender-based oppression as more than simply a momentary lapse in the overall progressive trajectory of liberal democracy? What does accountability look like when we acknowledge that oppression is systemic and structural rather individual? Perhaps the answer to these questions lies between cultures of impunity that always discount white culpability and a concept of offenders as monstrous aberrations that call forth harsh punitive and carceral solutions. Turning to Rowan's remarks once again, we find that one problem with rhetorics of accountability is that white subjects implicitly enjoy a privileged relationship with the law and cultural conceptions of *ethos*. In short, Rowan's preposterous defense prompts us to consider the rhetorical resources that white subjects might draw from to explain their racist speech and diminish their culpability. Indeed, as Robert Terrill and Joshua Gunn have both shown in their analyses of Trump's discourse, one defining mark of Trumpism has been the acceptance of responsibility without an ethic of accountability. White masculinity might even come to own its transgression but without any sense that it obligates them to do anything about it.

In one sense, Rowan's remarks conjure the cultural lore surrounding the so-called twinkie defense, a media myth derived from the trial of Dan White who murdered San Francisco Mayor George Moscone along with city supervisor and queer activist Harvey Milk. Although White's attorneys argued that his consumption of junk food was a symptom of his depression, the case for his reduced sentence was not based on the facile notion that junk food made him homicidal.[18] Yet, in this case, Rowan appropriates this mythology to suggest that racism is a physiological anomaly caused by misaligned body chemistry. Actor Roseanne Barr made a similar argument in defense of her racist tweets when she suggested that she had posted them while under the influence of the sleep drug Ambien.[19] Diminished capacity has also been articulated to social and cultural factors. For instance, the attorneys for Ethan Couch, a teenager who killed four in a drunk driving incident, argued that growing up white and affluent mitigated his ability to appreciate the consequences of his actions.[20] The news media even gave his disorder a clinical portmanteau: *affluenza*. Although this book has focused on the obscene outbursts of high-profile people and powerful celebrities, such incidents are all too commonplace in U.S. culture. What I have posited throughout this book is that white masculinity affords some the authority to define what counts as racism and misogyny alongside an arsenal of tropes and stereotypes that circumscribe how women and people of color are supposed to respond within the boundaries of white authority. Racist speech acts are more readily discounted where whiteness and/or manliness are virtually synonymous with good character. Culpability for racism is diminished, then, by its very own structural capacities to reproduce positive images of white men: fathers, Christians, community leaders, and so on. Such positive images are always predicated on a negative conception of difference— an image of people of color as an Other who lacks the essential traits and character that disqualify one from entering the ranks of the human. Hence, U.S. media culture presents a pastiche of people of color as criminals, cheats, delinquent fathers, welfare dependents, and troublemakers.[21] Indeed, it is a privilege for white subjects to make ethos claims and assume that their good character will be implicitly taken for granted. Rowan's appeals to his fatherly and Christian ethos are uttered in a context in which they are readily believable defenses against charges of bigotry.

Whiteness and white masculinity, then, can be thought of as a repertoire of both ethos and diminished capacity, which is to name a diffuse and shifting terrain of identity that evades accountability. As Ashley Noel Mack and Bryan J. McCann contend, "[Q]uestions of who deserves protection and whose actions warrant harsh punishment are tethered to racial, gender, and sexual hierarchies."[22] Here accountability lies not with the *self* but with the violence of the *Other*. Recall that Donald Trump's accountability was mitigated by the ideological scaffolding of rape culture and white victimhood. Mel Gibson's hate speech was discounted as lunacy even as he restaged a quintessential American racist melodrama. Donald Sterling's exposure shifted the issue of racism in professional sports to a question of diversity rather than the structures of racial capitalism. Smartphone-captured tirades eclipse the role of the spectator in structural racism. In all these cases, whiteness seeks to present itself as already always possessing a diminished capacity for responsibility: Billy Bush egged on Trump; Gibson, Hogan, and Sterling's comments were uttered in private conversations; Michael Richards was goaded by an unruly crowd; and ordinary people were pushed to the edge. In all these cases, structural and systemic oppression were never to blame. If whiteness is a metonymic stand-in for universal humanness, racism and misogyny are simply temporary deviations from the offender's otherwise pristine character.

But let us assume, for a moment, that these outbursts are somatic or unconscious rather than deliberate or ideational. Psychoanalysis teaches us that individual subjects are conduits for larger patterns of language and the unconscious. Often, people do things but have no clue as to why. That does not mean that obscene outbursts are random or without motive, even if they are spontaneous and confounding. But even if this were to somehow lessen individual culpability for racist speech acts, it poses a question as to why the unconscious would assemble racial signifiers when the mind and body are under duress? Indeed, it is the case that we are born into a language that predates our existence and lives long past our deaths. Upon entry into the Symbolic, we must therefore submit and conform our inchoate and ineffable desires to a system of signs that actively channel and shape those desires according to structural grammars, frequently in ways that are quite alienating. Language constitutes the subject according to the Other's discourse where the unconscious is, as Bruce Fink puts it, *"full of other people's talk, other people's conversations, and other people's goals, aspirations and fantasies* (insofar as they are expressed in words)."[23] Within psychoanalysis, "ego talk" (i.e., "*I* am not a racist") does not represent the statement of an active agent (the subject), but rather a "crystallization or sedimentation of ideal images" or an illusion of a coherence with which we idealize, cathect, and invest.[24] This "subject" is caught in nets of signifiers, or tropes, that are made up of arbitrary linguistic routes between signifiers and signified(s). As Christian Lundberg argues, tropes—metaphor and metonymy—are the worn symbolic pathways over which the ego has no control, despite being important sites of affective investment.[25] It is plausible to suggest that a subject's psychical investment in whiteness may not immediately register to them as a conscious desire (Michael Richards may have been genuinely confused by his own violently racist diatribe, but no less culpable for the damage he inflicted).

Rather than diminish their culpability, racist outbursts can be understood as reflections of how the Symbolic is saturated in racist signifiers and tropes that are inherited from the symbolic economy of colonialism and chattel slavery. Indeed, Hortense Spillers's conception of the "hieroglyphics of the flesh" names the process through which slavery both metonymically and physically encoded its symbolic order onto the bodies of the enslaved—the lash of the tongue and the whip both transformed human bodies into inhuman flesh.[26] The symbolic world that consigned the enslaved person to social death lives on, albeit in a more opaque and diffuse form, in the representational, economic, and political systems that organize our social world. This observation in no way diminishes one's culpability; quite the contrary. Instead, these irruptions speak to a racialized Symbolic and Imaginary in which we are all implicated. Rowan's reflexive turn to a historically resonate racial insult speaks to the durability of certain racial formations and how such formations are sustained at moments when latent racial tropology meets the affective intensity of white rage.

Although racist insults and rape jokes may seem spontaneous, it is only because they are spoken at a moment in which a perpetrator lashes out. However unlikely, it is possible that Rowan had never used that word, or at the very least, had never done so in a public setting or face-to-face confrontation. But he was certainly familiar enough with the word's violent history to understand its power to profoundly wound a young Black woman kneeling to spotlight the systematic murder of Black persons by the police. It was certainly not lost on him that such a racist insult is a tool that whites have used to name, dehumanize, and contain insolent and unruly manifestations of Blackness. Far from being random, racism is encoded and diffused into language itself, like a loaded weapon waiting to be used in moments of intense phobic reaction.[27] The racist insult and hate speech channel white masculine rage into a legible form, translating ineffable desires and felt intensities into language that constructs and organizes social reality.[28] It is therefore not a coincidence that an avowedly non-racist, non-sexist person or the person with a diminished capacity to appreciate the consequences of their speech find themselves suddenly deploying racist and misogynistic signifiers. There is, in fact, nothing sudden about it: the Symbolic is already composed of networks of racist and misogynistic tropes. And while certain signifying pathways might have become overgrown, they nonetheless leave remnants that the speaking subject might retrace without explicit cognitive awareness.

Consider how Blackness has come to signify death, decay, and dirt, while whiteness represents vitality, purity, and goodness. These associations are not accidental but, at the same time, they may not give pause to the user of such connotative terms as their associations have been naturalized and taken for granted within a long history of usage. So-called dog whistles capitalize on such inferential and metonymic associations; terms like "thug," "brute," "buck," and "welfare queen" operate as part of a racist code in which softer euphemisms stand in for more explicitly racist terminology.[29] The primal scene of their utterance is sometimes absent or even unknown to the speaker, but such terms nonetheless sustain an organized system of negative difference. Even though language *uses us*, the choice of terminology is anything but random. Like Gibson, Hogan, and Richards, Rowan used a racial epithet because it named an unacceptable expression of racial difference: a young Black woman in peaceful defiance of white authority. The term gave form to his rage by grafting a history of white perceptions onto the young woman's body, revoking her provisional humanity. His racism was at once spectacular for its embodiment of white rage but also banal because the Symbolic is saturated in racist signifiers.

The suggestion that such outbursts are out of character, irrational, or spontaneous underwrites the logics of white innocence or, more pointedly, whiteness as a diminished capacity for culpability.[30] Of course, the fact that language is full of other people's desires does not render one's capacity *diminished* but instead *distributed*. By distributed, I mean that the responsibility for racism transcends any one individual—it is a collective debt incurred by all white people that obligates both offenders and those who take offense to adopt a stance of anti-racism and dismantle the institutions and ideologies that sustain structural racism. By turning inward, both stakeholders might acknowledge the racist and misogynistic structures that reside within the rhetorical unconscious. Just as there is nothing outside of the Symbolic, which hits its absolute limit at the Real, we are inevitably socialized into a language that historically privileges white bodies, experiences, and norms. Racialization is, in other words, "scripted" according to templates or previous patterns of discourse that categorize, spatialize, and otherize according to recursive racial logics. Natalia Molino argues that "racial scripts refer to more than just a stereotype. They show how power is always at stake in racial categorization and how, once formed, those racial categories can easily be transferred to new groups. To put it simply, racism builds on past racial acts."[31] Scripting denotes the patterns of signification, or the tropes of negative difference that act as a kind of mental scaffolding that makes Otherness knowable and recognizable as race.[32] The racism and misogyny that seemingly irrupt into rational ego discourse can be understood as rehearsals of racist scripts inherited from a history of past iterations that structure white masculinity's relationship to Otherness—that render difference legible but not on its own terms. Responsibility at the level of structure begins with a recognition that we are all conduits for the racism and misogyny that structure the Symbolic.[33] We cannot therefore treat racism and misogyny as wholly rational categories, for they are byproducts of a fundamental *mis*recognition of whiteness and white masculinity as completeness or universal being; and Blackness, femininity, queerness, and transness as incomplete and abject. The compulsion to pin down racial and gender certainty is to cover over the gaps and fissures of a Symbolic realm that actually offers no such metaphysical assurances.[34] Postracialism and postfeminism constitute an organized misrecognition at a societal level so that white masculinity might evade knowledge of its own illusory identifications.

Notes

Introduction

1. David Lyon, *The Culture of Surveillance: Watching as a Way of Life* (Cambridge, UK: Polity, 2018), 2.
2. Michel Foucault, *Discipline and Punish: The Birth of the Prison* (New York: Vintage Books, 1977).
3. Liza Lin and Newley Purnell, "A World With a Billion Cameras Watching You Is Just Around the Corner," *Wall Street Journal*, December 6, 2019, https://www.wsj.com/articles/a-billion-surveillance-cameras-forecast-to-be-watching-within-two-years-11575565402.
4. Yves Citton, *The Ecology of Attention* (Cambridge, UK: Polity, 2017).
5. Rachel E. Dubrofsky and Antoine Hardy, "Performing Race in Flavor of Love and *The Bachelor*," *Critical Studies in Media Communication* 25, no. 4 (October 1, 2008): 373–92, https://doi.org/10.1080/15295030802327774.
6. See also Ralph Cintron, *Democracy as Fetish* (University Park: Pennsylvania State University Press, 2019).
7. Jodi Dean, *Publicity's Secret: How Technoculture Capitalizes on Democracy* (Ithaca, NY: Cornell University Press, 2002), 10.
8. Douglas Kellner, *Media Spectacle* (New York: Routledge, 2003); see also Douglas Kellner, *American Nightmare: Donald Trump, Media Spectacle, and Authoritarian Populism* (Rotterdam, the Netherlands: Sense Publishers, 2016).
9. Douglas Kellner, *Guys and Guns Amok: Domestic Terrorism and School Shootings from the Oklahoma City Bombing to the Virginia Tech Massacre* (Boulder, CO: Paradigm, 2008), 3. See also Guy Debord, *Society of the Spectacle* (Detroit: Black & Red, 2000).
10. Kevin Michael DeLuca and Jennifer Peeples, "From Public Sphere to Public Screen: Democracy, Activism, and the 'Violence' of Seattle," *Critical Studies in Media Communication* 19, no. 2 (June 1, 2002): 125–51, https://doi.org/10.1080/07393180216559.
11. See Citton, *The Ecology of Attention*.
12. Michael Kunzelman, "Capitol Rioters' Social Media Posts Influencing Sentencings," *Associated Press News*, December 11, 2021, https://apnews.com/article/media-prisons-social-media-capitol-siege-sentencing-0a60a821ce19635b70681faf86e6526e.
13. Henry A. Giroux, "Disturbing Pleasures: Murderous Images and the Aesthetics of Depravity," *Third Text* 26, no. 3 (2012): 259–73, https://doi.org/10.4324/9780203873250.
14. Giroux, "Disturbing Pleasures," 264.

15. See Mark Andrejevic, *I Spy: Surveillance and Power in the Interactive Era* (Lawrence: University Press of Kansas, 2007).

16. Tim Naftali, "Ronald Reagan's Long-Hidden Racist Conversation With Richard Nixon," *The Atlantic*, July 30, 2019, https://www.theatlantic.com/ideas/archive/2019/07/ronald-reagans-racist-conversation-richard-nixon/595102/.

17. Jacques Derrida, *The Beast and the Sovereign*, Vol. I, trans. Geoffrey Bennington (Chicago: University of Chicago Press, 2011).

18. Michael Warner, "Publics and Counterpublics," *Public Culture* 14, no. 1 (2002): 62.

19. Lauren Berlant, *Cruel Optimism* (Durham, NC: Duke University Press, 2011).

20. Sigmund Freud, *The Interpretation of Dreams: The Complete and Definitive Text*, trans. James Strachey (New York: Basic Books, 2010); Sigmund Freud and Peter Gay, *New Introductory Lectures on Psycho-Analysis*, ed. James Strachey (New York: W.W. Norton, 1990).

21. *Jouissance* is distinct from pleasure (*plaisir*). Freud's pleasure principle asserts that the ego protects the subject (and pleasure) against the excesses of the libido (Id). This homeostatic principle contrasts starkly with surplus enjoyment, that an overwhelming pleasure-in-pain exceeds governance by the pleasure principle. Žižek explains that "surplus-enjoyment is thus precisely that part of *jouissance* which resists being contained by the homeostasis, by the pleasure principle." See Slavoj Žižek, "Descartes and the Post-Traumatic Subject: On Catherine Malabou's Les Nouveaux Blessés and Other Autistic Monsters," *Qui Parle* 17, no. 2 (December 1, 2009): 21, https://doi.org/10.5250/quiparle.17.2.123; See also Sigmund Freud and James Strachey, *The Ego and the Id* (New York: W.W. Norton, 1962); and Jacques Lacan, *The Four Fundamental Concepts of Psycho-Analysis* (W.W. Norton, 1998).

22. See Lawrence Grossberg, *Cultural Studies in the Future Tense* (Durham, NC: Duke University Press, 2010).

23. Black studies scholars point out that theories of possessive individualism and democratic citizenship are rooted in the categorical disavowal of the humanness of racialized subjects that fundamentally excludes people of color from the rights enshrined in the nation's founding documents. White masculine violence done in the name of democracy is subsequently legitimized as a civilizing and defensive form of violence. See Charles W. Mills, *The Racial Contract* (Ithaca, NY: Cornell University Press, 1999); Charles W. Mills, *Black Rights/White Wrongs: The Critique of Racial Liberalism* (New York: Oxford University Press, 2017).

24. Raymond Williams, *Raymond Williams on Television: Selected Writings*, ed. Alan O'Connor (New York: Routledge, 1989), 4.

25. See Rachel E. Dubrofsky and Emily D. Ryalls, "The Hunger Games: Performing Not-Performing to Authenticate Femininity and Whiteness," *Critical Studies in Media Communication* 31, no. 5 (October 20, 2014): 395–409, https://doi.org/10.1080/15295036.2013.874038.

26. Kellen Browning and Taylor Lorenz, "Pro-Trump Mob Livestreamed Their Rampage, and Made Money Doing It" *New York Times*, January 8, 2021, https://www.nytimes.com/2021/01/08/technology/dlive-capitol-mob.html.

27. Caroline Levine, *Forms: Whole, Rhythm, Hierarchy, Network* (Princeton, NJ: Princeton University Press, 2015).

28. Paul McDonald, *The Star System: Hollywood's Production of Popular Identities* (New York: Columbia University Press, 2013).

29. See Alice E. Marwick, "Instafame: Luxury Selfies in the Attention Economy," *Public Culture* 27, no. 1 75 (January 2015): 137–60, https://doi.org/10.1215/08992363-2798 379; Alice E. Marwick, *Status Update: Celebrity, Publicity, and Branding in the Social Media Age* (New Haven, CT, and London: Yale University Press, 2015); and Alice E. Marwick, "You May Know Me From YouTube: (Micro-)Celebrity in Social Media," in *A Companion to Celebrity*, ed. P. David Marshall and Sean Redmond (Hoboken, NJ: John Wiley & Sons, 2015), 333–50.

30. Martin Conboy, "Foreword," in *The Tabloid Culture Reader*, ed. Biressi Anita and Nunn Heather (New York: McGraw-Hill, 2007), i, xv.

31. Anne Helen Petersen, "Smut Goes Corporate: TMZ and the Conglomerate, Convergent Face of Celebrity Gossip," *Television & New Media* 11, no. 1 (January 1, 2010): 62–81, https://doi.org/10.1177/1527476409338196.

32. Henry Jenkins, *Convergence Culture: Where Old and New Media Collide* (New York: NYU Press, 2008).

33. Sharon Marcus, "Celebrities and Publics in the Internet Era," *Public Culture* 27, no. 1 [75] (January 1, 2015): 2, https://doi.org/10.1215/08992363-2798319.

34. P. David Marshall, *Celebrity and Power: Fame in Contemporary Culture* (Minneapolis: University of Minnesota Press, 2014), xii.

35. Susan Murray and Laurie Ouellette, eds., *Reality TV: Remaking Television Culture* (New York: NYU Press, 2008).

36. Andrejevic, *I Spy*.

37. Casey Kelly, "Neocolonialism and the Global Prison in National Geographic's *Locked Up Abroad*," *Critical Studies in Media Communication* 29, no. 4 (October 1, 2012): 331–47, https://doi.org/10.1080/15295036.2011.645843.

38. Laura Grindstaff and Susan Murray, "Reality Celebrity: Branded Affect and the Emotion Economy," *Public Culture* 27, no. 1 (January 2015): 109–35, https://doi.org/10.1215/08992363-2798367.

39. See Sally Robinson, *Authenticity Guaranteed: Masculinity and the Rhetoric of Anti-Consumerism in American Culture* (Amherst: University of Massachusetts Press, 2018).

40. Claire Sisco King, *Washed in Blood: Male Sacrifice, Trauma, and the Cinema* (New Brunswick, NJ: Rutgers University Press, 2011).

41. Claire Sisco King, "It Cuts Both Ways: Fight Club, Masculinity, and Abject Hegemony," *Communication and Critical/Cultural Studies* 6, no. 4 (December 1, 2009): 371, https://doi.org/10.1080/14791420903335135.

42. Hegemonic masculinity refers to the traits and behaviors that constitute what counts as masculinity in a particular conjunctural moment. Those attributes that are hegemonic change over time, but the idea that masculinity is hegemonic rarely does. See R. W. Connell, *Masculinities* (Cambridge, UK: Polity, 2005).

43. Hamilton Carroll, *Affirmative Reaction: New Formations of White Masculinity* (Durham, NC: Duke University Press, 2011), 10.

44. Achille Mbembe, *Necropolitics* (Durham, NC: Duke University Press, 2019).

45. Paul Elliott Johnson, "The Art of Masculine Victimhood: Donald Trump's Demagoguery," *Women's Studies in Communication* 40, no. 3 (July 3, 2017): 229–50, https://doi.org/10.1080/07491409.2017.1346533; and Casey Ryan Kelly, "Donald J. Trump and the Rhetoric of Ressentiment," *Quarterly Journal of Speech* 106, no. 1 (January 2, 2020): 2–24, https://doi.org/10.1080/00335630.2019.1698756.

46. Kendall R. Phillips, *A Cinema of Hopelessness: The Rhetoric of Rage in 21st Century Popular Culture* (London: Palgrave Macmillan, 2021).

47. See Mark Andrejevic, "The Jouissance of Trump," *Television & New Media* 17, no. 7 (November 1, 2016): 651–55, https://doi.org/10.1177/1527476416652694; and Laurie Ouellette, "The Trump Show," *Television & New Media* 17, no. 7 (November 1, 2016): 647–50, https://doi.org/10.1177/1527476416652695.

48. Paul Elliott Johnson, *I, the People: The Rhetoric of Conservative Populism in the United States* (Tuscaloosa: University of Alabama Press, 2021), 14.

49. Johnson, *I, the People*, 15.

50. Darrel Wanzer-Serrano, "Barack Obama, the Tea Party, and the Threat of Race: On Racial Neoliberalism and Born Again Racism," *Communication, Culture & Critique* 4, no. 1 (March 1, 2011): 23–30, https://doi.org/10.1111/j.1753-9137.2010.01090.x; Vincent Pham, "Our Foreign President Barack Obama: The Racial Logics of Birther Discourses," *Journal of International and Intercultural Communication* 8, no. 2 (2015): 86–107.

51. See George Hawley, *Making Sense of the Alt-Right* (New York: Columbia University Press, 2017); and Heather Suzanne Woods and Leslie A. Hahner, *Make America Meme Again: The Rhetoric of the Alt-Right* (New York: Peter Lang, 2019).

52. Alexandra Minna Stern, *Proud Boys and the White Ethnostate: How the Alt-Right Is Warping the American Imagination* (Boston: Beacon Press, 2019).

53. Angela Nagle, *Kill All Normies: Online Culture Wars From 4Chan And Tumblr to Trump and the Alt-Right* (Washington, DC: Zero Books, 2017).

54. Casey R. Kelly, *Apocalypse Man: The Death Drive and the Rhetoric of White Masculine Victimhood* (Columbus: Ohio State University Press, 2020).

55. Joshua Gunn, *Political Perversion: Rhetorical Aberration in the Time of Trumpeteering* (Chicago: University of Chicago Press, 2020), 6.

56. Slavoj Žižek, *The Ticklish Subject: The Absent Centre of Political Ontology* (New York: Verso, 2000), 362.

57. See Rachel E. Dubrofsky, "Monstrous Authenticity: Trump's Whiteness," in *Theorizing the Communicative Power of Whiteness*, ed. D.M. MacIntosh, Dream A. Moon, and Thomas K. Nakayama (New York: Routledge, 2018), 155–75.

58. Brian L. Ott and Greg Dickinson, *The Twitter Presidency: Donald J. Trump and the Politics of White Rage* (New York: Routledge, 2019).

59. Laura Mulvey, "Visual Pleasure and Narrative Cinema," *Screen* 16, no. 3 (1975): 6–18, https://doi.org/10.1093/screen/16.3.6.

60. Although authors/speakers and audiences may encode or decode divergent meanings from any text, both intention and interpretation are structured by the structural dynamics of power. Audiences may adopt different reading strategies that read with or against the grain of a particular text, but they do so within the structural limits of knowledge, ideology, and experience. See John Fiske, *Television Culture* (New York: Routledge, 2010); Leah Ceccarelli, "Polysemy: Multiple Meanings in Rhetorical Criticism," *Quarterly Journal of Speech* 84, no. 4 (1998): 395, https://doi.org/10.1080/00335639809384229; Celeste Michelle Condit, "The Rhetorical Limits of Polysemy," *Critical Studies in Mass Communication* 6, no. 2 (1989): 103–22, https://doi.org/10.1080/15295038909366739.

61. David Theo Goldberg, *The Threat of Race: Reflections on Racial Neoliberalism* (Hoboken, NJ: John Wiley & Sons, 2011); and Ian Haney López, *Dog Whistle Politics: How Coded Racial Appeals Have Reinvented Racism and Wrecked the Middle Class* (New York: Oxford University Press, 2015).

62. Catherine Squires et al., "What Is This 'Post-' in Postracial, Postfeminist. . . (Fill in the Blank)?," *Journal of Communication Inquiry* 34, no. 3 (July 2010): 210–53, https://doi.org/10.1177/0196859910371375; Darrel Wanzer-Serrano, "Barack Obama, the Tea Party, and the Threat of Race: On Racial Neoliberalism and Born Again Racism," *Communication, Culture & Critique* 4, no. 1 (2011): 23–30, https://doi.org/10.1111/j.1753-9137.2010.01090.x.

63. Diane Negra, *What a Girl Wants?: Fantasizing the Reclamation of Self in Postfeminism* (New York: Routledge, 2009); Vicki Coppock, Deena Haydon, and Ingrid Richter, *The Illusions of Post-Feminism: New Women, Old Myths* (New York: Routledge, 2014); Yvonne Tasker and Diane Negra, eds., *Interrogating Postfeminism: Gender and the Politics of Popular Culture* (Durham, NC: Duke University Press Books, 2007).

64. Eric King Watts, "The Primal Scene of COVID-19: 'We're All in This Together,'" *Rhetoric, Politics, and Culture* 1, no. 1 (2021): 1–26.

65. Eric King Watts, "Postracial Fantasies, Blackness, and Zombies," *Communication and Critical/Cultural Studies* 14, no. 4 (2017): 318, https://doi.org/10.1080/14791420.2017.1338742.

66. Raka Shome, "Mapping the Limits of Multiculturalism in the Context of Globalization," *International Journal of Communication* 6 (February 15, 2012): 144–65.

67. Joshua Gunn, "Gunplay," Carroll C. Arnold Distinguished Lecture, November 9, 2018, https://www.natcom.org/sites/default/files/pages/2018NCA_ArnoldLecture.pdf.

68. Joshua Gunn, "Father Trouble: Staging Sovereignty in Spielberg's *War of the Worlds*," *Critical Studies in Media Communication* 25, no. 1 (March 2008): 12, https://doi.org/10.1080/15295030701849332.

69. Bruce Fink, *The Lacanian Subject: Between Language and Jouissance* (Princeton, N.J.: Princeton University Press, 1997).

70. Sigmund Freud, *Beyond the Pleasure Principle*, trans. James Strachey (New York: W.W. Norton, 1990).

71. Joan Copjec refigures Freud's exploration of the "death instinct" in *Beyond the Pleasure Principle*—or the notion that organic life always seeks to regress back to

inorganic matter—as a symbolic rather than biological process. In other words, desire is regressive in that the psyche seeks a return to the pre-Oedipal body that enjoyed unmediated access to the Real. See Joan Copjec, *Read My Desire: Lacan Against the Historicists* (New York: Verso, 2015).

72. Todd McGowan, *Enjoying What We Don't Have: The Political Project of Psychoanalysis* (Lincoln: University of Nebraska Press, 2013).

73. *Miller v. California* 413 U.S. 15 (1973).

74. Georges Bataille, *Erotism: Death and Sensuality* (San Francisco: City Lights Books, 1986), 17–18.

75. Terry Eagleton, *On Evil* (New Haven, CT: Yale University Press, 2011), 78.

76. Eagleton, *On Evil*, 78.

77. Joshua Gunn, "Death by Publicity: U.S. Freemasonry and the Public Drama of Secrecy," *Rhetoric & Public Affairs* 11, no. 2 (2008): 243–77, https://doi.org/10.1353/rap.0.0029.

78. John Berger, *Ways of Seeing* (New York: Penguin Books, 2008).

79. Laura Mulvey, "Visual Pleasure and Narrative Cinema," *Screen* 16, no. 3 (1975): 6–18, https://doi.org/10.1093/screen/16.3.6.

80. Todd McGowan, "Looking for the Gaze: Lacanian Film Theory and Its Vicissitudes," *Cinema Journal* 42, no. 3 (2003): 28–29.

81. Aristotle, *The Art of Rhetoric* (New York: HarperCollins, 2014), 7.

82. Raymie E. Mckerrow, "Critical Rhetoric: Theory and Praxis," *Communication Monographs* 56, no. 2 (June 1, 1989): 91–111, https://doi.org/10.1080/03637758909390253.

83. Kent A. Ono and John M. Sloop, "The Critique of Vernacular Discourse," *Communication Monographs* 62, no. 1 (March 1, 1995): 19–46, https://doi.org/10.1080/03637759509376346.

84. Michael Calvin McGee, "Text, Context, and the Fragmentation of Contemporary Culture," *Western Journal of Speech Communication: WJSC* 54, no. 3 (Summer 1990): 274–89.

85. For work on genre, see Karlyn Kohrs Campbell and Kathleen Hall Jamieson, *Form and Genre: Shaping Rhetorical Action* (Falls Church, VA: Speech Communication Association, 1978); Carolyn R. Miller, "Genre as Social Action," *Quarterly Journal of Speech* 70, no. 2 (May 1, 1984): 151–67, https://doi.org/10.1080/00335638409383686; Joshua Gunn, "Maranatha," *Quarterly Journal of Speech* 98, no. 4 (November 2012): 359–85, https://doi.org/10.1080/00335630.2012.714900.

86. Edwin Black, "The Second Persona," *Quarterly Journal of Speech* 56, no. 2 (April 1, 1970): 109–19, https://doi.org/10.1080/00335637009382992.

87. Lauren Berlant and Michael Warner, "Sex in Public," *Critical Inquiry* 24, no. 2 (January 1, 1998): 547, https://doi.org/10.1086/448884.

88. Berlant and Warner, "Sex in Public," 556.

89. Kenneth Burke, *A Rhetoric of Motives* (Berkeley: University of California Press, 1969).

90. Laura Kipnis, *How to Become a Scandal: Adventures in Bad Behavior* (New York: Metropolitan Books, 2010), 5, 4.

91. Edwin Black, "Secrecy and Disclosure as Rhetorical Forms," *Quarterly Journal of Speech* 74, no. 2 (1988): 136, https://doi.org/10.1080/00335638809383833.

92. Emphasis mine. Alenka Zupančič, *Why Psychoanalysis?: Three Interventions* (Natchitoches, LA: Northwestern State University Press, 2008), 7.

93. Zupančič, *Why Psychoanalysis?*, 8.

94. Calum Lister Matheson, "Psychotic Discourse: The Rhetoric of the Sovereign Citizen Movement," *Rhetoric Society Quarterly* 48, no. 2 (March 15, 2018): 187–206, https://doi.org/10.1080/02773945.2017.1306876.

95. Stuart Hall, *The Fateful Triangle: Race, Ethnicity, Nation*, ed. Kobena Mercer (Cambridge, MA: Harvard University Press, 2017).

96. Christian Lundberg, *Lacan in Public: Psychoanalysis and the Science of Rhetoric* (Tuscaloosa: University Alabama Press, 2012), 2.

97. Lundberg, *Lacan in Public*, 74

98. Barbara A. Biesecker, "No Time for Mourning: The Rhetorical Production of the Melancholic Citizen-Subject in the War on Terror," *Philosophy & Rhetoric* 40, no. 1 (2007): 152, https://doi.org/10.1353/par.2007.0009.

99. Michael Lane Bruner, *Rhetorical Unconsciousness and Political Psychoanalysis* (Columbia: University of South Carolina Press, 2019).

100. Christian Lundberg, "On Being Bound to Equivalential Chains," *Cultural Studies* 26, no. 2–3 (March 1, 2012): 299–318, https://doi.org/10.1080/09502386.2011.647641.

101. Christian Lundberg, "Enjoying God's Death: *The Passion of the Christ* and the Practices of an Evangelical Public," *Quarterly Journal of Speech* 95, no. 4 (November 2009): 387–411, https://doi.org/10.1080/00335630903296184.

102. Gunn, "Maranatha"; James P. McDaniel, "Fantasm: The Triumph of Form (an Essay on the Democratic Sublime)," *Quarterly Journal of Speech* 86, no. 1 (February 1, 2000): 48–66, https://doi.org/10.1080/00335630009384278.

103. Joshua Gunn, "On Social Networking and Psychosis," *Communication Theory* 28, no. 1 (February 1, 2018): 69–88, https://doi.org/10.1093/ct/qtx002; Joshua Gunn and Thomas Frentz, "Fighting for Father: Fight Club as Cinematic Psychosis," *Western Journal of Communication* 74, no. 3 (May 26, 2010): 269–91, https://doi.org/10.1080/10570311003767191; Matheson, "Psychotic Discourse"; Sarah Stone Watt, ""Rape Is a Four-Letter Word": Psychosis, Sexual Assault, and Abortion in the 2012 U.S. Election," *Women's Studies in Communication* 43, no. 3 (July 2, 2020): 225–46, https://doi.org/10.1080/07491409.2020.1740902.

104. E. Chebrolu, "The Racial Lens of Dylann Roof: Racial Anxiety and White Nationalist Rhetoric on New Media," *Review of Communication*, January 4, 2020, 1–22, https://doi.org/10.1080/15358593.2019.1708441; and Calum Matheson, "'What Does Obama Want of Me?' Anxiety and Jade Helm 15," *Quarterly Journal of Speech* 102, no. 2 (May 2016): 133–49, https://doi.org/10.1080/00335630.2016.1155127.

105. Joshua Gunn and David E. Beard, "On the Apocalyptic Sublime," *Southern Communication Journal* 65, no. 4 (September 1, 2000): 269–86, https://doi.org/10.1080/10417940009373176; and Calum Lister Matheson, *Desiring the Bomb: Communication, Psychoanalysis, and the Atomic Age* (Tuscaloosa: University of Alabama Press, 2018).

106. Janice Hocker Rushing, "Evolution of 'the New Frontier' in Alien and Aliens: Patriarchal Co-Optation of the Feminine Archetype," *Quarterly Journal of Speech* 75, no. 1 (February 1989): 1; Janice Hocker Rushing and Thomas S. Frentz, "The Frankenstein Myth in Contemporary Cinema," *Critical Studies in Mass Communication* 6, no. 1 (March 1989): 61; and Thomas S. Frentz and Janice Hocker Rushing, "Integrating Ideology and Archetype in Rhetorical Criticism, Part II: A Case Study of Jaws," *Quarterly Journal of Speech* 79, no. 1 (February 1993): 61.

107. Barbara A. Biesecker, "Rhetorical Studies and the 'New' Psychoanalysis: What's the Real Problem? Or Framing the Problem of the Real," *Quarterly Journal of Speech* 84, no. 2 (May 1, 1998): 222–40, https://doi.org/10.1080/00335639809384215.

108. Atilla Hallsby, "Imagine There's No President: The Rhetorical Secret and the Exposure of Valerie Plame," *Quarterly Journal of Speech* 101, no. 2 (May 2015): 359, https://doi.org/10.1080/00335630.2015.1024276.

109. Gayle Rubin, "The Traffic in Women: Notes on the 'Political Economy' of Sex," in *Toward an Anthropology of Women*, ed. Rayna R. Reiter (New York: Monthly Review Press, 1975), 157–210.

110. Lacan, *Four Fundamental Concepts*.

111. Thomas K. Nakayama and Robert L. Krizek, "Whiteness: A Strategic Rhetoric," *Quarterly Journal of Speech* 81, no. 3 (August 1995): 291, https://doi.org/10.1080/00335639509384117; and Joe R. Feagin and Eileen O'Brien, *White Men on Race: Power, Privilege, and the Shaping of Cultural Consciousness* (Boston: Beacon Press, 2003).

112. Kelly, *Apocalypse Man*.

113. Dyer, *White*, 10.

114. See Ashley Noel Mack and Tiara R. Na'puti, "'Our Bodies Are Not *Terra Nullius*': Building a Decolonial Feminist Resistance to Gendered Violence," *Women's Studies in Communication* 42, no. 3 (July 3, 2019): 347–70, https://doi.org/10.1080/07491409.2019.1637803.

115. María Lugones, "Toward a Decolonial Feminism," *Hypatia* 25, no. 4 (2010): 745.

116. Calvin L. Warren, *Ontological Terror: Blackness, Nihilism, and Emancipation* (Durham, NC: Duke University Press, 2018).

117. Fred Moten, *Stolen Life* (Durham, NC: Duke University Press, 2018), 16.

118. Matthew Houdek and Ersula J. Ore, "Cultivating Otherwise Worlds and Breathable Futures," *Rhetoric, Politics, and Culture* 1, no. 1 (Summer 2021): 86.

Chapter 1

1. "Mel Gibson's INSANE Racist, Screaming Rants EXPOSED," *RadarOnline*, August 12, 2016, https://radaronline.com/photos/mel-gibson-rants-audio-tapes-racist-swearing-screaming-fights-oksana-grigorieva/.

2. Elizabeth Wagmeister, "How Does Mel Gibson Still Have a Career?," *Variety*, July 2, 2020, https://variety.com/2020/film/news/mel-gibson-controversies-career-1234696080/.

3. Liza Grandia, "The Sober Racism of Mel Gibson's Apocalypto," *Common Dreams*, December 17, 2006, https://www.commondreams.org/views/2006/12/17/sober-rac ism-mel-gibsons-apocalypto; See also Gunn, "Maranatha."

4. Edgar, *Culturally Speaking*, 4.

5. Claire Sisco King and Joshua Gunn, "On a Violence Unseen: The Womanly Object and Sacrificed Man," *Quarterly Journal of Speech* 99, no. 2 (2013): 201, https://doi.org/10.1080/00335630.2013.777770.

6. Judith Butler, *Excitable Speech: A Politics of the Performative* (New York: Routledge, 1997); Helene A. Shugart, "Counterhegemonic Acts: Appropriation as a Feminist Rhetorical Strategy," *Quarterly Journal of Speech* 83, no. 2 (May 1997): 210.

7. John Durham Peters, *Courting the Abyss: Free Speech and the Liberal Tradition* (Chicago: University of Chicago Press, 2010), 6.

8. See Freud, "Mourning and Melancholia"; Sigmund Freud, "Mourning and Melancholia," in *The Standard Edition of the Complete Psychological Works of Sigmund Freud*, translated by James Strachey, 243–58, vol. XIV. (London: The Hogarth Press, 1964).

9. Robin James, *Resilience & Melancholy: Pop Music, Feminism, Neoliberalism* (Winchester, UK: Zero Books, 2015).

10. Judith Butler, "Melancholy Gender/Refused Identification," in *Constructing Masculnities*, ed. Maurice Berger, Brian Wallis, and Simon Watson (New York: Routledge, 2012), 21–36.

11. Dan Glaister, "*Seinfeld* Actor Lets Fly with Racist Tirade," *The Guardian*, November 22, 2006, https://www.theguardian.com/world/2006/nov/22/usa.danglaister.

12. I chose not to reprint racial epithets because of my own racial positionality and privilege. Even in the context of academic inquiry, the reproduction of racial epithets can have traumatic implications for readers. This is not to suggest that racial insults cannot be reappropriated, but rather as a white scholar, I am in no position to do so. See Ta-Nehisi Coates, "In Defense of a Loaded Word," *The New York Times*, November 23, 2013, https://www.nytimes.com/2013/11/24/opinion/sunday/coates-in-defense-of-a-loaded-word.html.

13. Katie Wilson Berg, "Hulk Hogan Fired from WWE After Reports of Racist Rant," *Hollywood Reporter*, July 25, 2015, https://www.hollywoodreporter.com/news/hulk-hogan-fired-wwe-reports-810894.

14. See "Primal Phantasies," in Jean Laplanche and Jean-Bertrand Pontalis, *The Language of Psycho-Analysis*, 6th ed. (New York: W.W. Norton, 1974), 331–33; see also Sigmund Freud, *The "Wolfman" and Other Cases* (New York: Penguin, 2003); and Sigmund Freud and Marie Bonaparte, *The Origins of Psychoanalysis: Letters to Wilhelm Fliess, Drafts and Notes, 1887–1902*, trans. James Strachey (New York: Basic Books, 1954).

15. Freud's theorized the primal scene as the moment a child witnesses parental coitus (or their belief of having witnessed it) but is unable to adequately understand what they have witnessed.

16. See Laplanche and Pontalis, *The Language of Psychoanalysis*, 19.

17. Frantz Fanon, *Black Skin, White Masks*, trans. Richard Philcox (New York: Grove Press, 2008); and Homi K. Bhabha, "The Other Question: The Stereotype and

Colonial Discourse," in *The Sexual Subject: A Screen Reader in Sexuality*, ed. Mandy Merck (London: Routledge, 1992), 312–31.

18. Bhabha, "The Other Question," 327.

19. Luz Calvo, "Racial Fantasies and the Primal Scene of Miscegenation," *International Journal of Psychoanalysis* 89, no. 1 (2008): 68, https://doi.org/10.1111/j.1745-8315.2007.00001.x.

20. Here, I borrow from Ronald L. Jackson's theory of cultural inscription that quite literally scripts and circumscribes the agental capacity of Black persons. See Ronald L. Jackson, *Scripting the Black Masculine Body: Identity, Discourse, and Racial Politics in Popular Media* (Albany: SUNY Press, 2006); by "flesh," I refer to Hortense Spillers's inquiry into the symbol system of slavery as dependent on a series of material practices applied to the body that impart not just physical pain and sorrow but white authority over Black people. Spillers writes that "these undecipherable markings on the captive body render a kind of hieroglyphics of the flesh whose severe disjunctures come to be hidden to the cultural seeing by skin" (p. 67). See "Mama's Baby, Papa's Maybe"; and Sylvia Wynter, "Unsettling the Coloniality of Being/Power/Truth/Freedom: Towards the Human, After Man, Its Overrepresentation—An Argument," *CR: The New Centennial Review* 3, no. 3 (2003): 257–337.

21. See Sharon Patricia Holland, *The Erotic Life of Racism* (Durham, NC: Duke University Press, 2012).

22. Chebrolu, "The Racial Lens of Dylann Roof."

23. See Ersula J. Ore, *Lynching: Violence, Rhetoric, and American Identity* (Jackson: University Press of Mississippi, 2019).

24. Barbara Welter, "The Cult of True Womanhood: 1820–1860," *American Quarterly* 18, no. 2 (1966): 151–74, https://doi.org/10.2307/2711179; Casey Ryan Kelly, "Feminine Purity and Masculine Revenge-Seeking in *Taken* (2008)," *Feminist Media Studies* 14, no. 3 (May 2014): 403–18, https://doi.org/10.1080/14680777.2012.740062.

25. Mary Bosworth and Jeanne Flavin, *Race, Gender, and Punishment: From Colonialism to the War on Terror* (New Brunswick, NJ: Rutgers University Press, 2007); Angela Yvonne Davis, *Women, Race, and Class* (New York: Vintage Books, 1983).

26. Collins, *Black Feminist Thought*.

27. Tamura Lomax, *Jezebel Unhinged: Loosing the Black Female Body in Religion and Culture* (Durham, NC: Duke University Press, 2018).

28. See Cheryl I. Harris, "Whiteness as Property," *Harvard Law Review* 106, no. 8 (1993): 1707–91, https://doi.org/10.2307/1341787.

29. Lacan argues that anxiety concerns uncertainty about the desire of the Other; therefore, proximity interrupts the fantasy by availing subjects that the Other's desire is incomprehensible and beyond their control. See Calum Matheson, "'What Does Obama Want of Me?' Anxiety and Jade Helm 15," *Quarterly Journal of Speech* 102, no. 2 (2016): 133–49, https://doi.org/10.1080/00335630.2016.1155127; and Jacques Lacan, *Anxiety: The Seminar of Jacques Lacan*, trans. A. R. Price, Book X ed. (Cambridge, UK: Polity, 2016).

30. Jared Sexton, *Amalgamation Schemes: Antiblackness and the Critique of Multiracialism* (Minneapolis: University of Minnesota Press, 2008), 25.

31. See Kaja Silverman, *The Acoustic Mirror: The Female Voice in Psychoanalysis and Cinema* (Bloomington: Indiana University Press, 1988).

32. See also Creed, *Phallic Panic*.

33. Mladen Dolar, *A Voice and Nothing More* (Cambridge, MA: MIT Press, 2006), 138.

34. See note 5 in Žižek, *The Plague of Fantasies*, 40.

35. For critical examinations of melodrama as the organizing genre for racial fantasies in U.S. public culture, see Elisabeth Robin Anker, *Orgies of Feeling: Melodrama and the Politics of Freedom* (Durham, NC: Duke University Press, 2014); Susan Gillman, *Blood Talk: American Race Melodrama and the Culture of the Occult* (Chicago: University of Chicago Press, 2003); and Linda Williams, *Playing the Race Card: Melodramas of Black and White from Uncle Tom to O. J. Simpson* (Princeton, NJ: Princeton University Press, 2002).

36. Kent A. Ono, *Contemporary Media Culture and the Remnants of a Colonial Past* (New York: Peter Lang, 2009).

37. See Leland S. Person, "The American Eve: Miscegenation and a Feminist Frontier Fiction," *American Quarterly* 37, no. 5 (1985): 668–85; Richard Slotkin, *Gunfighter Nation: The Myth of the Frontier in Twentieth-Century America* (Norman: University of Oklahoma Press, 1992); Richard Slotkin, *Regeneration Through Violence: The Mythology of the American Frontier, 1600–1860*, Norman: University of Oklahoma Press, 2000); Richard White and Patricia Nelson Limerick, *The Frontier in American Culture* (Berkeley: University of California Press, 1994).

38. Andrew Newman, *Allegories of Encounter: Colonial Literacy and Indian Captivities* (Chapel Hill: University of North Carolina Press, 2018).

39. Anderson, " 'Rhymes with Blunt.' "

40. Mulvey, "Visual Pleasure and Narrative Cinema."

41. See Michel Foucault, *Discipline and Punish: The Birth of the Prison* (New York: Vintage Books, 1977); and Michel Foucault, *The History of Sexuality*, Vol. 1 (New York: Random House, 1978).

42. I borrow this phrase from Richard Slotkin's history of violent frontier expansion in the American West. See Slotkin, *Regeneration Through Violence*.

43. See Freud, *Beyond the Pleasure Principle*, 13–14. Freud describes a game staged by a young boy to assert mastery over his displeasure of his mother's absence. The child used a wooden reel with a string attached to it to throw a toy out of view (yelling the word "fort" or "gone") and return it ("da" or "there"). The game serves as a metaphor in Freudian psychoanalysis for how the repetition compulsion domesticates and binds traumatic experiences.

44. See Watts, "Postracial."

45. Julia Kristeva, *The Power of Horror: An Essay on Abjection* (New York: Columbia University Press, 1982).

46. Charles R. Lawrence et al., eds., *Words That Wound: Critical Race Theory, Assaultive Speech, and the First Amendment* (Boulder, CO: Westview Press, 1993).

47. George Jerry Sefa Dei et al., *Playing the Race Card: Exposing White Power and Privilege* (New York: Peter Lang, 2004), 138–39.

48. Dei et al., *Race Card*, 140.

49. See Robin J. DiAngelo, *White Fragility: Why It's So Hard for White People to Talk about Racism* (Boston: Beacon Press, 2018); Carol Anderson, *White Rage: The Unspoken Truth of Our Racial Divide* (New York: Bloomsbury, 2016); and Bernadette Marie Calafell, *Monstrosity, Performance, and Race in Contemporary Culture* (New York: Peter Lang, 2015).

50. Mark Lawrence McPhail, *The Rhetoric of Racism Revisited: Reparations or Separation?* (Lanham, MD: Rowman & Littlefield, 2002), 16.

51. Calvin L. Warren, *Ontological Terror: Blackness, Nihilism, and Emancipation* (Durham, NC: Duke University Press Books, 2018).

52. Ashley Noel Mack and Bryan J. McCann, "Recalling Persky: White Rage and Intimate Publicity After Brock Turner," *Journal of Communication Inquiry* 43, no. 4 (October 1, 2019): 372–93, https://doi.org/10.1177/0196859919867265; Meta G. Carstarphen et al., "Rhetoric, Race, and Resentment: Whiteness and the New Days of Rage," *Rhetoric Review* 36, no. 4 (October 2017): 255–347, https://doi.org/10.1080/07350 198.2017.1355191.

53. Tommy Curry defines the "Buck" as "the mythological heterosexual Black male figure that emerged from slavery" whose masculinity is attributed to a patriarchal and hypersexual excess (p. 10). For more on the Buck, see *The Man-Not*, 10–19.

54. Fred Moten, *Stolen Life* (Durham, NC: Duke University Press, 2018), 134.

55. Trudier Harris, *Exorcising Blackness: Historical and Literary Lynching and Burning Rituals* (Bloomington: Indiana University Press, 1984).

56. See Bederman.

57. Michael Richards quoted in "'Kramer' Apologizes, Says He's Not Racist," *CBS News*, November 20. 2006, https://www.cbsnews.com/news/kramer-apologizes-says-hes-not-racist/.

58. See Holling, Moon, and Jackson Nevis, "Racist Violations"; and Tim Wise, *Speaking Treason Fluently: Anti-Racist Reflections From an Angry White Male* (Berkeley, CA: Soft Skull, 2008).

59. Holling, Moon, and Jackson Nevis, "Racist Violations," 261.

60. See Sara Ahmed, *Cultural Politics of Emotion* (Edinburgh: Edinburgh University Press, 2014); Brian Massumi, *Parables for the Virtual: Movement, Affect, Sensation* (Durham, NC: Duke University Press, 2002); Bryan J. McCann, "Affect, Black Rage, and False Alternatives in the Hip-Hop Nation," *Cultural Studies ↔ Critical Methodologies* 13, no. 5 (October 1, 2013): 408–18, https://doi.org/10.1177/15327 08613496392; Jenny Edbauer Rice, "The New 'New': Making a Case for Critical Affect Studies," *Quarterly Journal of Speech* 94, no. 2 (May 2008): 200–12, https://doi.org/ 10.1080/00335630801975434.

61. Fanon, *Black Skin*, 139.

62. Curry, *Man-Not*, 31–32.

63. Richard Delgado and Jean Stefancic, *Must We Defend Nazis?: Hate Speech, Pornography, and the New First Amendment* (New York: NYU Press, 1999), 8.

64. Ore, *Lynching*.

65. Doreen Fowler, "Faulkner's Return to the Freudian Father: Sanctuary Reconsidered," *MFS Modern Fiction Studies* 50, no. 2 (2004): 421, https://doi.org/10.1353/mfs.2004.0026.

66. Stephen L. Esquith, *The Political Responsibilities of Everyday Bystanders* (University Park: Penn State University Press, 2011), 46.

67. Sexton, *Amalgation Schemes*, 25.

68. bell hooks, *Black Looks: Race and Representation* (Boston: South End Press, 1992), 24.

69. hooks, *Black Looks*, 25.

70. Derek Hook, "Fanon via Lacan, or: Decolonization by Psychoanalytic Means. . . ?," *Journal of the British Society for Phenomenology* 51, no. 4 (October 1, 2020): 305–19, https://doi.org/10.1080/00071773.2020.1732575.

71. Peter Hudson, "The State and the Colonial Unconscious," *Social Dynamics* 39, no. 2 (June 1, 2013): 265, https://doi.org/10.1080/02533952.2013.802867.

72. Hudson, "Colonial Unconscious," 265.

73. See Sigmund Freud, *The "Wolfman" and Other Cases* (New York: Penguin, 2003); and Sigmund Freud, *The Origins of Psychoanalysis,* trans. James Strachey (New York: Basic Books, 1954).

74. Laplanche and Pontalis, *Psychoanalysis*, 335.

75. Bruce Fink, *The Lacanian Subject: Between Language and Jouissance* (Princeton, NJ: Princeton University Press, 1997).

76. Joshua Gunn, "Refitting Fantasy: Psychoanalysis, Subjectivity, and Talking to the Dead," *Quarterly Journal of Speech* 90, no. 1 (2004): 1–23, https://doi.org/10.1080/0033563042000206808.

77. Lee Barron, *Celebrity Cultures: An Introduction* (Thousand Oaks, CA: SAGE, 2014); and Clarissa Smith, Feona Attwood, and Brian McNair, *The Routledge Companion to Media, Sex and Sexuality* (New York: Routledge, 2017).

78. Clarissa Smith, Feona Attwood, and Brian McNair, *The Routledge Companion to Media, Sex and Sexuality* (New York: Routledge, 2017), 187.

79. Eriq Gardner, "Hulk Hogan Gets $115M Verdict Against Gawker at Sex Tape Trial" *Hollywood Reporter,*" March 16, 2016, https://www.hollywoodreporter.com/thr-esq/hulk-hogan-gets-115m-verdict-876768.

80. Hulk Hogan quoted in Reuven Blau, "Hulk Hogan's Bigoted Rant Revealed in Newly-Released Audio from Sex Tape," *New York Daily News,* April 14, 2016, https://www.nydailynews.com/news/national/hulk-hogan-bigoted-rant-revealed-new-sex-tape-audio-article-1.2601524.

81. Dana L. Cloud, "Hegemony or Concordance? The Rhetoric of Tokenism in `Oprah' Winfrey's Rags-to-Riches Biography," *Critical Studies in Mass Communication* 13, no. 2 (June 1996): 115; Herman Gray, *Watching Race: Television and the Struggle for Blackness* (Minneapolis: University of Minnesota Press, 2004).

82. See Mick Rouse, "Hulk Hogan Is Getting the Redemption Story He Never Earned," *GQ,* February 26, 2018, https://www.gq.com/story/hulk-hogan-is-getting-the-redemption-story-he-never-earned.

83. Marina Fang, "WWE Reinstates Hulk Hogan Into Hall of Fame After Racist Rant, Gawker Lawsuit," *Huffington Post*, July 17, 2018, https://www.huffpost.com/entry/hulk-hogan-reinstated-wwe-hall-of-fame_n_5b4e0b4fe4b0fd5c73bf587f.

84. Colin Gorenstein, "Hulk Hogan Is Baffled That He Can't Use the 'N-Word' While President Obama Can," *Salon*, July 27, 2015, https://www.salon.com/2015/07/27/hulk_hogan_is_baffled_that_he_cant_use_the_n_word_while_president_obama_can/.

85. Brooke Hogan quoted in Gorenstein, "Hulk Hogan."

86. Josh Lanier, "Hulk Hogan Shares Pro-Trump Message, Sparks Twitter Outrage," *Outsider*, October 28, 2020, https://outsider.com/news/trending/hulk-hogan-shares-pro-trump-message-sparks-twitter-outrage/.

87. Eric King Watts, "Border Patrolling and 'Passing' in Eminem's *8 Mile*," *Critical Studies in Media Communication* 22, no. 3 (2005): 187–206.

88. Alastair Bonnett, *White Identities: An Historical & International Introduction* (New York: Routledge, 2000).

89. See Wanzer-Serrano, "Barack Obama."

90. See also Goldberg, *The Threat of Race*.

91. Watts, "Border Patrolling," 191.

92. Hartman, *Scenes of Subjection*, 7.

93. Hartman, 7.

94. McGowan, *Enjoying*, 50.

95. McGowan, *Enjoying*, 50.

Chapter 2

1. Elgin Baylor, former NBA star and Clippers longtime general manager, filed a lawsuit against Sterling alleging racist hiring practices and salary disparities in the organization. Baylor's lawyers alleged that Sterling had the "vision of a Southern plantation-type structure." Nathan Fenno, "Elgin Baylor Lawsuit among Donald Sterling's Past Racial Issues," *Los Angeles Times*, April 27, 2014, https://www.latimes.com/sports/sportsnow/la-sp-sn-elgin-baylor-donald-sterling-20140426-story.html.

2. Thomas P. Oates, "The Erotic Gaze in the NFL Draft," *Communication & Critical/Cultural Studies* 4, no. 1 (March 2007): 74–90, https://doi.org/10.1080/14791420601138351; Thomas P. Oates, *Football and Manliness: An Unauthorized Feminist Account of the NFL* (Urbana: University of Illinois Press, 2017).

3. See Daniel A. Grano, "Michael Vick's 'Genuine Remorse' and Problems of Public Forgiveness," *Quarterly Journal of Speech* 100, no. 1 (February 2014): 81–104, https://doi.org/10.1080/00335630.2014.888460; Daniel A. Grano, "Ritual Disorder and the Contractual Morality of Sport: A Case Study in Race, Class, and Agreement," *Rhetoric & Public Affairs* 10, no. 3 (Fall 2007): 445–73.

4. Tom Goldman, "She Was Generous. She Was Also Racist. Should This Ballpark Carry Her Name?," *NPR*, June 10, 2020, https://www.npr.org/2020/06/10/873511957/a-stadium-name-once-meant-to-honor-now-offends.

5. Charles P. Pierce, "A Fan's Worst Nightmare: The Many Problems with Donald Sterling," *Grantland* (blog), April 28, 2014, https://grantland.com/features/donald-sterling-racism-nba-owner/.

6. "Suns Owner Robert Sarver Accused of Racism and Misogyny in Damning Report," *The Guardian*, November 4, 2021, https://www.theguardian.com/sport/2021/nov/04/suns-owner-robert-sarver-report-racism-sexism.

7. Cedric J. Robinson, *Black Marxism: The Making of the Black Radical Tradition*, 2nd ed. (Chapel Hill: University of North Carolina Press, 2005).

8. See William C. Rhoden, *Forty Million Dollar Slaves: The Rise, Fall, and Redemption of the Black Athlete* (New York: Three Rivers Press, 2010); and Billy Hawkins, *The New Plantation: Black Athletes, College Sports, and Predominantly White NCAA Institutions* (New York: Palgrave Macmillan, 2013).

9. See Linsay M. Cramer, "Cam Newton and Russell Westbrook's Symbolic Resistance to Whiteness in the NFL and NBA," *Howard Journal of Communications* 30, no. 1 (January 2019): 57–75, https://doi.org/10.1080/10646175.2018.1439421; Katherine L. Lavelle, "No Room for Racism: Restoration of Order in the NBA," *Communication & Sport* 4, no. 4 (December 2016): 424–41, https://doi.org/10.1177/216747951 5584046

10. *Never Scared*. Directed by Joel Gallen and performed by Chris Rock, 2004 HBO.

11. hooks, *Black Looks*, 23.

12. See Robert E. Terrill, "The Post-Racial and Post-Ethical Discourse of Donald J. Trump," *Rhetoric & Public Affairs* 20, no. 3 (Fall 2017): 493–510.

13. Harris, "Whiteness as Property."

14. Alexander G. Weheliye, *Habeas Viscus: Racializing Assemblages, Biopolitics, and Black Feminist Theories of the Human* (Durham, NC: Duke University Press, 2014).

15. See Oates, "The Erotic Gaze in the NFL Draft."

16. Michael Taussig, *Defacement: Public Secrecy and the Labor of the Negative* (Stanford, CA: Stanford University Press, 1999), 2.

17. Jack Bratich, "Public Secrecy and Immanent Security," *Cultural Studies* 20, no. 4–5 (July 1, 2006): 494, https://doi.org/10.1080/09502380600708937.

18. See E. Chebrolu, "The Racial Lens of Dylann Roof: Racial Anxiety and White Nationalist Rhetoric on New Media," *Review of Communication* 20, no. 1 (2020), 47–68, https://doi.org/10.1080/15358593.2019.1708441.

19. See James Baldwin, *The Fire Next Time* (New York: Knopf Doubleday, 1962).

20. Casey Ryan Kelly, "Donald J. Trump and the Rhetoric of White Ambivalence," *Rhetoric & Public Affairs* 23, no. 2 (2020): 195–223.

21. See Bernadette Marie Calafell, *Monstrosity, Performance, and Race in Contemporary Culture* (New York: Peter Lang, 2015); Rachel Alicia Griffin, "Problematic Representations of Strategic Whiteness and 'Post-Racial' Pedagogy: A Critical Intercultural Reading of *The Help*," *Journal of International & Intercultural Communication* 8, no. 2 (May 2015): 147–66, https://doi.org/10.1080/17513 057.2015.1025330; Thomas K. Nakayama and Robert L. Krizek, "Whiteness: A Strategic Rhetoric," *Quarterly Journal of Speech* 81, no. 3 (August 1, 1995): 291–309, https://doi.org/10.1080/00335639509384117.

22. Chebrolu, "Racial Lens."

23. See Matheson, "What Does Obama Want of Me?"

24. Jacques Lacan, *Anxiety: The Seminar of Jacques Lacan*, trans. A. R. Price (Malden, MA: Polity, 2016), 61.

25. Chebrolu, "Racial Lens," 55

26. Chebrolu, "Racial Lens," 57.

27. Homi K. Bhabha, *The Location of Culture* (New York: Routledge, 1994), 96.

28. Kalpana Seshadri-Crooks, *Desiring Whiteness: A Lacanian Analysis of Race* (New York: Routledge, 2000), 58.

29. See Atilla Hallsby, "Imagine There's No President: The Rhetorical Secret and the Exposure of Valerie Plame," *Quarterly Journal of Speech* 101, no. 2 (May 2015): 354–78, https://doi.org/10.1080/00335630.2015.1024276.

30. See Leslie Picca and Joe Feagin, *Two-Faced Racism: Whites in the Backstage and Frontstage* (New York: Routledge, 2007); and Kevin Hylton and Stefan Lawrence, "'For Your Ears Only!' Donald Sterling and Backstage Racism in Sport," *Ethnic and Racial Studies* 39, no. 15 (December 7, 2016): 2740–57, https://doi.org/10.1080/01419 870.2016.1177193.

31. Dave Zirin, *Bad Sports: How Owners Are Ruining the Games We Love* (New York: Simon and Schuster, 2010), 128.

32. Kevin B. Blackistone, "The Real Tragedy of Donald Sterling's Racism: It Took This Long for Us to Notice," *The Guardian*, April 28, 2014, https://www.theguardian.com/commentisfree/2014/apr/28/donald-sterling-racism-la-clippers-owner.

33. Fenno, "Elgin Baylor."

34. Joe R. Feagin, *The White Racial Frame: Centuries of Racial Framing and Counter-Framing* (New York: Routledge, 2013), 124.

35. Nancy Fraser, "Rethinking the Public Sphere: A Contribution to the Critique of Actually Existing Democracy," *Social Text* 25/26 (1990): 68.

36. Karma R. Chávez, "Counter-Public Enclaves and Understanding the Function of Rhetoric in Social Movement Coalition-Building," *Communication Quarterly* 59, no. 1 (2011): 124, https://doi.org/10.1080/01463373.2010.541333.

37. Jeff Tischauser and Kevin Musgrave, "Far-Right Media as Imitated Counterpublicity: A Discourse Analysis on Racial Meaning and Identity on Vdare. Com," *Howard Journal of Communications* 41, no. 3 (2020): 282–96, https://doi.org/10.1080/10646175.2019.1702124.

38. Feagin, *The White Racial Frame*, 124.

39. Kevin Hylton and Stefan Lawrence, "'For Your Ears Only!' Donald Sterling and Backstage Racism in Sport," *Ethnic and Racial Studies* 39, no. 15 (2016): 2749, https://doi.org/10.1080/01419870.2016.1177193.

40. Feagin, *The White Racial Frame*, 12.

41. "Donald Sterling," *Forbes*, accessed February 21, 2021, https://www.forbes.com/profile/donald-sterling/.

42. Adrian Glick Kudler, "The Revealing Map of Donald Sterling's 162 LA Properties," *Curbed LA*, April 29, 2014, https://la.curbed.com/maps/the-revealing-map-of-donald-sterlings-162-la-properties.

43. David R. Roediger, *The Wages of Whiteness: Race and the Making of the American Working Class* (New York: Verso, 1999); and W. E. B. Du Bois, *Black Reconstruction in America, 1860–1880* (New York: Free Press, 1998).

44. I borrow this term from Charles W. Mills, who argues that the racial contract is a more apt description of the social contract as developed in the works of Enlightenment philosophies of possessive individualism. See Charles W. Mills, *The Racial Contract* (Ithaca, NY: Cornell University Press, 1999); and Charles Wade Mills, *Black Rights/ White Wrongs: The Critique of Racial Liberalism* (New York: Oxford University Press, 2017).

45. Terrill, "The Post-Racial."

46. Eduardo Bonilla-Silva, *Racism Without Racists: Color-Blind Racism and the Persistence of Racial Inequality in the United States* (Lanham, MD: Rowman & Littlefield, 2010).

47. See Harris, "Whiteness as Property."

48. See Griffin, "Problematic Representations of Strategic Whiteness and 'Post-Racial' Pedagogy"; Dreama G. Moon, "'Be/Coming' White and the Myth of White Ignorance: Identity Projects in White Communities," *Western Journal of Communication* 80, no. 3 (2016): 282–303, https://doi.org/10.1080/10570 314.2016.1143562; Thomas K. Nakayama and Judith N. Martin, *Whiteness: The Communication of Social Identity* (Thousand Oaks, CA: SAGE, 1999); Tammie M. Kennedy, Joyce Irene Middleton, and Krista Ratcliffe, *Rhetorics of Whiteness: Postracial Hauntings in Popular Culture, Social Media, and Education* (Carbondale: Southern Illinois University Press, 2017); Michael G. Lacy, "Exposing the Spectrum of Whiteness: Rhetorical Conceptions of White Absolutism," *Communication Yearbook* 32 (May 2008): 277–311; George Lipsitz, *Possessive Investment in Whiteness* (Philadelphia: Temple University Press, 1998); and Aimee Carrillo Rowe and Sheena Malhotra, "(Un)Hinging Whiteness," *International & Intercultural Communication Annual* 29 (2006): 166–92.

49. See Stephanie L. Hartzell, "Whiteness Feels Good Here: Interrogating White Nationalist Rhetoric on Stormfront," *Communication and Critical/Cultural Studies*, March 26, 2020, 1–20, https://doi.org/10.1080/14791420.2020.1745858.

50. Eric L. Goldstein, *The Price of Whiteness: Jews, Race, and American Identity* (Princeton, NJ: Princeton University Press, 2008)4.

51. Goldstein, *The Price of Whiteness*, 5.

52. "Who Is Donald Sterling and How Did He Become Synonymous with Bigotry?," *Haaretz*, April 30, 2014, https://www.haaretz.com/jewish/who-is-donald-sterling-1.5246727; and "L.A. Jewish Leader: Clippers Owner Donald Sterling Is Not Part of Jewish Community," *J.: The Jewish News of Northern California*, May 2, 2014, https://www.jweekly.com/2014/05/02/l-a-jewish-leader-clippers-owner-donald-sterling-is-not-part/.

53. "Who Is Donald Sterling."

54. Carol Hartsell, "Bill Maher Argues for Privacy, Free Speech in Wake of Donald Sterling Scandal," *The Huffington Post*, May 10, 2014, https://www.huffpost.com/entry/bill-maher-donald-sterling_n_5301576.

55. See "Revenge of the Other Woman! V. Stiviano Pal Leaked Tape of Donald Sterling's Racist Rant Because His Wife Sued Her, Source Claims," *Radar Online*, May 5, 2014, https://radaronline.com/exclusives/2014/05/v-stiviano-leaked-tape-donald-sterling-wife-sued-her/.

56. Marc J. Spears, "The Distressing Lack of Black Leadership in the NBA," *The Undefeated*, June 1, 2016, https://theundefeated.com/features/the-distressing-lack-of-black-leadership-in-the-nba/.

57. James Baldwin, *The Fire Next Time* (New York: Knopf Doubleday, 2013), 95.

58. *Blackballed*, season 1, episode 4, "Property," directed by Marc Jacobs, May 18, 2020, Quibi; and *The Donald Sterling Affair: 30 for 30 Podcast*, "Property," hosted by Ramona Shelburn, podcast audio, August 20, 2019, https://30for30podcasts.com/sterling/.

59. Stephen A. Smith quoted in *Blackballed*.

60. Jonathan Abrams, "Elgin Baylor and His Lawsuit Against the Clippers," *New York Times*, May 29, 2009, https://www.nytimes.com/2009/03/27/sports/basketball/27baylor.html.

61. Marc J. Spears, "Inside the Clippers' Final Days with Donald Sterling as Owner," *The Undefeated*, April 24, 2019, https://theundefeated.com/features/inside-los-angeles-clippers-final-days-with-donald-sterling-as-owner/.

62. See Zirin, *Bad Sports*.

63. Adam Silver quoted in "Full Transcript of Adam Silver on Donald Sterling Ban," *USA Today*, April 29, 2014, https://www.usatoday.com/story/sports/nba/2014/04/29/adam-silver-commissioner-opening-statement-donald-sterling/8467947/.

64. Linsay M. Cramer, "Postracism Mythology: NBA Commissioner Adam Silver's 'Heroic' Banishment of Racism From the NBA," *Communication & Sport* 7, no. 3 (June 2019): 271–91, https://doi.org/10.1177/2167479518769895.

65. Lavelle, "No Room for Racism," 425.

66. Donald Sterling quoted in "Donald Sterling Apology: 'I'll Never Do It Again,'" *The Chicago Tribune*, May 14, 2014, https://www.chicagotribune.com/sports/bulls/chi-donald-sterling-apology-20140511-story.html.

67. Karma R. Chávez, *The Borders of AIDS: Race, Quarantine, and Resistance* (Seattle: University of Washington Press, 2021).

68. Jeffrey A. Bennett, *Banning Queer Blood: Rhetorics of Citizenship, Contagion, and Resistance* (Tuscaloosa: University Alabama Press, 2015), 36.

69. See Bryant Keith Alexander, *Performing Black Masculinity: Race, Culture, and Queer Identity* (Lanham, MD: Rowman Altamira, 2006).

Chapter 3

1. Roland S. Martin, "Roland's Instructions For Recording Encounters With Crazy A$$ White People For Android & IOS," *#Roland Martin Unfiltered*, August 3, 2019, https://www.youtube.com/watch?v=VnBWdMR6_Bo.

2. Ore, *Lynching*, 50.

3. Ore, *Lynching*, 18.

4. Nathan Stormer, "All Diseased Things Are Critics," *Communication and the Public* 5, no. 1–2 (March 1, 2020): 74–82, https://doi.org/10.1177/2057047320950642.

5. Derek Hook, "What Is 'Enjoyment as a Political Factor'?," *Political Psychology* 38, no. 4 (2017): 614.

6. Stormer, "All Diseased Things Are Critics," 80.

7. Kevin DeLuca and Jennifer Peeples observed that screens now mediate public life, which introduces a new attentional economy in which only shocking "image events" can cut through the flak of a ceaseless flow of images on the "public screen." See Kevin Michael DeLuca and Jennifer Peeples, "From Public Sphere to Public Screen: Democracy, Activism, and the 'Violence' of Seattle," *Critical Studies in Media Communication* 19, no. 2 (June 1, 2002): 125–51, https://doi.org/10.1080/0739318 0216559.

8. Safiya Umoja Noble, *Algorithms of Oppression: How Search Engines Reinforce Racism* (New York: NYU Press, 2018).

9. See Mark Andrejevic, *Reality TV: The Work of Being Watched* (Lanham, MD: Rowman & Littlefield, 2004); Susan Murray and Laurie Ouellette, eds., *Reality TV: Remaking Television Culture* (New York: NYU Press, 2008); Laurie Ouellette and James Hay, *Better Living Through Reality TV: Television and Post-Welfare Citizenship* (Malden, MA: Wiley-Blackwell, 2008).

10. McDonald, *The Star System*; Richard Dyer, *Heavenly Bodies: Film Stars and Society* (New York: Routledge, 2013).

11. Marwick, "Instafame."

12. Marwick, *Status Update*, 14.

13. Jenkins, *Convergence Culture*.

14. Dubrofsky, "Monstrous Authenticity: Trump's Whiteness."

15. "Hate Speech Policy—YouTube Help," accessed August 24, 2021, https://support.goo gle.com/youtube/answer/2801939?hl=en.

16. Hook, "What Is 'Enjoyment as a Political Factor'?," 609.

17. Williams, *Raymond Williams on Television*, 47.

18. See Sigmund Freud and Peter Gay, *Inhibitions, Symptoms and Anxiety*, ed. James Strachey, the standard ed. (New York: W.W. Norton, 1990); Sigmund Freud and Peter Gay, *New Introductory Lectures on Psycho-Analysis*, ed. James Strachey, the standard ed. (New York: W.W. Norton, 1990).

19. Frank B. Wilderson III, *Red, White & Black: Cinema and the Structure of U.S. Antagonisms* (Durham, NC: Duke University Press, 2010), 7.

20. Fanon, *Black Skin, White Masks*.

21. Jared Sexton, "Afro-Pessimism: The Unclear Word," *Rhizomes: Cultural Studies in Emerging Knowledge*, no. 29 (2016), https://doi.org/10.20415/rhiz/029.e02.

22. Seventy percent of videos viewed on YouTube are algorithm-recommended content. See Nicky Rettke, "Drive Results with New Direct Response Solutions on YouTube," *Google Ads and Commerce* (blog), June 18, 2020. https://blog. google/products/ads/new-ways-to-drive-action/?_ga=2.122735113.366374 710.1611185634-867922050.1611185634&_gac=1.184789851.1611271695.

CjwKCAiA6aSABhApEiwA6Cbm_0ZIYIKsU4Pd9_mXwJwmJhKUNjEtQ4lFp-
SzRZendLORVEEUUORWCBoCImkQAvD_BwE.

23. Brooke Auxier and Monica Anderson, "Social Media Use in 2021," *Pew Research Center: Internet, Science & Tech*, April 7, 2021, https://www.pewresearch.org/internet/2021/04/07/social-media-use-in-2021/.

24. Jenni Hokka, "PewDiePie, Racism and YouTube's Neoliberalist Interpretation of Freedom of Speech," *Convergence* 27, no. 1 (February 1, 2021): 142–60, https://doi.org/10.1177/1354856520938602.

25. Ariadna Matamoros-Fernández, "Platformed Racism: The Mediation and Circulation of an Australian Race-Based Controversy on Twitter, Facebook and YouTube," *Information, Communication & Society* 20, no. 6 (June 3, 2017): 930–46, https://doi.org/10.1080/1369118X.2017.1293130.

26. Matamoros-Fernández, "Platform Racism," 931.

27. See also Safiya Umoja Noble, *Algorithms of Oppression: How Search Engines Reinforce Racism* (New York: NYU Press, 2018).

28. Steve Martinot and Jared Sexton, "The Avant-Garde of White Supremacy," *Social Identities* 9, no. 2 (June 1, 2003): 169–81, https://doi.org/10.1080/1350463032000101542.

29. Martinot and Sexton, "Avante-Garde," 175.

30. W. E. B. Du Bois, *Black Reconstruction in America, 1860–1880* (New York: Free Press, 1998); David R. Roediger, *The Wages of Whiteness: Race and the Making of the American Working Class* (New York: Verso, 1999).

31. Eduardo Bonilla-Silva, *Racism Without Racists: Color-Blind Racism and the Persistence of Racial Inequality in the United States* (Lanham, MD: Rowman & Littlefield, 2010), 15.

32. The good/bad person dichotomy tends to obscure the structural nature of racism. Robin J. DeAngelo argues that "although individual racist acts do occur, these acts are part of a larger system of interlocking dynamics. The focus on individual incidences masks the personal, interpersonal, cultural, historical, and structural analysis that is necessary to challenge this larger system." Robin J. DiAngelo, *White Fragility: Why It's So Hard for White People to Talk about Racism* (Boston: Beacon Press, 2018), 73.

33. Hasan Abi, "INSANE Racist Freak-out at a Walmart," August 6, 2021, https://www.youtube.com/watch?v=azomt8t9fks&t=243s.

34. "Another Day, Another INSANE RACIST FREAKOUT at Walmart," *The Majority Report with Sam Seder*, August 1, 2017, https://www.youtube.com/watch?v=-TN0abDlBEw.

35. "Racist Lunatic Harasses Gas Station Worker," *TYT Sports*, January 25, 2021, https://www.youtube.com/watch?v=qc2nmS5XKSQ.

36. "'Come F*ing See Me . . .': Crazy A$$ Racist Harasses Black Neighbor, Crowd Shows Up At His Door," *Roland Martin Unfiltered*, July 7, 2021, https://www.youtube.com/watch?v=1FB6NH2xlxs&t=521s.

37. "WTH?!? Crazy Racist Man Hurls N-Word At a Black Woman During a Road-Rage Incident," *Roland Martin Unfiltered*, November 12, 2019, https://www.youtube.com/watch?v=TAKjQm8vijA&t=132s.

38. See Richard Seymour, *The Twittering Machine* (New York: Verso Books, 2020), 169.

39. Robyn Wiegman argues that white hegemony is actually maintained by its disidentification with segregationist white supremacy insofar as it allows subjects to disavow the awful inheritance of white supremacy that manifests in everyday privileges that seem disconnected—even as they are contiguous—from structural racism and anti-blackness. See Robyn Wiegman, *Object Lessons* (Durham, NC: Duke University Press Books, 2012).

40. Anderson, *White Rage*, 3.

41. Ashley Noel Mack and Bryan J. McCann, "Recalling Persky: White Rage and Intimate Publicity After Brock Turner," *Journal of Communication Inquiry* 43, no. 4 (October 1, 2019): 372–93, https://doi.org/10.1177/0196859919867265.

42. Cady Lang, "How the Karen Meme Confronts History of White Womanhood," *TIME Magazine*, July 6, 2020, https://time.com/5857023/karen-meme-history-meaning/.

43. Imani Perry, *Vexy Thing: On Gender and Liberation* (Durham, NC: Duke University Press Books, 2018).

44. Kathleen M. Blee, *Women of the Klan: Racism and Gender in the 1920s* (Oakland: University of California Press, 2009).

45. Hasan Abi is a leftist political commentator and one of the most followed Internet gamers on the platform Twitch. Abi was born in Turkey and raised in New Jersey. He has worked for the *Young Turks* and *The Huffington Post*.

46. Jeanne Theoharis, *A More Beautiful and Terrible History: The Uses and Misuses of Civil Rights History* (Boston: Beacon Press, 2018).

47. Thomas J. Sugrue, *Sweet Land of Liberty: The Forgotten Struggle for Civil Rights in the North*, illustrated ed. (New York: Random House, 2009).

48. Brian J. Purnell and Jeanne Theoharis, "Charlottesville Belies Racism's Deep Roots in the North," *The Conversation*, August 16, 2018, http://theconversation.com/charlott esville-belies-racisms-deep-roots-in-the-north-101567.

49. Fanon, *Black Skin, White Masks*, 133.

50. E. Chebrolu, "The Racial Lens of Dylann Roof: Racial Anxiety and White Nationalist Rhetoric on New Media," *Review of Communication*, January 4, 2020, 1–22, https://doi.org/10.1080/15358593.2019.1708441; Hortense J. Spillers, "Mama's Baby, Papa's Maybe: An American Grammar Book," *Diacritics* 17, no. 2 (1987): 65–81, https://doi.org/10.2307/464747.

51. Copjec, *Read My Desire*, 143.

52. Hartzell, "Whiteness Feels Good Here."

53. Williams, "Film Bodies."

54. See Linda Williams, *Hard Core: Power, Pleasure, and the "Frenzy of the Visible"* (Berkeley: University of California Press, 1989); Helen Hester, *Beyond Explicit: Pornography and the Displacement of Sex* (Albany: SUNY Press, 2014).

55. Gunn, "Maranatha."

56. Gunn, "Maranatha," 367.

57. Grindstaff and Murray, "Reality Celebrity," 117.

58. Martinot and Sexton, "Avant-Garde," 178.

59. "Elderly White Man Hurls Racial Insults At Black Postal Worker in North Texas," *Roland Martin Unfiltered*, August 24, 2019, https://www.youtube.com/watch?v=vwBj bv2-Hwg.

60. "Pennsylvania Woman Goes on Racist Rant in Walmart," *International Newz*, https://www.youtube.com/watch?v=f-8is2Nc1Bk&list=PL qFlTn7OkI1blGtXJYe9IkG9tVU JWCEP&index=2.

61. "Racist White Man Gets Beat Up After Calling Black Guy <Expletive> Outside the Cheesecake Factory," December 20, 2016, https://www.youtube.com/watch?v=neOt WcN1Ebw.

62. "Twisted Tea Smack—Original Video," *Desirable to Watch*, December 24, 2020, https://www.youtube.com/watch?v=TJXrewjTN_Y.

63. Christian Lundberg, "Enjoying God's Death: The Passion of the Christ and the Practices of an Evangelical Public," *Quarterly Journal of Speech* 95, no. 4 (November 2009): 402, https://doi.org/10.1080/00335630903296184.

64. Sigmund Freud, *The Interpretation of Dreams: The Complete and Definitive Text*, trans. James Strachey (New York: Basic Books, 2010); See also Robin Wood, *Hollywood from Vietnam to Reagan . . . and Beyond* (New York: Columbia University Press, 2003).

65. Bonilla-Silva, *Racism Without Racists*, 8.

66. David Theo Goldberg, *The Threat of Race: Reflections on Racial Neoliberalism* (New York: John Wiley & Sons, 2011); see also Darrel Wanzer-Serrano, "Barack Obama, the Tea Party, and the Threat of Race: On Racial Neoliberalism and Born Again Racism," *Communication, Culture & Critique* 4, no. 1 (March 1, 2011): 23–30, https://doi.org/10.1111/j.1753-9137.2010.01090.x.

67. See Richard Delgado and Jean Stefancic, *Must We Defend Nazis?: Hate Speech, Pornography, and the New First Amendment* (New York: NYU Press, 1999).

68. Michael Omi and Howard Winant, *Racial Formation in the United States: From the 1960s to the 1990s* (New York: Psychology Press, 1994).

69. Grindstaff and Murray, "Reality Celebrity," 109.

70. Grindstaff and Murray, "Reality Celebrity," 110.

71. Sara Ahmed, *Cultural Politics of Emotion* (Edinburgh: Edinburgh University Press, 2014), 44.

72. André Brock Jr., *Distributed Blackness: African American Cybercultures* (New York: NYU Press, 2020), 1.

73. See Curry, *The Man-Not*.

Chapter 4

1. Donald J. Trump quoted in David A. Fahrenthold, "Trump Recorded Having Extremely Lewd Conversation about Women in 2005," *Washington Post*, October 8, 2016, https://www.washingtonpost.com/politics/trump-recorded-having-extremely-lewd-conversation-about-women-in-2005/2016/10/07/3b9ce776-8cb4-11e6-bf8a-3d26847eeed4_story.html .

2. Trump quoted in Fahrenthold, "Trump Recorded."

3. Steve Bannon quoted in Matt Flegenheimer, "What Donald Trump's 'Access Hollywood' Weekend Says About 2020," *The New York Times*, July 12, 2020, https://www.nytimes.com/2020/07/12/us/politics/donald-trump-access-hollywood.html.

4. Giorgio Agamben, *State of Exception* (Chicago: University of Chicago Press, 2008).

5. Sigmund Freud, *Totem and Taboo: Resemblances Between the Psychic Lives of Savages and Neurotics* (New York: Moffat, Yard, 1918).

6. See also Sigmund Freud, *Civilization and Its Discontents*, trans. James Strachey (New York: W.W. Norton, 2010).

7. Freud, *Totem and Taboo*, 285.

8. Freud, *Totem and Taboo*, 286.

9. Freud, *Totem and Taboo*, 287–88.

10. Jacques Lacan, *Ecrits: The First Complete Edition in English* (New York: W.W. Norton, 2006), 423.

11. See Joshua Gunn and Thomas Frentz, "Fighting for Father: Fight Club as Cinematic Psychosis," *Western Journal of Communication* 74, no. 3 (May 26, 2010): 269–91, https://doi.org/10.1080/10570311003767191; Joshua Gunn, "On Social Networking and Psychosis," *Communication Theory* 28, no. 1 (2018): 69–88, https://doi.org/10.1093/ct/qtx002; Matheson, "Psychotic Discourse"; Jacques Lacan, *Seminar of Jacques Lacan: The Psychoses*, trans. Jacques-Alain Miller and Russell Grigg, reprint ed. (New York: W.W. Norton, 1997).

12. Sarah Stone Watt, "'Rape Is a Four-Letter Word': Psychosis, Sexual Assault, and Abortion in the 2012 U.S. Election," *Women's Studies in Communication* 43, no. 3 (July 2, 2020): 229, https://doi.org/10.1080/07491409.2020.1740902.

13. Watt, "Psychosis," 229.

14. See Joshua Gunn, "On Political Perversion," *Rhetoric Society Quarterly* 48, no. 2 (2018): 161–86, https://doi.org/10.1080/02773945.2018.1428766; and Gunn, *Political Perversion*.

15. Slavoj Žižek, *The Ticklish Subject: The Absent Centre of Political Ontology* (New York: Verso, 2000), 362.

16. See Eric King Watts, "'Zombies Are Real': Fantasies, Conspiracies, and the Post-Truth Wars," *Philosophy & Rhetoric* 51, no. 4 (2018): 441–70.

17. Dana L. Cloud, *Reality Bites: Rhetoric and the Circulation of Truth Claims in U.S. Political Culture* (Columbus: Ohio State University Press, 2018).

18. Copjec, *Read My Desire*, 142.

19. Hal Foster, "Père Trump," *October Magazine*, January 2017, 5.

20. Žižek characterizes the repetition of footage of the World Trade Center collapsing on September 11, 2001, as precisely this form of enjoyment: "[T]he same shots were repeated *ad nauseam,* and the uncanny satisfaction we got from it was *jouissance* at its purest." See Slavoj Žižek, *Welcome to the Desert of the Real* (New York: Verso, 2002), 12.

21. Sigmund Freud, *Group Psychology and the Analysis of the Ego*, trans. James Strachey (New York: W.W. Norton, 2018), 51.

22. Freud, *Group Psychology*, 51.

23. Stephanie Coontz, *The Way We Never Were: American Families and the Nostalgia Trap*, reprint ed. (New York: Basic Books, 1993).

24. Jeffrey R. Dudas, *Raised Right: Fatherhood in Modern American Conservatism* (Palo Alto, CA: Stanford University Press, 2017).

25. Lauren Berlant, *The Queen of America Goes to Washington City: Essays on Sex and Citizenship* (Durham, NC: Duke University Press, 1997); see also Lauren Berlant and Michael Warner, "Sex in Public," *Critical Inquiry* 24, no. 2 (1998): 547–66, https://doi.org/10.1086/448884.

26. See Paul Apostolidis and Juliet A. Williams, *Public Affairs: Politics in the Age of Sex Scandals* (Durham, NC: Duke University Press, 2004); and Hinda Mandell, *Sex Scandals, Gender, and Power in Contemporary American Politics* (Santa Barbara, CA: ABC-CLIO, 2017).

27. Ryan Neville-Shepard and Meredith Neville-Shepard, "The Pornified Presidency: Hyper-Masculinity and the Pornographic Style in U.S. Political Rhetoric," *Feminist Media Studies* 21, no. 7 (2021): 1193–208, https://doi.org/10.1080/14680777.2020.1786429. See also Karrin Vasby Anderson, "'Rhymes with Blunt': Pornification and U.S. Political Culture," *Rhetoric & Public Affairs* 14, no. 2 (2011): 327–68, https://doi.org/10.1353/rap.2010.0228.

28. Donald J. Trump quoted in Gregory Krieg King, "Donald Trump Defends Size of His Penis," *CNN*, March 4, 2016, https://www.cnn.com/2016/03/03/politics/donald-trump-small-hands-marco-rubio/index.html.

29. Susan Jeffords, *Hard Bodies: Hollywood Masculinity in the Reagan Era* (New Brunswick, NJ: Rutgers University Press, 1994); and Aidan Smith, *Gender, Heteronormativity, and the American Presidency* (New York: Routledge, 2017).

30. Clark Mindok, "Full List of the Women Who Have Accused President Donald Trump of Sexual Assault," *The Independent*, October 9, 2019, https://www.independent.co.uk/news/world/americas/us-politics/trump-sexual-assault-allegations-all-list-misconduct-karen-johnson-how-many-a9149216.html.

31. Amanda Nell Edgar, *Culturally Speaking: The Rhetoric of Voice and Identity in a Mediated Culture* (Columbus: Ohio State University Press, 2019).

32. Bruce Fink, *The Lacanian Subject: Between Language and Jouissance* (Princeton, NJ: Princeton University Press, 1997), 9.

33. Fink, *The Lacanian Subject*, 9.

34. Joan Copjec, *Imagine There's No Woman: Ethics and Sublimation* (Cambridge, MA: MIT Press, 2004).

35. See Heather Suzanne Woods and Leslie A. Hahner, *Make America Meme Again: The Rhetoric of the Alt-Right* (New York: Peter Lang, 2019); and Angela Nagle, *Kill All Normies: Online Culture Wars From 4Chan and Tumblr to Trump and the Alt-Right* (Washington, DC: Zero Books, 2017).

36. Donald J. Trump, "Remarks by President Trump on the Election," November 5, 2020, https://trumpwhitehouse.archives.gov/briefings-statements/remarks-president-trump-election/.

37. Graig Graziosi, "Nevada Man Storms Press Conference to Accuse Biden of Stealing the Election," *The Independent*, November 5, 2020, https://www.independent.co.uk/

news/world/americas/us-election-2020/us-election-joe-biden-nevada-results-b1600500.html.

38. Stanley Milgram, *Obedience to Authority: An Experimental View* (New York: Harper Perennial, 2009).

39. Katie Shepherd, "Trump Cheers Supporters Who Swarmed a Biden Bus in Texas: 'These Patriots Did Nothing Wrong,'" *Washington Post*, November 2, 2020, https://www.washingtonpost.com/nation/2020/11/02/trump-caravan-biden-bus/.

40. Jay Yarow, "Peter Thiel Perfectly Summed Up Donald Trump in a Few Sentences," *CNBC*, November 9, 2016, https://www.cnbc.com/2016/11/09/peter-thiel-perfectly-summed-up-donald-trump-in-one-paragraph.html.

41. Luce Irigaray, *This Sex Which Is Not One* (Ithaca, NY: Cornell University Press, 1985) 25.

42. Irigaray, *Sex*, 25.

43. See also Casey Ryan Kelly, "Donald J. Trump and the Rhetoric of Ressentiment," *Quarterly Journal of Speech* 106, no. 1 (2020): 2–24, https://doi.org/10.1080/00335630.2019.1698756.

44. Paul E. Johnson points out how Trump uses sexual humiliation metaphors to characterize foreign nations taking advantage of the United States in trade deals. See Paul Elliott Johnson, "The Art of Masculine Victimhood: Donald Trump's Demagoguery," *Women's Studies in Communication* 40, no. 3 (2017): 229–50, https://doi.org/10.1080/07491409.2017.1346533.

45. Donald J. Trump quoted in "President Donald Trump delivers remarks at a Make America Great Again rally, Southaven, Mississippi," *Federal News Service*, October 2, 2018, nexis-uni.

46. See Dubrofsky, "Monstrous Authenticity."

47. The feminization thesis—that U.S. culture has been emasculated by overbearing women, feminine values, and governmental regulation—put forward by the conservative movement is explored in greater depth in Katie L. Gibson and Amy L. Heyse, "'The Difference Between a Hockey Mom and a Pit Bull': Sarah Palin's Faux Maternal Persona and Performance of Hegemonic Masculinity at the 2008 Republican National Convention," *Communication Quarterly* 58, no. 3 (2010): 235–56, https://doi.org/10.1080/01463373.2010.503151; Katie L. Gibson and Amy L. Heyse, "Depoliticizing Feminism: Frontier Mythology and Sarah Palin's 'The Rise of The Mama Grizzlies,'" *Western Journal of Communication* 78, no. 1 (2014): 97–117, https://doi.org/10.1080/10570314.2013.812744; and Sally Robinson, *Authenticity Guaranteed: Masculinity and the Rhetoric of Anti-Consumerism in American Culture* (Amherst: University of Massachusetts Press, 2018).

48. See Michael S. Kimmel, *Manhood in America: A Cultural History* (New York: Oxford University Press, 2012); and Michael Kimmel, *Angry White Men: American Masculinity at the End of an Era* (New York: Nation Books, 2013).

49. See Hamilton Carroll, *Affirmative Reaction: New Formations of White Masculinity* (Durham, NC: Duke University Press, 2011); and Michelle Rodino-Colocino, "Flexing Italian American Masculinity and White Diversity on Man Caves," *Women's Studies in Communication* 41, no. 3 (2018): 246–68, https://doi.org/10.1080/07491409.2018.1502703.

50. Fox News focused on the "weaponizing" of the tape as evidence of media bias against Trump. For an example of this kind of coverage, see Brian Flood, "Billy Bush Says 'Everybody' at NBC Knew about Notorious 'Access Hollywood' Tape before It Leaked," *Fox News*, September 9, 2019, https://www.foxnews.com/media/billy-bush-says-everybody-at-nbc-knew-about-notorious-access-hollywood-tape-before-it-leaked.

51. See Billy Bush, "Yes, Donald Trump, You Said That," *New York Times*, December 3, 2017, https://www.nytimes.com/2017/12/03/opinion/billy-bush-trump-access-hollywood-tape.html.

52. Freud, *Group Psychology*, 51.

53. See Petersen, "Smut Goes Corporate."

54. I borrow this term from Gayle Rubin, *Deviations: A Gayle Rubin Reader* (Durham, NC: Duke University Press, 2011).

55. Kenneth Burke, *A Rhetoric of Motives* (Berkeley: University of California Press, 1969), 13.

56. Todd McGowan, *Capitalism and Desire: The Psychic Cost of Free Markets* (New York: Columbia University Press, 2016).

57. Tara Isabella Burton, "Trump-Allied Pastor: Reagan Was a Womanizer Too," *Vox*, July 23, 2018, https://www.vox.com/2018/7/23/17603524/robert-jeffress-defends-trump-adultery-reagan.

58. Mike Pence quoted in "Here's the List of GOP Responses to Trump's Vulgar Comments about Groping Women," *PBS NewsHour*, October 7, 2016, https://www.pbs.org/newshour/politics/headline-republicans-react-trump-comments-objectifying-women.

59. Jeb Bush quoted in "Here's the List."

60. Mitch McConnel quoted in Jessica Contrera, "As 'the Fathers of Daughters,' They Were Offended by Harassment. But What Did That Really Mean?," *Washington Post*, October 13, 2017, https://www.washingtonpost.com/lifestyle/style/as-the-fathers-of-daughters-they-were-offended-by-harassment-but-what-did-that-really-mean/2017/10/13/c1991f70-aed7-11e7-9e58-e6288544af98_story.html.

61. Ben Carson quoted in "Here's the List."

62. Ted Cruz quoted in "Here's the List."

63. Mitt Romney quoted in "Here's the List."

64. Irigaray, *This Sex Which Is Not One*, 31.

65. Carole Pateman, *The Sexual Contract* (Palo Alto, CA: Stanford University Press, 1988).

66. Iris Marion Young, "The Logic of Masculinist Protection: Reflections on the Current Security State," *Signs* 29, no. 1 (2003): 2, https://doi.org/10.1086/375708.

Epilogue

1. This phrase is borrowed from Slavoj Žižek, *The Metastases of Enjoyment: On Women and Causality* (New York: Verso, 2006). See also Barbara A. Biesecker, "Whither

Ideology? Toward a Different Take on Enjoyment as a Political Factor," *Western Journal of Communication* 75, no. 4 (July 1, 2011): 445–50, https://doi.org/10.1080/10570314.2011.588904.

2. Hook, "What Is 'Enjoyment as a Political Factor'?," 605.
3. McGowan, *Enjoying*, 113.
4. See Kelly, "Ressentiment."
5. Kaja Silverman, *Male Subjectivity at the Margins* (New York: Routledge, 1992).
6. Eagleton, *On Evil*, 109.
7. Lisa A. Flores, *Deportable and Disposable: Public Rhetoric and the Making of the Illegal Immigrant* (University Park: Penn State Press, 2020), 75. See also Ore, *Lynching*.
8. Zupančič, *Why Psychoanalysis?*, 8.
9. McGowan, *Enjoying*, 6. See also Zupančič, *Ethics of the Real*.
10. See McGowan, *Capitalism and Desire*.
11. Jack Bratich and Sarah Banet-Weiser, "From Pick-Up Artists to Incels: Con(Fidence) Games, Networked Misogyny, and the Failure of Neoliberalism," *International Journal of Communication* 13 (2019): 5003–27.
12. John Rajchman, "Lacan and the Ethics of Modernity," *Representations*, no. 15 (1986): 43, https://doi.org/10.2307/2928391.
13. As Ashley Noel Mack and Bryan J. McCann observe, framing predators as "monsters" disavows the ways in which they align with the structural norms of race and gender violence. Instead, they "recognize them as especially putrid reflections of the norms that structure White cisheteropatriarchy and sanction pervasive gendered violence in U.S. culture" (pp. 2–3).

    Ashley Noel Mack and Bryan J. McCann, "'Harvey Weinstein, Monster': Antiblackness and the Myth of the Monstrous Rapist," *Communication and Critical/Cultural Studies* 18, no. 2 (2021): 103–120, https://doi.org/10.1080/14791420.2020.1854802.
14. Maria Cramer, "Announcer Caught on Open Mic Using Racial Slur at Basketball Game," *New York Times*, March 13, 2021, https://www.nytimes.com/2021/03/13/us/norman-oklahoma-announcer-matt-rowan.html.
15. See David Remnick, "The Racial Demagoguery of Trump's Assaults on Colin Kaepernick and Steph Curry," *The New Yorker*, September 23, 2017, https://www.newyorker.com/news/daily-comment/the-racial-demagoguery-of-trumps-assaults-on-colin-kaepernick-and-steph-curry.
16. Matt Rowan quoted in "Announcer."
17. Matt Rowan quoted in "Announcer."
18. Carol Pogash, "Myth of the 'Twinkie Defense'/The Verdict in the Dan White Case Wasn't Based on His Ingestion of Junk Food," *San Francisco Chronicle*, November 23, 2003, https://www.sfgate.com/health/article/Myth-of-the-Twinkie-defense-The-verdict-in-2511152.php.
19. David Bauder, "Roseanne Barr Blames Ambien for Racist Tweet. The Drug Maker Responds," *PBS NewsHour*, May 30, 2018, https://www.pbs.org/newshour/arts/roseanne-barr-blames-ambien-for-racist-tweet-the-drug-maker-responds.

20. Daniel Victor, "Ethan Couch, 'Affluenza Teen' Who Killed 4 While Driving Drunk, Is Freed," *The New York Times*, April 2, 2018, https://www.nytimes.com/2018/04/02/us/ethan-couch-affluenza-jail.html.

21. Curry, *The Man-Not*.

22. Ashley Noel Mack and Bryan J. McCann, "Recalling Persky: White Rage and Intimate Publicity After Brock Turner," *Journal of Communication Inquiry* 43, no. 4 (October 1, 2019): 376, https://doi.org/10.1177/0196859919867265.

23. Fink, *The Lacanian* Subject, 10. Emphasis in original.

24. Fink, *The Lacanian Subject*, 36.

25. Lundberg, *Lacan*.

26. Spillers, "Mama's Baby," 67.

27. I borrow this phrase from Robert A. Williams who argues that dangerous racist and anti-indigenous ideologies are latent within U.S. legal rhetoric on sovereignty and citizenship, continually rearing their ugly head even when it seems like such terms and concepts have vanished. See Robert A. Williams Jr., *Like a Loaded Weapon: The Rehnquist Court, Indian Rights, and the Legal History of Racism in America* (Minneapolis: University of Minnesota Press, 2005).

28. See Ahmed, *Cultural Politics of Emotion*.

29. Ian Haney López, *Dog Whistle Politics: How Coded Racial Appeals Have Reinvented Racism and Wrecked the Middle Class* (Oxford: Oxford University Press, 2015).

30. Michael G. Lacy, "White Innocence Heroes: Recovery, Reversals, Paternalism, and David Duke," *Journal of International & Intercultural Communication* 3, no. 3 (August 2010): 206–27, https://doi.org/10.1080/17513057.2010.487221.

31. Natalia Molina, *How Race Is Made in America: Immigration, Citizenship, and the Historical Power of Racial Scripts* (Berkeley: University of California Press, 2014), 23.

32. Jackson, *Scripting the Black Masculine Body*.

33. On the phallocentricism of language, see Helene Cixous, "The Laugh of the Medusa," *Signs: Journal of Women in Culture and Society* 1, no. 4 (1976): 875–93. See also Barbara A. Biesecker, "Towards a Transactional View of Rhetorical and Feminist Theory: Rereading Helene Cixous's 'The Laugh of the Medusa,'" *Southern Communication Journal* 57, no. 2 (March 1, 1992): 86–96, https://doi.org/10.1080/10417949209372856.

34. Christopher Lane, ed., *The Psychoanalysis of Race* (New York: Columbia University Press, 1998).

Selected Bibliography

Agamben, Giorgio. *State of Exception*. Chicago: University of Chicago Press, 2008.

Ahmed, Sara. *Cultural Politics of Emotion*. Edinburgh: Edinburgh University Press, 2014.

Alexander, Bryant Keith. *Performing Black Masculinity: Race, Culture, and Queer Identity*. Lanham, MD: Rowman Altamira, 2006.

Anderson, Carol. *White Rage: The Unspoken Truth of Our Racial Divide*. New York: Bloomsbury, 2016.

Andrejevic, Mark. *I Spy: Surveillance and Power in the Interactive Era*. Lawrence: University Press of Kansas, 2007.

Andrejevic, Mark. *Reality TV: The Work of Being Watched*. Lanham, MD: Rowman & Littlefield, 2004.

Andrejevic, Mark. "The Jouissance of Trump." *Television & New Media* 17, no. 7 (November 1, 2016): 651–55. https://doi.org/10.1177/1527476416652694.

Anker, Elisabeth Robin. *Orgies of Feeling: Melodrama and the Politics of Freedom*. Durham, NC: Duke University Press, 2014.

Apostolidis, Paul, and Juliet A. Williams. *Public Affairs: Politics in the Age of Sex Scandals*. Durham, NC: Duke University Press, 2004.

Aristotle. *The Art of Rhetoric*. New York: HarperCollins, 2014.

Baldwin, James. *The Fire Next Time*. New York: Knopf Doubleday, 2013.

Barron, Lee. *Celebrity Cultures: An Introduction*. Thousand Oaks, CA: SAGE, 2014.

Bataille, Georges. *Erotism: Death and Sensuality*. San Francisco: City Lights Books, 1986.

Bederman, Gail. *Manliness and Civilization: A Cultural History of Gender and Race in the United States, 1880–1917*. Chicago: University of Chicago Press, 2008.

Bennett, Jeffrey A. *Banning Queer Blood: Rhetorics of Citizenship, Contagion, and Resistance*. Tuscaloosa: University Alabama Press, 2015.

Berger, John. *Ways of Seeing*. New York: Penguin Books Limited, 2008.

Berlant, Lauren. *Cruel Optimism*. Durham, NC: Duke University Press, 2011.

Berlant, Lauren. *The Queen of America Goes to Washington City: Essays on Sex and Citizenship*. Durham, NC: Duke University Press, 1997.

Berlant, Lauren, and Michael Warner. "Sex in Public." *Critical Inquiry* 24, no. 2 (January 1, 1998): 547–66. https://doi.org/10.1086/448884.

Bhabha, Homi K. *The Location of Culture*, 2nd ed. New York: Routledge, 2004.

Biesecker, Barbara A. "No Time for Mourning: The Rhetorical Production of the Melancholic Citizen-Subject in the War on Terror." *Philosophy & Rhetoric* 40, no. 1 (April 16, 2007): 147–69. https://doi.org/10.1353/par.2007.0009.

Biesecker, Barbara A. "Rhetorical Studies and the 'New' Psychoanalysis: What's the Real Problem? Or Framing the Problem of the Real." *Quarterly Journal of Speech* 84, no. 2 (May 1, 1998): 222–40. https://doi.org/10.1080/00335639809384215.

Biesecker, Barbara A. "Towards a Transactional View of Rhetorical and Feminist Theory: Rereading Helene Cixous's 'The Laugh of the Medusa.'" *Southern Communication Journal* 57, no. 2 (March 1, 1992): 86–96. https://doi.org/10.1080/10417949209372856.

Biesecker, Barbara A. "Whither Ideology? Toward a Different Take on Enjoyment as a Political Factor." *Western Journal of Communication* 75, no. 4 (July 1, 2011): 445–50. https://doi.org/10.1080/10570314.2011.588904.

Black, Edwin. "Secrecy and Disclosure as Rhetorical Forms." *Quarterly Journal of Speech* 74, no. 2 (May 1, 1988): 133–50. https://doi.org/10.1080/00335638809383833.

Black, Edwin. "The Second Persona." *Quarterly Journal of Speech* 56, no. 2 (April 1, 1970): 109–19. https://doi.org/10.1080/00335637009382992.

Blee, Kathleen M. *Women of the Klan: Racism and Gender in the 1920s*. Oakland: University of California Press, 2009.

Bonilla-Silva, Eduardo. *Racism Without Racists: Color-Blind Racism and the Persistence of Racial Inequality in the United States*. Lanham, MD: Rowman & Littlefield, 2010.

Bonnett, Alastair. *White Identities: An Historical & International Introduction*. New York: Routledge, 2018.

Bosworth, Mary, and Jeanne Flavin. *Race, Gender, and Punishment: From Colonialism to the War on Terror*. New Brunswick, NJ: Rutgers University Press, 2007.

Bratich, Jack. "Public Secrecy and Immanent Security." *Cultural Studies* 20, no. 4–5 (July 1, 2006): 493–511. https://doi.org/10.1080/09502380600708937.

Bratich, Jack, and Sarah Banet-Weiser. "From Pick-Up Artists to Incels: Con(Fidence) Games, Networked Misogyny, and the Failure of Neoliberalism." *International Journal of Communication* 13 (2019): 5003–27.

Brock, André, Jr. *Distributed Blackness: African American Cybercultures*. New York: NYU Press, 2020.

Bruner, Michael Lane. *Rhetorical Unconsciousness and Political Psychoanalysis*. Columbia: University of South Carolina Press, 2019.

Burke, Kenneth. *A Rhetoric of Motives*. Berkeley: University of California Press, 1969.

Butler, Judith. *Excitable Speech: A Politics of the Performative*. New York: Routledge, 1997.

Butler, Judith. "Melancholy Gender/Refused Identification." In *Constructing Masculinities*, edited by Maurice Berger, Brian Wallis, and Simon Watson, 21–36. New York: Routledge, 2012.

Calafell, Bernadette Marie. *Monstrosity, Performance, and Race in Contemporary Culture*. New York: Peter Lang, 2015.

Calvo, Luz. "Racial Fantasies and the Primal Scene of Miscegenation." *International Journal of Psychoanalysis* 89, no. 1 (February 1, 2008): 55–70. https://doi.org/10.1111/j.1745-8315.2007.00001.x.

Campbell, Karlyn Kohrs, and Kathleen Hall Jamieson. *Form and Genre: Shaping Rhetorical Action*. Falls Church, VA: Speech Communication Association, 1978.

Carroll, Hamilton. *Affirmative Reaction: New Formations of White Masculinity*. Durham, NC: Duke University Press, 2011.

Carstarphen, Meta G., Kathleen E. Welch, Wendy K. Z. Anderson, Davis W. Houck, Mark L. McPhail, David A. Frank, Rachel C. Jackson, et al. "Rhetoric, Race, and Resentment: Whiteness and the New Days of Rage." *Rhetoric Review* 36, no. 4 (October 2017): 255–347. https://doi.org/10.1080/07350198.2017.1355191.

Ceccarelli, Leah. "Polysemy: Multiple Meanings in Rhetorical Criticism." *Quarterly Journal of Speech* 84, no. 4 (November 1998): 395. https://doi.org/10.1080/00335639809384229.

Chávez, Karma R. *The Borders of AIDS: Race, Quarantine, and Resistance*. Seattle: University of Washington Press, 2021.

Chávez, Karma R. "Counter-Public Enclaves and Understanding the Function of Rhetoric in Social Movement Coalition-Building." *Communication Quarterly* 59, no. 1 (January 2011): 1–18. https://doi.org/10.1080/01463373.2010.541333.

Chebrolu, E. "The Racial Lens of Dylann Roof: Racial Anxiety and White Nationalist Rhetoric on New Media." *Review of Communication* 20, no. 1 (January 4, 2020): 47–68. https://doi.org/10.1080/15358593.2019.1708441.

Cintron, Ralph. *Democracy as Fetish*. University Park: Penn State Press, 2019.

Citton, Yves. *The Ecology of Attention*. Cambridge, UK: Polity, 2017.

Cixous, Helene. "The Laugh of the Medusa." *Signs: Journal of Women in Culture and Society* 1, no. 4 (1976): 875–93.

Cloud, Dana L. "Hegemony or Concordance? The Rhetoric of Tokenism in 'Oprah' Winfrey's Rags-to-Riches Biography." *Critical Studies in Mass Communication* 13, no. 2 (June 1996): 115.

Cloud, Dana L. *Reality Bites: Rhetoric and the Circulation of Truth Claims in U.S. Political Culture*. Columbus: Ohio State University Press, 2018.

Collins, Patricia Hill. *Black Feminist Thought: Knowledge, Consciousness, and the Politics of Empowerment*. New York: Routledge, 2008.

Conboy, Martin. "Foreword." In *The Tabloid Culture Reader*, edited by Biressi Anita and Nunn Heather, XV–XVI. Maidenhead, UK: McGraw-Hill, 2007.

Condit, Celeste Michelle. "The Rhetorical Limits of Polysemy." *Critical Studies in Mass Communication* 6, no. 2 (June 1, 1989): 103–22. https://doi.org/10.1080/1529503890 9366739.

Connell, R. W. *Masculinities*. London: Polity, 2005.

Coontz, Stephanie. *The Way We Never Were: American Families and the Nostalgia Trap*, reprint ed. New York: Basic Books, 1993.

Copjec, Joan. *Imagine There's No Woman: Ethics and Sublimation*. Cambridge, MA: MIT Press, 2004.

Copjec, J. *Read My Desire: Lacan Against the Historicists*. New York: Verso, 2015.

Coppock, Vicki, Deena Haydon, and Ingrid Richter. *The Illusions of Post-Feminism: New Women, Old Myths*. New York: Routledge, 2014.

Cramer, Linsay M. "Cam Newton and Russell Westbrook's Symbolic Resistance to Whiteness in the NFL and NBA." *Howard Journal of Communications* 30, no. 1 (January 2019): 57–75. https://doi.org/10.1080/10646175.2018.1439421.

Cramer, Linsay M. "Postracism Mythology: NBA Commissioner Adam Silver's 'Heroic' Banishment of Racism From the NBA." *Communication & Sport* 7, no. 3 (June 2019): 271–91. https://doi.org/10.1177/2167479518769895.

Creed, Barbara. *Phallic Panic: Film, Horror and the Primal Uncanny*. Carlton, AU: Melbourne University, 2005.

Curry, Tommy J. *The Man-Not: Race, Class, Genre, and the Dilemmas of Black Manhood*. Philadelphia: Temple University Press, 2017.

Davis, Angela Yvonne. *Women, Race, and Class*. New York: Vintage Books, 1983.

Dean, Jodi. *Publicity's Secret: How Technoculture Capitalizes on Democracy*. Ithaca, NY: Cornell University Press, 2002.

Debord, Guy. *Society of the Spectacle*. Detroit: Black & Red, 2000.

Dei, George Jerry Sefa, Leeno Luke Karumanchery, Nisha Karumanchery, and Nisha Karumanchéry Luik. *Playing the Race Card: Exposing White Power and Privilege*. New York: Peter Lang, 2004.

Delgado, Richard, and Jean Stefancic. *Must We Defend Nazis?: Hate Speech, Pornography, and the New First Amendment.* New York: NYU Press, 1999.

DeLuca, Kevin Michael, and Jennifer Peeples. "From Public Sphere to Public Screen: Democracy, Activism, and the 'Violence' of Seattle." *Critical Studies in Media Communication* 19, no. 2 (June 1, 2002): 125–51. https://doi.org/10.1080/0739318 0216559.

Derrida, Jacques. *The Beast and the Sovereign: Vol. I.* Translated by Geoffrey Bennington. Chicago: University of Chicago Press, 2011.

DiAngelo, Robin J. *White Fragility: Why It's So Hard for White People to Talk about Racism.* Boston: Beacon Press, 2018.

Dolar, Mladen. *A Voice and Nothing More.* Cambridge, MA: MIT Press, 2006.

Du Bois, W. E. B. *Black Reconstruction in America, 1860–1880.* New York: Free Press, 1998.

Dubrofsky, Rachel E. "Monstrous Authenticity: Trump's Whiteness." In *Theorizing the Communicative Power of Whiteness,* edited by D.M. MacIntosh, Dream A. Moon, and Thomas K. Nakayama, 155–75. New York: Routledge, 2018.

Dubrofsky, Rachel E., and Antoine Hardy. "Performing Race in Flavor of Love and The Bachelor." *Critical Studies in Media Communication* 25, no. 4 (October 1, 2008): 373–92. https://doi.org/10.1080/15295030802327774.

Dubrofsky, Rachel E., and Emily D. Ryalls. "The Hunger Games: Performing Not-Performing to Authenticate Femininity and Whiteness." *Critical Studies in Media Communication* 31, no. 5 (October 20, 2014): 395–409. https://doi.org/10.1080/15295 036.2013.874038.

Dudas, Jeffrey R. *Raised Right: Fatherhood in Modern American Conservatism.* Palo Alto, CA: Stanford University Press, 2017.

Dyer, Richard. *Heavenly Bodies: Film Stars and Society.* New York: Routledge, 2013.

Dyer, Richard. *White: Essays on Race and Culture.* London and New York: Routledge, 1997.

Eagleton, Terry. *On Evil.* New Haven, CT: Yale University Press, 2011.

Edgar, Amanda Nell. *Culturally Speaking: The Rhetoric of Voice and Identity in a Mediated Culture.* Columbus: Ohio State University Press, 2019.

Esquith, Stephen L. *The Political Responsibilities of Everyday Bystanders.* University Park: Penn State Press, 2011.

Fanon, Frantz. *Black Skin, White Masks.* Translated by Richard Philcox. New York: Grove Press, 2008.

Feagin, Joe R. *The White Racial Frame: Centuries of Racial Framing and Counter-Framing.* New York: Routledge, 2013.

Feagin, Joe R., and Eileen O'Brien. *White Men on Race: Power, Privilege, and the Shaping of Cultural Consciousness.* Boston: Beacon Press, 2003.

Fink, Bruce. *The Lacanian Subject: Between Language and Jouissance.* Princeton, NJ: Princeton University Press, 1997.

Fiske, John. *Television Culture.* New York: Routledge, 2010.

Flores, Lisa A. *Deportable and Disposable: Public Rhetoric and the Making of the Illegal Immigrant.* University Park: Penn State Press, 2020.

Foucault, Michel. *Discipline and Punish: The Birth of the Prison.* New York: Vintage Books, 1977.

Foucault, Michel. *The History of Sexuality: Vol. 1.* New York: Random House, 1978.

Fowler, Doreen. "Faulkner's Return to the Freudian Father: Sanctuary Reconsidered." *MFS Modern Fiction Studies* 50, no. 2 (2004): 411–34. https://doi.org/10.1353/mfs.2004.0026.

Fraser, Nancy. "Rethinking the Public Sphere: A Contribution to the Critique of Actually Existing Democracy." *Social Text* 25/26 (1990): 56–80.

Frentz, Thomas S., and Janice Hocker Rushing. "Integrating Ideology and Archetype in Rhetorical Criticism, Part II: A Case Study of Jaws." *Quarterly Journal of Speech* 79, no. 1 (February 1993): 61.

Freud, Sigmund. *Beyond the Pleasure Principle*. New York: International Psycho-analytical Press, 1922.

Freud, Sigmund. *Beyond the Pleasure Principle*. Translated by James Strachey. New York: W.W. Norton, 1990.

Freud, Sigmund. *Group Psychology and the Analysis of the Ego*. Translated by James Strachey. New York: W.W. Norton, 2018.

Freud, Sigmund. "Mourning and Melancholia." In *The Standard Edition of the Complete Psychological Works of Sigmund Freud: Vol. XIV*, translated by James Strachey, 243–58. London: Hogarth Press, 1964.

Freud, Sigmund. *The Interpretation of Dreams: The Complete and Definitive Text*. Translated by James Strachey. New York: Basic Books, 2010.

Freud, Sigmund. *The "Wolfman" and Other Cases*. New York: Penguin, 2003.

Freud, Sigmund, and Marie Bonaparte. *The Origins of Psychoanalysis: Letters to Wilhelm Fliess, Drafts and Notes, 1887–1902*. Whitefish, MT: Literary Licensing, 2013.

Freud, Sigmund, and Abraham Arden Brill. *Totem and Taboo: Resemblances Between the Psychic Lives of Savages and Neurotics*. New York: Moffat, Yard, 1918.

Freud, Sigmund, and Peter Gay. *Inhibitions, Symptoms and Anxiety*. Edited by James Strachey, standard ed. New York: W.W. Norton, 1990.

Freud, Sigmund, and Peter Gay. *New Introductory Lectures on Psycho-Analysis*. Edited by James Strachey, standard ed. New York: W.W. Norton, 1990.

Freud, Sigmund, Christopher Hitchens, and Peter Gay. *Civilization and Its Discontents*. Edited by James Strachey, reprint ed. New York: W.W. Norton, 2010.

Freud, Sigmund, and James Strachey. *The Ego and the Id*. New York: W.W. Norton, 1962.

Gibson, Katie L., and Amy L. Heyse. "Depoliticizing Feminism: Frontier Mythology and Sarah Palin's 'The Rise of The Mama Grizzlies.'" *Western Journal of Communication* 78, no. 1 (February 1, 2014): 97–117. https://doi.org/10.1080/10570314.2013.812744.

Gibson, Katie L., and Amy L. Heyse. "'The Difference Between a Hockey Mom and a Pit Bull': Sarah Palin's Faux Maternal Persona and Performance of Hegemonic Masculinity at the 2008 Republican National Convention." *Communication Quarterly* 58, no. 3 (July 2010): 235–56. https://doi.org/10.1080/01463373.2010.503151.

Gillman, Susan. *Blood Talk: American Race Melodrama and the Culture of the Occult*. Chicago: University of Chicago Press, 2003.

Giroux, Henry A. "Disturbing Pleasures." *Third Text* 26, no. 3 (November 12, 2012): 259–73. https://doi.org/10.4324/9780203873250.

Goldberg, David Theo. *The Threat of Race: Reflections on Racial Neoliberalism*. Hoboken, NJ: John Wiley & Sons, 2011.

Goldstein, Eric L. *The Price of Whiteness: Jews, Race, and American Identity*. Princeton, N.J.: Princeton University Press, 2008.

Grano, Daniel A. "Michael Vick's 'Genuine Remorse' and Problems of Public Forgiveness." *Quarterly Journal of Speech* 100, no. 1 (February 2014): 81–104. https://doi.org/10.1080/00335630.2014.888460.

Grano, Daniel A. "Ritual Disorder and the Contractual Morality of Sport: A Case Study in Race, Class, and Agreement." *Rhetoric & Public Affairs* 10, no. 3 (Fall 2007): 445–73.

Gray, Herman. *Watching Race: Television and the Struggle for Blackness*. Minneapolis: University of Minnesota Press, 2004.

Griffin, Rachel Alicia. "Problematic Representations of Strategic Whiteness and 'Post-Racial' Pedagogy: A Critical Intercultural Reading of *The Help*." *Journal of International & Intercultural Communication* 8, no. 2 (May 2015): 147–66. https://doi.org/10.1080/17513057.2015.1025330.

Grindstaff, Laura, and Susan Murray. "Reality Celebrity: Branded Affect and the Emotion Economy." *Public Culture* 27, no. 1 (January 2015): 109–35. https://doi.org/10.1215/08992363-2798367.

Grossberg, Lawrence. *Cultural Studies in the Future Tense*. Durham, NC: Duke University Press, 2010.

Gunn, Joshua. "Death by Publicity: U.S. Freemasonry and the Public Drama of Secrecy." *Rhetoric & Public Affairs* 11, no. 2 (2008): 243–77. https://doi.org/10.1353/rap.0.0029.

Gunn, Joshua. "Father Trouble: Staging Sovereignty in Spielberg's *War of the Worlds*." *Critical Studies in Media Communication* 25, no. 1 (March 2008): 1–27. https://doi.org/10.1080/15295030701849332.

Gunn, Joshua. "Gunplay." Carroll C. Arnold Distinguished Lecture, November 9, 2018. https://www.natcom.org/sites/default/files/pages/2018NCA_ArnoldLecture.pdf.

Gunn, Joshua. "Maranatha." *Quarterly Journal of Speech* 98, no. 4 (November 2012): 359–85. https://doi.org/10.1080/00335630.2012.714900.

Gunn, Joshua. "On Political Perversion." *Rhetoric Society Quarterly* 48, no. 2 (March 15, 2018): 161–86. https://doi.org/10.1080/02773945.2018.1428766.

Gunn, Joshua. "On Social Networking and Psychosis." *Communication Theory* 28, no. 1 (February 1, 2018): 69–88. https://doi.org/10.1093/ct/qtx002.

Gunn, Joshua. *Political Perversion: Rhetorical Aberration in the Time of Trumpeteering*. Chicago: University of Chicago Press, 2020.

Gunn, Joshua. "Refitting Fantasy: Psychoanalysis, Subjectivity, and Talking to the Dead." *Quarterly Journal of Speech* 90, no. 1 (February 2004): 1–23. https://doi.org/10.1080/0033563042000206808.

Gunn, Joshua, and David E. Beard. "On the Apocalyptic Sublime." *Southern Communication Journal* 65, no. 4 (September 1, 2000): 269–86. https://doi.org/10.1080/10417940009373176.

Gunn, Joshua, and Thomas Frentz. "Fighting for Father: Fight Club as Cinematic Psychosis." *Western Journal of Communication* 74, no. 3 (May 26, 2010): 269–91. https://doi.org/10.1080/10570311003767191.

Hall, Stuart, and Henry Louis Gates Jr. *The Fateful Triangle: Race, Ethnicity, Nation*. Edited by Kobena Mercer. Cambridge, MA: Harvard University Press, 2017.

Hallsby, Atilla. "Imagine There's No President: The Rhetorical Secret and the Exposure of Valerie Plame." *Quarterly Journal of Speech* 101, no. 2 (May 2015): 354–78. https://doi.org/10.1080/00335630.2015.1024276.

Harris, Cheryl I. "Whiteness as Property." *Harvard Law Review* 106, no. 8 (1993): 1707–91. https://doi.org/10.2307/1341787.

Harris, Trudier. *Exorcising Blackness: Historical and Literary Lynching and Burning Rituals*. Bloomington: Indiana University Press, 1984.

Hartman, Saidiya V. *Scenes of Subjection: Terror, Slavery, and Self-Making in Nineteenth-Century America*. New York: Oxford University Press, 1997.

Hartzell, Stephanie L. "Whiteness Feels Good Here: Interrogating White Nationalist Rhetoric on Stormfront." *Communication and Critical/Cultural Studies* 17, no. 2 (March 26, 2020): 129–48. https://doi.org/10.1080/14791420.2020.1745858.

Hawkins, Billy. *The New Plantation: Black Athletes, College Sports, and Predominantly White NCAA Institutions*. New York: Palgrave Macmillan, 2013.

Hawley, George. *Making Sense of the Alt-Right*. New York: Columbia University Press, 2017.

Hester, Helen. *Beyond Explicit: Pornography and the Displacement of Sex*. Albany: SUNY Press, 2014.

Hill, Mike. *Whiteness: A Critical Reader*. New York: NYU Press, 1997.

Holland, Sharon Patricia. *The Erotic Life of Racism*. Durham, NC: Duke University Press, 2012.

Holling, Michelle A., Dreama G. Moon, and Alexandra Jackson Nevis. "Racist Violations and Racializing Apologia in a Post-Racism Era." *Journal of International and Intercultural Communication* 7, no. 4 (2014): 260–86. https://doi.org/10.1080/17513 057.2014.964144.

Hook, Derek. "Fanon via Lacan, or: Decolonization by Psychoanalytic Means . . . ?" *Journal of the British Society for Phenomenology* 51, no. 4 (October 1, 2020): 305–19. https://doi.org/10.1080/00071773.2020.1732575.

Hook, Derek. "What Is 'Enjoyment as a Political Factor'?" *Political Psychology* 38, no. 4 (2017): 605–20.

hooks, bell. *Black Looks: Race and Representation*. Boston: South End Press, 1992.

Houdek, Matthew, and Ersula J. Ore. "Cultivating Otherwise Worlds and Breathable Futures." *Rhetoric, Politics, and Culture* 1, no. 1 (Summer 2021): 85–95.

Hudson, Peter. "The State and the Colonial Unconscious." *Social Dynamics* 39, no. 2 (June 1, 2013): 263–77. https://doi.org/10.1080/02533952.2013.802867.

Hylton, Kevin, and Stefan Lawrence. "'For Your Ears Only!' Donald Sterling and Backstage Racism in Sport." *Ethnic and Racial Studies* 39, no. 15 (December 7, 2016): 2740–57. https://doi.org/10.1080/01419870.2016.1177193.

Irigaray, Luce. *This Sex Which Is Not One*. Ithaca, NY: Cornell University Press, 1985.

Jackson, Ronald L. *Scripting the Black Masculine Body: Identity, Discourse, and Racial Politics in Popular Media*. Albany: SUNY Press, 2006.

James, Robin. *Resilience & Melancholy: Pop Music, Feminism, Neoliberalism*. Winchester, UK: Zero Books, 2015.

Jeffords, Susan. *Hard Bodies: Hollywood Masculinity in the Reagan Era*. New Brunswick, NJ: Rutgers University Press, 1994.

Jenkins, Henry. *Convergence Culture: Where Old and New Media Collide*. New York: NYU Press, 2008.

Johnson, Paul Elliott. *I, the People: The Rhetoric of Conservative Populism in the United States*. Tuscaloosa: University of Alabama Press, 2021.

Johnson, Paul Elliott. "The Art of Masculine Victimhood: Donald Trump's Demagoguery." *Women's Studies in Communication* 40, no. 3 (July 3, 2017): 229–50. https://doi.org/ 10.1080/07491409.2017.1346533.

Kellner, Douglas. *American Nightmare: Donald Trump, Media Spectacle, and Authoritarian Populism*. Rotterdam, the Netherlands: Sense Publishers, 2016.

Kellner, Douglas. *Guys and Guns Amok: Domestic Terrorism and School Shootings from the Oklahoma City Bombing to the Virginia Tech Massacre*. New York: Routledge, 2008.

Kellner, Douglas. *Media Spectacle*. New York: Routledge, 2003.

Kelly, Casey R. *Apocalypse Man: The Death Drive and the Rhetoric of White Masculine Victimhood*. Columbus: Ohio State University Press, 2020. https://ohiostatepress.org/books/titles/9780814214329.html.

Kelly, Casey R. "Donald J. Trump and the Rhetoric of Ressentiment." *Quarterly Journal of Speech* 106, no. 1 (January 2, 2020): 2–24. https://doi.org/10.1080/00335630.2019.1698756.

Kelly, Casey R. "Donald J. Trump and the Rhetoric of White Ambivalence." *Rhetoric & Public Affairs* 23, no. 2 (August 6, 2020): 195–223.

Kelly, Casey R. "Feminine Purity and Masculine Revenge-Seeking in *Taken* (2008)." *Feminist Media Studies* 14, no. 3 (May 2014): 403–18. https://doi.org/10.1080/14680777.2012.740062.

Kelly, Casey R. "Neocolonialism and the Global Prison in *National Geographic*'s Locked Up Abroad." *Critical Studies in Media Communication* 29, no. 4 (October 1, 2012): 331–47. https://doi.org/10.1080/15295036.2011.645843.

Kennedy, Tammie M., Joyce Irene Middleton, and Krista Ratcliffe. *Rhetorics of Whiteness: Postracial Hauntings in Popular Culture, Social Media, and Education*. Carbondale: Southern Illinois University Press, 2017.

Kimmel, Michael. *Angry White Men: American Masculinity at the End of an Era*. New York: Nation Books, 2013.

Kimmel, Michael. *Manhood in America: A Cultural History*. New York: Oxford University Press, 2012.

King, Claire Sisco. *Washed in Blood: Male Sacrifice, Trauma, and the Cinema*. New Brunswick, NJ: Rutgers University Press, 2011.

King, Claire Sisco. "It Cuts Both Ways: Fight Club, Masculinity, and Abject Hegemony." *Communication and Critical/Cultural Studies* 6, no. 4 (December 1, 2009): 366–85. https://doi.org/10.1080/14791420903335135.

King, Claire Sisco, and Joshua Gunn. "On a Violence Unseen: The Womanly Object and Sacrificed Man." *Quarterly Journal of Speech* 99, no. 2 (May 2013): 200–08. https://doi.org/10.1080/00335630.2013.777770.

Kipnis, Laura. *How to Become a Scandal: Adventures in Bad Behavior*. New York: Metropolitan Books, 2010.

Kristeva, Julia. *The Power of Horror: An Essay on Abjection*. New York: Columbia University Press, 1982.

Lacan, Jacques. *Anxiety: The Seminar of Jacques Lacan*, Book X ed. Translated by A. R. Price. Malden, MA: Polity, 2016.

Lacan, Jacques. *Seminar of Jacques Lacan: The Psychoses*, reprint ed. Translated by Jacques-Alain Miller and Russell Grigg. New York: W.W. Norton, 1997.

Lacan, Jacques. *The Four Fundamental Concepts of Psycho-Analysis*. New York: W.W. Norton, 1998.

Lacan, Jacques. *Ecrits: The First Complete Edition in English*. New York: W.W. Norton, 2006.

Lacy, Michael G. "Exposing the Spectrum of Whiteness: Rhetorical Conceptions of White Absolutism." *Communication Yearbook* 32 (May 2008): 277–311.

Lacy, Michael G. "White Innocence Heroes: Recovery, Reversals, Paternalism, and David Duke." *Journal of International & Intercultural Communication* 3, no. 3 (August 2010): 206–27. https://doi.org/10.1080/17513057.2010.487221.

Lane, Christopher, ed. *The Psychoanalysis of Race*. New York: Columbia University Press, 1998.

Laplanche, Jean, and Jean-Bertrand Pontalis. *The Language of Psycho-Analysis*. New York: W. W. Norton, 1974.

Lavelle, Katherine L. "No Room for Racism: Restoration of Order in the NBA." *Communication & Sport* 4, no. 4 (December 2016): 424–41. https://doi.org/10.1177/2167479515584046.

Lawrence, Charles R., Mari J. Matsuda, Richard Delgado, and Kimberlè Williams Crenshaw, eds. *Words That Wound: Critical Race Theory, Assaultive Speech, and the First Amendment*. Boulder, CO: Westview Press, 1993.

Levine, Caroline. *Forms: Whole, Rhythm, Hierarchy, Network*. Princeton, NJ: Princeton University Press, 2015.

Lipsitz, George. *Possessive Investment in Whiteness*. Philadelphia: Temple University Press, 1998.

Lomax, Tamura. *Jezebel Unhinged: Loosing the Black Female Body in Religion and Culture*. Durham, NC: Duke University Press, 2018.

López, Ian Haney. *Dog Whistle Politics: How Coded Racial Appeals Have Reinvented Racism and Wrecked the Middle Class*. New York: Oxford University Press, 2015.

Lugones, María. "Toward a Decolonial Feminism." *Hypatia* 25, no. 4 (2010): 742–59.

Lundberg, Christian. "Enjoying God's Death: The Passion of the Christ and the Practices of an Evangelical Public." *Quarterly Journal of Speech* 95, no. 4 (November 2009): 387–411. https://doi.org/10.1080/00335630903296184.

Lundberg, Christian. *Lacan in Public: Psychoanalysis and the Science of Rhetoric*. Tuscaloosa: University Alabama Press, 2012.

Lundberg, Christian. "On Being Bound to Equivalential Chains." *Cultural Studies* 26, no. 2–3 (March 1, 2012): 299–318. https://doi.org/10.1080/09502386.2011.647641.

Lyon, David. *The Culture of Surveillance: Watching as a Way of Life*. Cambridge, UK: Polity, 2018.

Mack, Ashley Noel, and Bryan J. McCann. "'Harvey Weinstein, Monster': Antiblackness and the Myth of the Monstrous Rapist." *Communication and Critical/Cultural Studies* 18, no. 2 (February 25, 2021): 103–20. https://doi.org/10.1080/14791420.2020.1854802.

Mack, Ashley Noel, and Bryan J. McCann. "Recalling Persky: White Rage and Intimate Publicity After Brock Turner." *Journal of Communication Inquiry* 43, no. 4 (October 1, 2019): 372–93. https://doi.org/10.1177/0196859919867265.

Mack, Ashley Noel, and Tiara R. Na'puti. "'Our Bodies Are Not *Terra Nullius*': Building a Decolonial Feminist Resistance to Gendered Violence." *Women's Studies in Communication* 42, no. 3 (July 3, 2019): 347–70. https://doi.org/10.1080/07491409.2019.1637803.

Mandell, Hinda. *Sex Scandals, Gender, and Power in Contemporary American Politics*. Santa Barbara, CA: ABC-CLIO, 2017.

Marcus, Sharon. "Celebrities and Publics in the Internet Era [Special Issue]." *Public Culture* 27, no. 1 [75] (January 1, 2015): 1–195. https://doi.org/10.1215/08992363-2798319.

Marshall, P. David. *Celebrity and Power: Fame in Contemporary Culture*. Minneapolis: University of Minnesota Press, 2014.

Martinot, Steve, and Jared Sexton. "The Avant-Garde of White Supremacy." *Social Identities* 9, no. 2 (June 1, 2003): 169–81. https://doi.org/10.1080/1350463032000101542.

Marwick, Alice E. "Instafame: Luxury Selfies in the Attention Economy." *Public Culture* 27, no. 1 [75] (January 2015): 137–60. https://doi.org/10.1215/08992363-2798379.

Marwick, Alice E. *Status Update: Celebrity, Publicity, and Branding in the Social Media Age*. New Haven, CT, and London: Yale University Press, 2015.

Marwick, Alice E. "You May Know Me From YouTube: (Micro-)Celebrity in Social Media." In *A Companion to Celebrity*, edited by P. David Marshall and Sean Redmond. Hoboken, NJ: John Wiley & Sons, 2015.

Massumi, Brian. *Parables for the Virtual: Movement, Affect, Sensation*. Durham, NC: Duke University Press Books, 2002.

Matamoros-Fernández, Ariadna. "Platformed Racism: The Mediation and Circulation of an Australian Race-Based Controversy on Twitter, Facebook and YouTube." *Information, Communication & Society* 20, no. 6 (June 3, 2017): 930–46. https://doi.org/10.1080/1369118X.2017.1293130.

Matheson, Calum Lister. *Desiring the Bomb: Communication, Psychoanalysis, and the Atomic Age*. Tuscaloosa: University of Alabama Press, 2018.

Matheson, Calum Lister. "Psychotic Discourse: The Rhetoric of the Sovereign Citizen Movement." *Rhetoric Society Quarterly* 48, no. 2 (March 15, 2018): 187–206. https://doi.org/10.1080/02773945.2017.1306876.

Matheson, Calum Lister. "'What Does Obama Want of Me?' Anxiety and Jade Helm 15." *Quarterly Journal of Speech* 102, no. 2 (May 2016): 133–49. https://doi.org/10.1080/00335630.2016.1155127.

Mbembe, Achille. *Necropolitics*. Durham, NC: Duke University Press, 2019.

McCann, Bryan J. "Affect, Black Rage, and False Alternatives in the Hip-Hop Nation." *Cultural Studies ↔ Critical Methodologies* 13, no. 5 (October 1, 2013): 408–18. https://doi.org/10.1177/1532708613496392.

McDaniel, James P. "Fantasm: The Triumph of Form (an Essay on the Democratic Sublime)." *Quarterly Journal of Speech* 86, no. 1 (February 1, 2000): 48–66. https://doi.org/10.1080/00335630009384278.

McDonald, Paul. *The Star System: Hollywood's Production of Popular Identities*. New York: Columbia University Press, 2013.

McGee, Michael Calvin. "Text, Context, and the Fragmentation of Contemporary Culture." *Western Journal of Speech Communication: WJSC* 54, no. 3 (Summer 1990): 274–89.

McGowan, Todd. *Capitalism and Desire: The Psychic Cost of Free Markets*. New York: Columbia University Press, 2016.

McGowan, Todd. *Enjoying What We Don't Have: The Political Project of Psychoanalysis*. Lincoln: University of Nebraska Press, 2013.

McGowan, Todd. "Looking for the Gaze: Lacanian Film Theory and Its Vicissitudes." *Cinema Journal* 42, no. 3 (2003): 27–47.

Mckerrow, Raymie E. "Critical Rhetoric: Theory and Praxis." *Communication Monographs* 56, no. 2 (June 1, 1989): 91–111. https://doi.org/10.1080/03637758909390253.

Milgram, Stanley. *Obedience to Authority: An Experimental View*. New York: Harper Perennial, 2009.

Miller, Carolyn R. "Genre as Social Action." *Quarterly Journal of Speech* 70, no. 2 (May 1, 1984): 151–67. https://doi.org/10.1080/00335638409383686.

Mills, Charles W. *The Racial Contract*. Ithaca, NY: Cornell University Press, 1999.

Mills, Charles W. *Black Rights/White Wrongs: The Critique of Racial Liberalism*. New York: Oxford University Press, 2017.

Molina, Natalia. *How Race Is Made in America: Immigration, Citizenship, and the Historical Power of Racial Scripts*. Berkeley: University of California Press, 2014.

Moon, Dreama G. "'Be/Coming' White and the Myth of White Ignorance: Identity Projects in White Communities." *Western Journal of Communication* 80, no. 3 (June 5, 2016): 282–303. https://doi.org/10.1080/10570314.2016.1143562.

Moten, Fred. *Stolen Life*. Durham, NC: Duke University Press Books, 2018.

Mulvey, Laura. "Visual Pleasure and Narrative Cinema." *Screen* 16, no. 3 (September 21, 1975): 6–18. https://doi.org/10.1093/screen/16.3.6.

Murray, Susan, and Laurie Ouellette, eds. *Reality TV: Remaking Television Culture*. 2nd ed. New York: NYU Press, 2008.

Naftali, Tim. "Ronald Reagan's Long-Hidden Racist Conversation With Richard Nixon." *The Atlantic*, July 30, 2019. https://www.theatlantic.com/ideas/archive/2019/07/ronald-reagans-racist-conversation-richard-nixon/595102/.

Nagle, Angela. *Kill All Normies: Online Culture Wars From 4Chan and Tumblr to Trump and the Alt-Right*. Washington, DC: Zero Books, 2017.

Nakayama, Thomas K., and Robert L. Krizek. "Whiteness: A Strategic Rhetoric." *Quarterly Journal of Speech* 81, no. 3 (August 1, 1995): 291–309. https://doi.org/10.1080/00335639509384117.

Nakayama, Thomas K., and Judith N. Martin. *Whiteness: The Communication of Social Identity*. Thousand Oaks, CA: SAGE, 1999.

Negra, Diane. *What a Girl Wants?: Fantasizing the Reclamation of Self in Postfeminism*. New York: Routledge, 2009.

Neville-Shepard, Ryan, and Meredith Neville-Shepard. "The Pornified Presidency: Hyper-Masculinity and the Pornographic Style in U.S. Political Rhetoric." *Feminist Media Studies* 21, no. 7 (June 27, 2020): 1193–208. https://doi.org/10.1080/14680777.2020.1786429.

Newman, Andrew. *Allegories of Encounter: Colonial Literacy and Indian Captivities*. Chapel Hill: University of North Carolina Press Books, 2018.

Noble, Safiya Umoja. *Algorithms of Oppression: How Search Engines Reinforce Racism*. New York: NYU Press, 2018.

Oates, Thomas P. *Football and Manliness: An Unauthorized Feminist Account of the NFL*. Urbana: University of Illinois Press, 2017.

Oates, Thomas P. "The Erotic Gaze in the NFL Draft." *Communication & Critical/Cultural Studies* 4, no. 1 (March 2007): 74–90. https://doi.org/10.1080/14791420601138351.

Omi, Michael, and Howard Winant. *Racial Formation in the United States: From the 1960s to the 1990s*. London: Psychology Press, 1994.

Ono, Kent A. *Contemporary Media Culture and the Remnants of a Colonial Past*. New York: Peter Lang, 2009.

Ono, Kent A., and John M. Sloop. "The Critique of Vernacular Discourse." *Communication Monographs* 62, no. 1 (March 1, 1995): 19–46. https://doi.org/10.1080/03637759509376346.

Ore, Ersula J. *Lynching: Violence, Rhetoric, and American Identity*. Jackson: University Press of Mississippi, 2019.

Ott, Brian L., and Greg Dickinson. *The Twitter Presidency: Donald J. Trump and the Politics of White Rage*. New York: Routledge, 2019.

Ouellette, Laurie. "The Trump Show." *Television & New Media* 17, no. 7 (November 1, 2016): 647–50. https://doi.org/10.1177/1527476416652695.

Ouellette, Laurie, and James Hay. *Better Living Through Reality TV: Television and Post-Welfare Citizenship*. Malden, MA: Wiley-Blackwell, 2008.

Pateman, Carole. *The Sexual Contract*. Cambridge, UK: Polity, 2018.

Perry, Imani. *Vexy Thing: On Gender and Liberation*. Durham, NC: Duke University Press, 2018.

Person, Leland S. "The American Eve: Miscegenation and a Feminist Frontier Fiction." *American Quarterly* 37, no. 5 (1985): 668–85.

Peters, John Durham. *Courting the Abyss: Free Speech and the Liberal Tradition*. Chicago: University of Chicago Press, 2010.

Petersen, Anne Helen. "Smut Goes Corporate: TMZ and the Conglomerate, Convergent Face of Celebrity Gossip." *Television & New Media* 11, no. 1 (January 1, 2010): 62–81. https://doi.org/10.1177/1527476409338196.

Pham, Vincent. "Our Foreign President Barack Obama: The Racial Logics of Birther Discourses." *Journal of International and Intercultural Communication* 8, no. 2 (2015): 86–107.

Phillips, Kendall R. *A Cinema of Hopelessness: The Rhetoric of Rage in 21st Century Popular Culture*. London: Palgrave Macmillan, 2021.

Picca, Leslie, and Joe Feagin. *Two-Faced Racism: Whites in the Backstage and Frontstage*. New York: Routledge, 2007.

Rajchman, John. "Lacan and the Ethics of Modernity." *Representations* 4, no. 15 (1986): 42–56. https://doi.org/10.2307/2928391.

Rhoden, William C. *Forty Million Dollar Slaves: The Rise, Fall, and Redemption of the Black Athlete*. New York: Three Rivers Press, 2010.

Rice, Jenny Edbauer. "The New 'New': Making a Case for Critical Affect Studies." *Quarterly Journal of Speech* 94, no. 2 (May 2008): 200–12. https://doi.org/10.1080/00335630801975434.

Robinson, Cedric J., and Robin D. G. Kelley. *Black Marxism: The Making of the Black Radical Tradition*, 2nd ed. Chapel Hill: University of North Carolina Press, 2005.

Robinson, Sally. *Authenticity Guaranteed: Masculinity and the Rhetoric of Anti-Consumerism in American Culture*. Amherst: University of Massachusetts Press, 2018.

Rodino-Colocino, Michelle. "Flexing Italian American Masculinity and White Diversity on Man Caves." *Women's Studies in Communication* 41, no. 3 (August 2018): 246–68. https://doi.org/10.1080/07491409.2018.1502703.

Roediger, David R. *The Wages of Whiteness: Race and the Making of the American Working Class*. New York: Verso, 1999.

Rowe, Aimee Carrillo, and Sheena Malhotra. "(Un)Hinging Whiteness." *International & Intercultural Communication Annual* 29 (October 2006): 166–92.

Rubin, Gayle. *Deviations: A Gayle Rubin Reader*. Durham, NC: Duke University Press, 2011.

Rubin, Gayle. "The Traffic in Women: Notes on the 'Political Economy' of Sex." In *Toward an Anthropology of Women*, edited by Rayna R. Reiter, 157–210. New York: Monthly Review Press, 1975.

Rushing, Janice Hocker. "Evolution of 'the New Frontier' in Alien and Aliens: Patriarchal Co-Optation of the Feminine Archetype." *Quarterly Journal of Speech* 75, no. 1 (February 1989): 1.

Rushing, Janice Hocker, and Thomas S. Frentz. "The Frankenstein Myth in Contemporary Cinema." *Critical Studies in Mass Communication* 6, no. 1 (March 1989): 61.

Seshadri-Crooks, Kalpana. *Desiring Whiteness: A Lacanian Analysis of Race*. London and New York: Routledge, 2000.

Sexton, Jared. "Afro-Pessimism: The Unclear Word." *Rhizomes: Cultural Studies in Emerging Knowledge*, no. 29 (2016). https://doi.org/10.20415/rhiz/029.e02.

Sexton, Jared. *Amalgamation Schemes: Antiblackness and the Critique of Multiracialism*. Minneapolis: University of Minnesota Press, 2008.

Seymour, Richard. *The Twittering Machine*. New York: Verso Books, 2020.

Shome, Raka. "Mapping the Limits of Multiculturalism in the Context of Globalization." *International Journal of Communication* 6, no. 0 (February 15, 2012): 22.

Shugart, Helene A. "Counterhegemonic Acts: Appropriation as a Feminist Rhetorical Strategy." *Quarterly Journal of Speech* 83, no. 2 (May 1997): 210.

Silverman, Kaja. *Male Subjectivity at the Margins*. New York: Routledge, 1992.

Silverman, Kaja. *The Acoustic Mirror: The Female Voice in Psychoanalysis and Cinema*. 5th or later ed. Bloomington: Indiana University Press, 1988.

Slotkin, Richard. *Gunfighter Nation: The Myth of the Frontier in Twentieth-Century America*. Norman: University of Oklahoma Press, 1992.

Slotkin, Richard. *Regeneration Through Violence: The Mythology of the American Frontier, 1600–1860*. Norman: University of Oklahoma Press, 2000.

Smith, Aidan. *Gender, Heteronormativity, and the American Presidency*. New York: Routledge, 2017.

Smith, Clarissa, Feona Attwood, and Brian McNair. *The Routledge Companion to Media, Sex and Sexuality*. New York: Routledge, 2017.

Spillers, Hortense J. "Mama's Baby, Papa's Maybe: An American Grammar Book." *Diacritics* 17, no. 2 (1987): 65–81. https://doi.org/10.2307/464747.

Squires, Catherine, Eric King Watts, Mary Douglas Vavrus, Kent A. Ono, Kathleen Feyh, Bernadette Marie Calafell, and Daniel C. Brouwer. "What Is This 'Post-' in Postracial, Postfeminist. . . (Fill in the Blank)?" *Journal of Communication Inquiry* 34, no. 3 (July 2010): 210–53. https://doi.org/10.1177/0196859910371375.

Stern, Alexandra Minna. *Proud Boys and the White Ethnostate: How the Alt-Right Is Warping the American Imagination*. Boston: Beacon Press, 2019.

Stone Watt, Sarah. "Rape Is a Four-Letter Word": Psychosis, Sexual Assault, and Abortion in the 2012 U.S. Election." *Women's Studies in Communication* 43, no. 3 (July 2, 2020): 225–46. https://doi.org/10.1080/07491409.2020.1740902.

Stormer, Nathan. "All Diseased Things Are Critics." *Communication and the Public* 5, no. 1–2 (March 1, 2020): 74–82. https://doi.org/10.1177/2057047320950642.

Sugrue, Thomas J. *Sweet Land of Liberty: The Forgotten Struggle for Civil Rights in the North*. New York: Random House, 2009.

Tasker, Yvonne, and Diane Negra, eds. *Interrogating Postfeminism: Gender and the Politics of Popular Culture*. Durham, NC: Duke University Press, 2007.

Taussig, Michael. *Defacement: Public Secrecy and the Labor of the Negative*. Stanford, CA: Stanford University Press, 1999.

Terrill, Robert E. "The Post-Racial and Post-Ethical Discourse of Donald J. Trump." *Rhetoric & Public Affairs* 20, no. 3 (Fall 2017): 493–510.

Theoharis, Jeanne. *A More Beautiful and Terrible History: The Uses and Misuses of Civil Rights History*. Boston: Beacon Press, 2018.

Tischauser, Jeff, and Kevin Musgrave. "Far-Right Media as Imitated Counterpublicity: A Discourse Analysis on Racial Meaning and Identity on Vdare.Com." *Howard Journal of Communications* 41, no. 3 (2020): 282–96. https://doi.org/10.1080/10646175.2019.1702124.

Wanzer-Serrano, Darrel. "Barack Obama, the Tea Party, and the Threat of Race: On Racial Neoliberalism and Born Again Racism." *Communication, Culture & Critique* 4, no. 1 (March 1, 2011): 23–30. https://doi.org/10.1111/j.1753-9137.2010.01090.x.

Warner, Michael. "Publics and Counterpublics." *Public Culture* 14, no. 1 (2002): 49–90.

Warren, Calvin L. *Ontological Terror: Blackness, Nihilism, and Emancipation*. Durham, NC: Duke University Press, 2018.

Watts, Eric King. "Border Patrolling and 'Passing' in Eminem's *8 Mile*." *Critical Studies in Media Communication* 22, no. 3 (2005): 187–206.

Watts, Eric King. "The Primal Scene of COVID-19: 'We're All in This Together.'" *Rhetoric, Politics, and Culture* 1, no. 1 (2021): 1–26.

Watts, Eric King. "'Zombies Are Real': Fantasies, Conspiracies, and the Post-Truth Wars." *Philosophy & Rhetoric* 51, no. 4 (2018): 441–70.

Weheliye, Alexander G. *Habeas Viscus: Racializing Assemblages, Biopolitics, and Black Feminist Theories of the Human*. Durham, NC: Duke University Press, 2014.

Welter, Barbara. "The Cult of True Womanhood: 1820–1860." *American Quarterly* 18, no. 2 (1966): 151–74. https://doi.org/10.2307/2711179.

White, Richard, and Patricia Nelson Limerick. *The Frontier in American Culture*. Oakland: University of California Press, 1994.

Wilderson, Frank B. *Red, White & Black: Cinema and the Structure of U.S. Antagonisms*. Durham, NC: Duke University Press, 2010.

Wiegman, Robyn. *Object Lessons*. Durham, NC: Duke University Press, 2012.

Williams, Linda. "Film Bodies: Gender, Genre, and Excess." *Film Quarterly* 44, no. 4 (1991): 2–13. https://doi.org/10.2307/1212758.

Williams, Linda. *Hard Core: Power, Pleasure, and the "Frenzy of the Visible."* Oakland: University of California Press, 1989.

Williams, Linda. *Playing the Race Card: Melodramas of Black and White from Uncle Tom to O. J. Simpson*, revised ed. Princeton, NJ: Princeton University Press, 2002.

Williams, Raymond. *Raymond Williams on Television: Selected Writings*. Edited by Alan O'Connor. New York: Routledge, 1989.

Williams. Robert A. *Like a Loaded Weapon: The Rehnquist Court, Indian Rights, and the Legal History of Racism in America*. Minneapolis: University of Minnesota Press, 2005.

Wise, Tim. *Speaking Treason Fluently: Anti-Racist Reflections From an Angry White Male*. New York and Berkeley, CA: Publishers Group West for Soft Skull, 2008.

Wood, Robin. *Hollywood from Vietnam to Reagan . . . and Beyond*. New York: Columbia University Press, 2003.

Woods, Heather Suzanne, and Leslie A. Hahner. *Make America Meme Again: The Rhetoric of the Alt-Right*. New York: Peter Lang, 2019.

Wynter, Sylvia. "Unsettling the Coloniality of Being/Power/Truth/Freedom: Towards the Human, After Man, Its Overrepresentation—An Argument." *CR: The New Centennial Review* 3, no. 3 (2003): 257–337.

Young, Iris Marion. "The Logic of Masculinist Protection: Reflections on the Current Security State." *Signs* 29, no. 1 (2003): 1–25. https://doi.org/10.1086/375708.

Zirin, Dave. *Bad Sports: How Owners Are Ruining the Games We Love*. New York: Simon and Schuster, 2010.

Žižek, Slavoj. "Descartes and the Post-Traumatic Subject: On Catherine Malabou's *Les Nouveaux Blessés and Other Autistic Monsters*." *Qui Parle* 17, no. 2 (December 1, 2009): 123–47. https://doi.org/10.5250/quiparle.17.2.123.

Žižek, Slavoj. *The Metastases of Enjoyment: On Women and Causality*. New York: Verso, 2006.

Žižek, Slavoj. *The Plague of Fantasies*. New York: Verso, 1997.

Žižek, Slavoj. *The Ticklish Subject: The Absent Centre of Political Ontology*. New York: Verso, 2000.

Žižek, Slavoj. *Welcome to the Desert of the Real!: Five Essays on September 11 and Related Dates*. New York: Verso, 2002.

Zupančič, Alenka. *Ethics of the Real: Kant and Lacan*. London: Verso, 2012.

Zupančič, Alenka. *Why Psychoanalysis?: Three Interventions*. Uppsala, Sweden: Uppsala University Press, 2008.

Index